Sharia and Justice

Sharia and Justice

An Ethical, Legal, Political, and
Cross-Cultural Approach

Edited by
Abbas Poya

DE GRUYTER

ISBN 978-3-11-068322-6
e-ISBN (PDF) 978-3-11-057459-3
e-ISBN (EPUB) 978-3-11-057359-6

Library of Congress Control Number: 2018941741

Bibliographic information published by the Deutsche Nationalbibliothek
The Deutsche Nationalbibliothek lists this publication in the Deutsche Nationalbibliografie; detailed bibliographic data are available on the Internet at http://dnb.dnb.de.

This volume is text- and page-identical with the hardback published in 2018.
Cover image: Abstract colorful oil painting on canvas, Gurgen Bakhshetyan/Shutterstock.com
Printing and binding: CPI books GmbH, Leck

www.degruyter.com

Table of Contents

Introduction — 1

Rumee Ahmed
Ordinary Justice: A Theology of Islamic Law as a Social Contract — 13

Abbas Poya
Conditions for a Good World
The Concept of Comprehensive Justice by Abū al-Ḥasan al-Māwardī (972–1058) — **39**

Werner Ende
Justice as a Political Principle in Islam — 59

Ziba Mir-Hosseini
Justice and Equality and Muslim Family Laws: New Ideas, New Prospects — 73

Mathias Rohe
Islamic Law and Justice — 105

Abbas Poya
***Jihād* and Just War Theory: A Conceptual Analysis — 135**

Bernd Ladwig
The Islamic Veil and Justice — 151

Name Index — 177

Subject Index — 179

Short Biographies — 181

Introduction

I

According to Muslim belief, Sharia cannot be but just.[1] God is just and so is His legislation; this statement is recurrent among Muslim scholars.[2] Nevertheless, there are most probably many Muslims, who in some cases may consider themselves victims of unjust treatment by states that follow Sharia law. This does not only apply to critical Muslims, who believe that certain regulations of a traditional version of Sharia are out of time and in need of reform, such as corporal punishment and discrimination against women in regard to inheritance law and to their role as witnesses. Also those Muslims, who unexceptionally approve of Sharia law in its traditional form, do in some cases feel that they or their fellow citizens are treated unfairly by the state. The perceived injustice of the Muslim ruler of the state, even if he subscribed to the same religious orientation, was often enough a cause for waging wars against fellow believers.[3] The following anecdote illustrates the struggle of the human mind — despite or maybe because of the belief in the existence of an order of justice in creation and in a just God — in the face of *human* tragedy:

---

1 All different streams within Islam agree on this, even if they put forward different explanations of what justice is. The Muʿtazilites believed that God cannot act but justly and that His actions are subjected to the same moral standards that are applied to human behaviour. According to the Ashʿarites, God is just due to His omnipotence. Everything He does is just, even if human beings might consider it to be otherwise. Contrary to the positions of these two theological schools, the Ḥanbalis argued that God is in fact capable of doing evil, but due to His grace He committed himself to act justly. This shows that regardless of the different approaches to the concept of divine justice, they all conclude that the divine actions are just.

2 Aḥmad Shuʿayb Lamdī, for example, begins his recently published book by saying: 'Praise be to God, the just, the one who acts justly and the one who has given His creation existence according to a just measure, and has sent prophets, laws and books according to just scales, i.e. to justice.' See Aḥmad Shuʿayb Lamdī, *Maqṣad al-ʿadl ʿinda Ibn Taymiyya: Al-ʿadl al-dīnī wa al-dunyawī fī l-naṣṣ wa l-wāqiʿ* (Beirut, Cairo, Riyadh: al-Shabaka al-ʿarabiyya li-l-abḥāth wa an-nashr, 2014), 9.

3 The Muʿtazilites, for example, who otherwise opposed the legitimacy of militant acts against the ruling class, supported under the leadership of Abū Muḥammad Bashīr al-Raḥḥāl the revolt of Muḥammad al-Nafs al-Zakiyya (d. 762) against the Abbasid caliph al-Manṣūr (r. 754–775). Even though he refused to fight fellow believers, he nevertheless 'obviously considered fighting Mansur to be legitimate. For he did not bring justice.' Josef van Ess, *Theologie und Gesellschaft im 2. und 3. Jahrhundert Hidschra: Eine Geschichte des religiösen Denkens im frühen Islam*, 6 vols. (Berlin: De Gruyter, 1991), 2/329–330.

https://doi.org/10.1515/9783110574593-001

> A story is told that a certain prophet used to worship God on a high mountain, beneath which was a spring of running water. By day he used to sit out of sight on the mountain top, reciting the Name of Almighty God, and he would look down at those who came to the spring. One day, while he was doing this, he saw a horseman ride up, dismount and drink, after which he rested. This man had put down a bag which had been fastened round his neck and which was full of dinars, but when he rode away he left it behind. Another man then came there and when he had drunk from the spring, he took the bag with the money in it and left safely. He was followed to the spring by a woodcutter, who was carrying a heavy load of firewood on his back. He sat down to drink, and at this point the rider came back anxiously and asked him where the bag was that had been there. 'I know nothing about a bag,' said the woodcutter, at which the rider drew his sword and killed him with a blow. The rider then searched through his clothes but found nothing and went off, leaving the corpse there. The prophet said: 'Lord, one man has taken a thousand dinars and another has been killed unjustly.' God then sent him a revelation, telling him: 'Concern yourself with your worship, for the ordering of the kingdom is no concern of yours. The father of this rider had forcibly plundered a thousand dinars from the father of the second man, and I allowed the son to recover his father's money, while the woodcutter had killed the rider's father, and I allowed the son to avenge his father.' The prophet said: 'There is no god but You, Glory be to You, Who are the knower of secrets.'[4]

In this anecdote, the tension between the order of creation, which is believed to be just, and the perceived injustice that occurred through divine intervention has been resolved; an exceptional case. In ordinary situations that happen to human beings/Muslims this tension persists, so the struggle endures to (re-)establish a just order. From this perspective, theological efforts, debates and processes within Islam may be perceived as a constant reflection of the current status (amongst others those of legal nature) and the search for alternative solutions that are more just. Hereby, justice is not considered a true possibility in actual history, but an ideal that is to be pursued but never fully attained; hence Sharia law is characterised by an ongoing dynamic. Justice, then, becomes what Jacques Derrida called 'eternal' justice,[5] or, in the terminology of Rainer Forst, an inescapable desire and likewise unattainable ideal.[6]

---

4 *The Arabian Nights: Tales of 1001 Nights*, trans. Malcolm C. Lyons with Ursula Lyons, introduced and annotated by Robert Irwin, 3 vols. (London: Penguin Books, 2011), 2/353 (Night 478).

5 Derrida looks into the relation between law and justice and tries to carve out space for justice beyond law. He aims for a concept of justice that is of a general form and is not to be equated with law, but changes and expands it constantly by taking into account the specificities of the other (fellow human beings?). See Jacques Derrida, *Gesetzeskraft: Der 'mystische Grund der Autorität'* (Frankfurt am Main: Suhrkamp, 1991), 51.

6 Forst considers law-enforcement as the place in which justice remains attainable; he argues, however, that disruptions with the existing law are occurring constantly and thereby the law is expanded in the sense of a higher justice. See Rainer Forst, 'Die Ungerechtigkeit der Gerechtigkeit: Normative Dialektik nach Ibsen, Cavell und Adorno', in *Kritik der Rechtfertigungsverhält-*

The paradox that lies in affirming the existence of a just order and perceiving injustice within that same order triggered much discussion about the concept of justice in various Islamic disciplines.

II

By and large, within Islamic thought the concept of justice is discussed within three larger thematic areas: First, theology (e.g. freedom of will, divine justice); Secondly, theory of the state/social ethics (e.g. traits of the ruler, just internal order of the polity); Thirdly, law (e.g. traits of judges and witnesses, and since modern times also questions related to the economic system and equality between women and men, Muslim and non-Muslim citizens, etc.).

Already in the Quran we find the terms *ʿadl* and *qisṭ*. They are not used in a terminological, but in a rather unspecific way in the sense of justice: 'He is maintaining [creation] in justice' (Q. 3:18); 'Indeed, Allah commands you [...] that when you judge between people to judge with justice' (Q. 4:58); 'Indeed, Allah loves those who act justly' (Q. 49:9). Altogether, the Quran takes a definite stance in favour of justice, but does not elaborate on what this means in practice.[7] It is precisely this clear stance on justice, however, that has shaped the discussions on the concept of justice up until our days and has led to general agreement on the importance of maintaining justice – despite differences as to how this should be achieved.

The following may serve as a short introduction to the larger thematic areas, in which the term justice is discussed:

A) Theology: Regarding the issue of *qadar* (i.e. the question whether human acts are subject to God's determination or based on free choice), the proponents of free will advocated their position by referring to the fact that God is just (*ʿadl*, *ʿādil*). They found it unimaginable that a just God would punishes men for acts they are predetermined to do.[8]

---

nisse: Perspektiven einer kritischen Theorie der Politik, ed. Rainer Forst (Berlin: Suhrkamp, 2011), 193.

7 On the issue of justice in the Quran see Daud Rahbar, *God of Justice: A Study in Ethical Doctrine of the Qurʾan* (Leiden: Brill, 1960); Nasr Hamid Abu Zayd, 'Der Begriff "Gerechtigkeit" nach dem Koran', accessed August 1, 2017, https://them.polylog.org/3/fan-de.htm; Abdoldjavad Falaturi, 'Gerechtigkeit im Islam', accessed August 1, 2017, http://www.ahlebeyt.ch/de/index.php/bibliothek/122-gerechtigkeit-im-islam.

8 See van Ess, *Theologie und Gesellschaft im 2. und 3. Jahrhundert Hidschra*, 1/199–200 and 2/250.

Nowhere does the Quran use the term *ʿadl* nor the term *qisṭ* or any of their possible variations as a designation of God. The Quranic advocacy of justice is, however, is so strong that the predicate *muqsiṭ* and the noun *ʿadl* in the sense of 'the Just' are included into the post-Quranic list of the 99 most beautiful names of God.

A further aspect of theological reflection on the concept of justice concerned the issue of theodicy, i.e. the question why a just God allows evil and suffering to exist in the world. Muslim scholars have proposed various answers, of which that of the Ashʿarites is the most common. According to them, natural events and the depth of God's wisdom are fathomless.[9]

B) Theory of state and social ethics: Beside the theological questions, which were unarguably interconnected with political issues, it was most often the socio-political dimension of justice that the people were preoccupied with. Van Ess notices that the term *ʿadl* is found in early Islamic texts most often as a reference to justice in the sense of a this-worldly social order. When opposition groups like the Kharijites, the Shiites, and also the Muʿtazilites called for justice, they did so, according to van Ess, in order to express their disapproval of the political authorities. Even the concept of the *mahdī*, an eschatological figure who will fill the world with justice, is to be understood within this wider context.[10] Most publications of the modern era discuss the concept of justice in the sense of a this-worldly social postulate and only rarely as a divine attribute relevant to human salvation in the hereafter; as can be seen, for example, in the work of the famous theoretician of the Muslim Brotherhood Sayyid Quṭb (1906–1966) entitled *al-ʿAdāla al-ijtimāʿiyya fī-l-Islām* (social justice in Islam).

We notice a strong engagement with the political and social aspects of the concept of justice especially in the works on the theory of the state and of social theory, which constitute a specific literary genre (*adab*)[11] within the Islamic tradition. One of the most prominent and widely-read authors until today is Abū al-Ḥasan al-Māwardī (972–1058). Beside his work on the theory of the state, entitled

---

9 See Birgit Krawietz, 'Gerechtigkeit als Leitidee islamischen Rechts', in *Islam und Rechtsstaat: Zwischen Scharia und Säkularisierung*, ed. Birgit Krawietz and Helmut Reifeld (Berlin: Konrad-Adenauer-Stiftung e.V., 2008), 41. For more on this issue see Eric Ormsby, *Theodicy in Islamic Thought: The Dispute over al-Ghazali's 'Best of All Possible Worlds'* (Princeton: Princeton University Press, 1984); Mehmet A. Aydin, 'Das Problem der Theodizee', in *Der aufgeklärte Islam. Aufkommen — Ideen — Niederschlag: Das Paradigma Said Nursi*, ed. Cäcilia Schmitt (Stuttgart: Basis-Verlag, 2007).

10 See van Ess, *Theologie und Gesellschaft im 2. und 3. Jahrhundert Hidschra*, 4/507–508.

11 For a thoroughgoing analysis of the term *adab* see: Hartmut Fähndrich, 'Der Begriff "adab" und sein literarischer Niederschlag', in *Neues Handbuch der Literaturwissenschaft, vol. 5: Orientalisches Mittelalter*, ed. Wolfhart Heinrichs (Wiesbaden: Aula, 1990).

al-Aḥkām al-sulṭāniyya (The rules of rulership), he also authored a book on social ethics, called *Adab al-dunyā wa al-dīn* (Codes of conduct in this world and in religion). In both of these works he discusses the concept of justice but more especially in the latter one he develops a concept a 'universal justice' (*al-ʿadl al-shāmil*), which will be discussed in one of the contributions to the volume at hand.

C) Legal doctrine: With regard to Islamic law, Birgit Krawietz states 'that debates on justice became more frequent in the Islamic modernity than in the preceding centuries.'[12] She is correct when it comes to the question of where to localise the usage of the concept of justice within Islamic law. Traditionally, the term justice in Islamic law appears in the context of the discussion of certain professions, such as jurists, judges, medical doctors and prayer-leaders, who are expected to adhere to high standards of justice. Witnesses, who carry out important and responsible duties at that time, are expecially commanded to act justly. In modern times, in contrast, the term justice appears in many different contexts, be they of a social, economic, or political nature as well as regarding criminal law and civil rights.[13] In the case where one takes the discussion to be about the basic attitude, in the sense of a fundamentally justice-oriented law system, one will find instruments in legal theory that may support such an orientation. Among the most important of these instruments are, for example, the principle of public welfare (*maṣlaḥa*) and juristic preference (*istiḥsān*),[14] whereby the general public interest, customs and habits amounts to a point of reference in the law-making process. The famous Ḥanbali jurist Ibn Qayyim al-Jawziyya (1292–1350) made it very clear that whoever ignores the habits and customs of the community while issuing legal judgements is misled and leads astray.[15] Legal instruments just as *al-ṭāʿa bi-ḥasab al-ṭāqa* (performance of obligations being conditional upon capability / reasonability) and *lā-ḍarar wa-lā-ḍirār* (no harm being inflicted or reciprocated) facilitate the adaption of Islamic law to changing needs and in a changing environment. In line with the former principle, the ill or infirm, for example, may be relieved from certain religious obligations.[16] The latter principle serves, for example, to combat fraudulent activities in sales or rental agreements.[17] It is this basic orientation of Sharia that ʿAbdul-

12 Krawietz, 'Gerechtigkeit als Leitidee islamischen Rechts', 37.

13 Ibid., 42–43.

14 Both terms are discussed by Wahba al-Zuhaylī, *Uṣūl al-fiqh al-islāmī*, 2 vols. (Dār al-fikr: Damascus, 1986), 2/735–827.

15 See ʿAbd al-Munʿim al-Nimr, *al-Ijtihād* (Cairo: Dār al-surūq, 1986), 70.

16 See Muḥammad Ṣidqī b. Aḥmad al-Būrnū al-Ghazzī, *Mawsūʿat al-qawāʿid al-fiqhiyya*, 13 vols. (Beirut: Muʿassasat al-risāla, 1997), 6/301–302.

17 See ibid., 6/256.

karīm Surūsh (b. 1945) has in mind when he argues that Sharia law follows justice and not the other way round.[18] Even before him, the jurist Murtaḍā Muṭahharī (1919–1979) considered justice as the touch-stone and reason for existence of Sharia.[19] The mechanisms to establish a just order are inherent to Sharia law; a fact that Krawietz also points at while discussing procedural justice in Islam: 'The properness of procedures prevail within the legal interpretation and application.' Furthermore, she notices regarding the 'written Islamic legal opinion, fatwa' that it is not an expression of arbitrariness or vigilantism, but of legitimizing procedures suitable for everyday life.[20]

Against this background, the reference to justice by many contemporary jurists is logically consistent. Being aware of this general orientation they try to react to new challenges by using some of the mechanisms that have been mentioned above. Taking the principle of justice as a point of departure, they are endeavouring to find answers that fit our times with regard to issues such as, for example, the application of corporal punishment, sex discrimination with respect to inheritance, or discrimination of citizens based on religious affiliation. Beyond that, issues of economics are also being rethought and reinterpreted in the same manner.[21]

III

The discussion about the relationship between Sharia and justice is also a discussion of how Islamic norms should be negotiated within Western secular states. To what extent might the state, which is obliged to respect its citizens and to interact with them justly, take Islamic norms into consideration? This general question is heatedly discussed within different thematic contexts, from polygamy, child marriage, education (shaking hands between sexes, swimming instruction for girls, etc.) up to the issue of halal meat (slaughter according to Islamic rites versus animal welfare legislation, and the availability of halal meat in school and staff canteens).

The issue of the veil is probably the most emblematic of all those issues debated within this context and the one which challenges the commandment of justice expressed in European constitutions. This is not the place to discuss

18 'Adulkarīm Surūsh, *Rūshanfikrī wa dīndārī* (Tehran: Mu'assasa-ye farhangi-ye ṣirāṭ, 1986), 47.
19 Cf. Murtaḍā Muṭahharī, *Barrasī-i iğmālī-i mabānī-i iqtiṣād-i islāmī*, (Qom: Intishārāt-i ḥikmat, 1990), 14.
20 Cf. Krawietz, 'Gerechtigkeit als Leitidee islamischen Rechts', 43.
21 See ibid., 44–47.

the question of whether wearing a veil constitutes a religious obligation or not, even if many Muslim women believe this to be the case. This poses the valid question of treating veiled women differently from others within the working world, for example in the professional world of teaching, medicine or the non-professional world of train conductor or factory worker.

According to the latest legal ruling of the European Court of Justice (ECJ) dating to March 2017 – given as a joint judgment in the cases of two women in France and Belgium – a ban on staff wearing veils is legal on condition that it is part of the company's general policy barring all religious symbols.[22] This ruling shows how difficult it is for the judges to keep the balance between justice as a universal principle and current legislation; therefore, it is worthwhile having a closer look at the two cases.

In the Belgian case, the judges decided in favour of the plaintiff, Samira Achbita. She had worked as a receptionist in a Belgian security company for three years. In April 2006, she informed her employer to intend to wear the veil not only in free-time but also at work. She was told that she could not do so because this violated the company's rule requiring philosophical and religious neutrality in their employees' attire. Achbita was dismissed and provided with severance pay; she however took the matter to the court.

The ECJ confirmed the general legality of the company's internal policy. According to the judges, it does not constitute direct discrimination due to religion or ideology, which is prohibited by an EU Directive that aims at establishing a general framework for *equal treatment in employment* and occupation. The court stressed in its reasoning that '[a]n employer's wish to project an image of neutrality towards customers relates to the freedom to conduct a business [...] is, in principle, legitimate, notably where the employer involves in its pursuit of that aim only those workers who are required to come into contact with the employer's customers.'[23] However, the rule must be applied systematically to all employees regardless of religion or world view.

Furthermore, the Belgian courts have to check, whether the employer could have assigned to Samira A. a post not involving any visual contact with customers rather than dismissing her. In both cases, it is now on the national courts to issue final rulings on the grounds of the decision of the ECJ.

The second case is somewhat different: Asma Bougnaoui worked as a design engineer for a French company from 2007. Less than a year later, she was dis-

22 The press release of the EJC provides more details: http://curia.europa.eu/jcms/upload/docs/application/pdf/2017-03/cp170030de.pdf.
23 Case C-157/15 *Achbita* v. G4 S, para. 38.

missed. This happened due to her refusal of the company's request for her to take off her veil, after a client from Toulouse complained about it. Bougnaoui then sued her employer for discrimination. The will to comply with the special wishes of customers does not provide sufficient ground for banning the veil. Such a ban has to be based on an internal policy that prohibits wearing any visible signs of one's political, philosophical or religious beliefs. Whether this policy was in place is not clear. In case it was not, such a ban could only be dictated by the nature of the Bougnaoui's work itself that requires it to be carried out by workers who do not wear the veil. The ECJ sent this question on to the French courts for further investigation.[24]

The above-mentioned case regarding legal disputes on the issue of wearing the veil at work shows on the one hand that wearing the veil is considered to have a political connotation rather than being merely a religious act like praying or fasting. Even though the legal ruling of the ECJ does not address this political aspect explicitly, the political signal sent by the veil to the public is indeed part of the legal decision. On the other hand, the case illustrates how complex the embellishment of the relationship between justice and legal system may be in secular contexts.

IV

Any anthology including the one at hand has to limit its view on certain aspects of the ambivalent relationship between sharia and justice that have been outlined above. In the first article that has an introductory character, Mathias Rohe starts from the assumption that law in general constitutes an important, if not the most important instrument for maintaining justice, and that this is true also regarding the Islamic Culture. Rohe confirms that theoretical elaborations on the principle of justice are rare in Islamic thought; the study of case-by-case decisions does, however, reveal the general dynamic within Islamic Law for maintaining justice. By giving examples from the economic, political and social realm, Rohe shows how Islamic legal systems are subject to the contingencies of the times and their changing circumstances. He identifies this as the intrinsic potential of sharia to be adapted to the changing mandates of justice; and he illustrates this by elaborating on the relationship between the sexes. Rohe also addresses a further aspect of the debate, which is the question of the just treatment of Muslim citizens by secular states. With reference to some pre-

24 For further details see note 22 above.

modern and modern authors he states that in Islam justice is the decisive factor for legitimizing political rule. Hence, Rohe concludes: 'On the basis of this maxim, Islam and a secular constitutional state can be convincingly reconciled in an overlapping search for justice.'

In his contribution 'Ordinary Justice: A Theology of Islamic Law as a Social Contract', Rumee Ahmad moves in the opposite direction by stating that there is a long history of jurists who held that Islamic law was not a just moral code at all, and that following it does not lead to salvation. Laws in this conception, are neither just nor unjust; rather, they are only relatively just and based on the spiritual state of the practitioner. Ahmad discusses in his paper one such group of scholars, the early Ḥanafi school of Islamic law, which promoted a notion of Islamic legal justice that is different from those to which we are used. For these Muslim jurists, Islamic law did not have a metaphysical component, and though early Ḥanafis thought laws to be important, they did not think them central to salvation. Importantly, while early Ḥanafis believed that individual laws might be more or less just depending on circumstances, they did not believe that justice itself was to be found in laws. Thus, neither following the laws slavishly nor adapting them to changing mores would result in justice in this world nor felicity in the life hereafter. Understanding how and why will require closer study, and will give us new insights into how broadly justice can be conceived with respect to Islamic law. For such Ḥanafis it does not make sense to ask whether Islamic law is inherently just or unjust, because justice is itself an unattainable and incomprehensible concept that can only be understood and enacted by God. Believers are not tasked with establishing justice on Earth, nor are they capable of doing so. The early Ḥanafis were abundantly clear about this, and their writings left little ambiguity on the subject. Yet, modern scholarship is slow to accept their claims at face value, most probably because they challenge popular, modern notions about 'true' Islam and Muslims, and about the uniquely spiritual nature of Islamic law. A reconsideration of early Ḥanafi legal thought seriously opens up the discussion around Islam and justice, and brings us closer to the simple notion that Islamic legal justice might mean different things to the many different Muslims around the world.

Abbas Poya focuses in his article on the concept of justice in the classical period of Islam. Taking the example of Abū al-Ḥasan al-Māwardī (972–1058), he tries to show how the Muslim scholars' understanding of justice developed from being merely an attribute of God to being a social ethical concept. Al-Māwardī, a respected and acknowledged jurist, judge and diplomat considered justice to be a profane issue and argued for this in a rational or pragmatic manner. According to him, justice is necessary to the functioning of a society. In a first step, he distinguishes three axes of social relations: 1) the relationship between those who are ranked above to those who are below and 2) vice versa, and 3) and the relationship of those who are equally ranked. Interaction on all of these axes has to be just, otherwise all will be harmed regardless of their hierarchical position. Hence, al-Māwardī does not consider justice to be fully attainable, but to be an ongoing process.

In his article, which has already been published in German, Werner Ende discusses justice as a political organising principle in Islam. He bases his study on the 'fact' that there are notions of justice in Islam and that they played a crucial role from the very beginning within the thought of many Muslims. Ende dates the rise of debates on justice to not later than the death of the prophet Muhammad (d. 632), when different parties argued against each other about the conditions and, among other thing, the justice of the successor of the prophet. Even though many Muslims do not consider the further historical development as a triumphal procession of law and justice, their notions of rule and political order are nevertheless informed by their desire for just relationships. The claim that political leaders have to be just is not only to be found in legal works of religious scholars, but specific literary genres developed, in which the rights and obligations of rulers are laid down. After discussing some historical and legal examples, Ende confirms the assumption held by many Muslims that Islam strives for justice in actual fact and that Muslims have so far not or not fully been able to accomplish this goal. According to Ende, this assumption has led to antagonistic attitudes: one is pessimistic and passive, the other is politically rebellious and active.

The contribution 'Justice and Equality and Muslim Family Laws: New Ideas, New Prospects' is a reprint generously granted by its author Ziba Mir-Hosseini. In this article, she explores the question of how the idea of justice, which is indeed present in Islamic legal theory, goes against the gender inequality embedded in Islamic legal norms. Following up on this, she asks how the idea of justice may open up possibilities for reforming these Islamic legal norms. With reference to two statements of the great Ḥanbali scholar Ibn Qayyim al-Jawziyya (d. 1350) she shows that the avowal of a scholar to justice as a yardstick by which to measure Islamic norms, does not necessarily that he equates men and women in the modern sense. While Ibn Qayyim states at one point that 'any rule that departs from justice to injustice [...] cannot be part of Sharia', he nevertheless also states that 'the wife is her husband's prisoner, a prisoner being akin to a slave'.[25] A modern understanding of justice helps contemporary authors to rethink legal norms to

---

25 Quoted in Ziba Mir-Hosseini: *Justice and Equality and Muslim Family Laws: New Ideas, New Prospects*, in: this volume, 1.

promote gender equality. She makes this change of views apparent on the basis of two treatises: 'Women in the Shari'a and in Our Society' (1930) by the Tunisian religious reform thinker Tahir Haddad (d. 1935), and the 'The Status of Women in Islam: A Modernist Interpretation' (1982) by the Pakistani reform thinker Fazlur Rahman (1919 – 1988). The 'two reform texts [...] negotiate and bridge the chasm, the dissonance, between contemporary notions of justice and gender rights and those informed by classical fiqh rulings and lay the groundwork for an egalitarian family law.'[26]

In his second article, entitled '*Jihād* and Just War Theory: A Conceptual Analysis', Abbas Poya engages with the question whether, and if so to what extent, the Arabic Islamic concept of *jihād* might be understood in the sense of just war. On the one hand, the author identifies a conceptual contradiction between the act of war and just acts; as war, according to him, cannot be but unjust provided that justice is understood as a universal and cosmopolitan concept. On the other hand, the issue of 'just wars' has been part of legal, ethical and philosophical debates ever since the inception of Islam. The article provides a concise elaboration on the term *jihād* in Arabic and in classical and modern Islamic literature and arrives at the following conclusions: The concept of *jihād* as understood in Islamic law has a combative dimension. While often interpreted as defensive especially in modern times, there are many scholars who regarded *jihād* as offensive warfare. In view of the current international law, such an understanding is, however, irresponsible and untenable. Only if *jihād* is understood as a defensive act against aggression, will it be able to contribute – due to its rich theoretical tradition – to today's heatedly debated issue of 'just war'.

The final contribution to the anthology at hand takes a look at the question of how a secular state acts towards Islamic legal norms that are deemed to be acceptable. With reference to the discussions on the veil, Bernd Ladwig shows how complex the answer to this question is. In so doing, Ladwig addresses the normative solution to the problem of the veil especially within the German context. On the whole, Ladwig sums up three different answers that might be given to the question of whether a teacher should be allowed to wear the veil in school. One group holds the opinion that the principle of neutrality of the state would not preclude allowing a teacher to wear the veil, as it is just like the nun's habit and the cross. However, as the wearing of the veil is incompatible with 'Christian and occidental educational and cultural values' it should nevertheless be banned and this response also argues for a general ban on all religious signs in schools except during religious classes. The third and final answer

26 Ibid, 2.

pleads for general permission for teachers to wear the veil during all classes. In the author's view, justice as a normative basis subscribes to the third view and hence he argues that a teacher should be allowed to wear the veil in school.

Bibliography

Abu Zayd, Nasr Hamid. 'Der Begriff "Gerechtigkeit" nach dem Koran'. Accessed August 1, 2017. https://them.polylog.org/3/fan-de.htm.

Aydin, Mehmet A. 'Das Problem der Theodizee'. In *Der aufgeklärte Islam. Aufkommen — Ideen — Niederschlag: Das Paradigma Said Nursi*. Edited by Cäcilia Schmitt, 285–301. Stuttgart: Basis-Verlag, 2007.

Būrnū al-Ghazzī, Muḥammad Ṣidqī b. Aḥmad al-. *Mawsūʿat al-qawāʿid al-fiqhiyya*. 13 vols. Beirut: Muʿassasat al-risāla, 1997.

Derrida, Jacques. *Gesetzeskraft: Der 'mystische Grund der Autorität'*. Frankfurt am Main: Suhrkamp, 1991.

Ess, Josef van. *Theologie und Gesellschaft im 2. und 3. Jahrhundert Hidschra: Eine Geschichte des religiösen Denkens im frühen Islam*. 6 vols. Berlin: De Gruyter, 1991.

Fähndrich, Hartmut. 'Der Begriff "adab" und sein literarischer Niederschlag'. In *Neues Handbuch der Literaturwissenschaft, vol. 5: Orientalisches Mittelalter*. Edited by Wolfhart Heinrichs, 326–45. Wiesbaden: Aula, 1990.

Falaturi, Abdoldjavad. 'Gerechtigkeit im Islam'. Accessed August 1, 2017. http://www.ahlebeyt.ch/de/index.php/bibliothek/122-gerechtigkeit-im-islam.

Forst, Rainer. 'Die Ungerechtigkeit der Gerechtigkeit: Normative Dialektik nach Ibsen, Cavell und Adorno'. In *Kritik der Rechtsfertigungsverhältnisse: Perspektiven einer kritischen Theorie der Politik*. Edited by Rainer Forst, 181–95. Berlin: Suhrkamp, 2011.

Krawietz, Birgit. 'Gerechtigkeit als Leitidee islamischen Rechts'. In *Islam und Rechtsstaat: Zwischen Scharia und Säkularisierung*. Edited by Birgit Krawietz and Helmut Reifeld, 37–52. Berlin: Konrad-Adenauer-Stiftung e.V., 2008.

Lamdī, Aḥmad Shuʿayb. *Maqṣad al-ʿadl ʿinda Ibn Taymiyya: Al-ʿadl al-dīnī wa al-dunyawī fī l-naṣṣ wa l-wāqiʿ*. Beirut, Cairo, Riyadh: al-Shabaka al-ʿarabiyya li-l-abḥāth wa an-nashr, 2014.

Muṭahharī, Murtaḍā. *Barrasī-i ijmālī-i mabānī-i iqtiṣād-i islāmī*, Qom: Intishārāt-i ḥikmat, 1990.

Nimr, ʿAbd al-Munʿim al-. *al-Ijtihād*. Cairo: Dār al-shurūq, 1986.

Ormsby, Eric. *Theodicy in Islamic Thought: The Dispute over al-Ghazali's 'Best of All Possible Worlds'*. Princeton: Princeton University Press, 1984.

Rahbar, Daud. *God of Justice: A Study in Ethical Doctrine of the Qurʾan*. Leiden: Brill, 1960.

Surūsh, ʿAbdulkarīm. *Rūshanfikrī wa dīndārī*. Tehran: Muʾassasa-i farhangī-i ṣirāṭ, 1986.

The Arabian Nights: Tales of 1001 Nights. Translated by Malcolm C. Lyons with Ursula Lyons, introduced and annotated by Robert Irwin. 3 vols. London: Penguin Books, 2011.

Zuhaylī, Wahba al-. *Uṣūl al-fiqh al-islāmī*. 2 vols. Dār al-fikr: Damascus, 1986.

Rumee Ahmed

Ordinary Justice: A Theology of Islamic Law as a Social Contract

'Justice' is an incredibly difficult word to define, not least because the term means different things to different people. One person's justice might be another's oppression, and justice seems to shift meaning whenever one either gains or loses power. This is now a widely accepted truth, and political philosophers have busied themselves not so much with the question of whether there are multiple conceptions of justice, but with what informs those different conceptions.[1]

We should therefore expect that diverse Muslim groups throughout history defined justice in multiple ways. This is no doubt true, and yet Islamic legal justice is regularly depicted – both in popular rhetoric and in scholarship on the subject – as working in only one of two ways. The first has to do with submission, and according to this presumption Islamic justice is achieved only when Muslims submit to an ancient law developed by elite, male scholars. The ancient law that they promulgated contains an exclusive standard of justice, making all other systems of law illegitimate and, by definition, unjust. In this framework, Muslims work toward justice when they follow the law as outlined by pious Muslim predecessors, and they work toward injustice when they either disobey or misinterpret it.[2]

The second way that Islamic legal justice is presumed to work has to do with critique. In this presumption, 'justice' is a Divine measuring stick according to which Islamic laws are judged. God, in this way of thinking, is just and demands

1 Drucilla Cornell, *At the Heart of Freedom: Feminism, Sex, and Equality* (Princeton: Princeton University Press, 1998); Alasdair MacIntyre, *Whose Justice? Which Rationality* (Notre Dame, IN: University of Notre Dame Press, 1988); John Rawls, *A Theory of Justice* (Cambridge, MA: Harvard University Press, 1998); Amrtya Sen, *The Idea of Justice* (Cambridge, MA: Harvard University Press, 2009); and many, many more.

2 See for example, M. Cherif Bassiouni, *The Shariʿa and Islamic Criminal Justice in Time of War and Peace* (Cambridge: Cambridge University Press, 2014); Harry Dammer and Jay Albanese, *Comparative Criminal Justice Systems* (Belmont, CA: Wadsworth, 2014), 58–62; Hisham Ramadan, ed., *Understanding Islamic Law: From Classical to Contemporary* (Lanham, MD: AltaMira, 2006); Joseph Schacht, 'Law and Justice in Islam', in *The Cambridge History of Islam, volume 2B: Islamic Society and Civilization*, ed. P. M. Hold, Ann Lambton and Bernard Lewis (Cambridge: Cambridge University Press, 2008).

The author would like to thank the Stanford Humanities Center for the time and resources to complete this article, and Dr. Ayesha S. Chaudhry for her invaluable feedback.

https://doi.org/10.1515/9783110574593-002

justice, and Islamic law is simply a way of realizing that justice on Earth. Thus, Islamic law is only legitimate when it serves the cause of justice, and it is illegitimate when it subverts justice. Historical Islamic laws are therefore always subject to critique, and when they no longer function in a way that leads to a just society, they should be considered un-Islamic and replaced with new, more just laws.[3] Justice, in this second conception, determines what is or is not Islamic law, not the other way around.

In the first way of thinking about Islamic justice, having to do with submission, Islamic laws are historical artifacts that are inherently just, and they are presumed to remain just in perpetuity. In the second way of thinking about Islamic justice, having to do with critique, Islamic laws are only Islamic insofar as they are able to provide justice. Though they may appear to be polar opposites, these two modern conceptions of Islamic justice are in fact flip sides of the same coin, both fraught with Orientalist tropes, both relying on two fundamental, unproved assumptions about Islamic law.

The first assumption is that Islamic law is supposed to manifest and represent Divine justice on Earth. The law, whether comprised of static historical legal opinions or principles that provide critique, is always presumed to reflect the divine; thus, following the law and/or its principles will lead individuals and society to godliness. The second assumption is that Islamic law is primarily metaphysical. That is, it is assumed that following Islamic law will bring metaphysical benefits, especially salvation and God's favour. This casts Islamic law as primarily salvific, operating on a different level than, say, Danish law or Canadian law.

The reader might think that these two assumptions are fair and should be given; that Islamic law necessarily has a metaphysical element in a way that Danish and Canadian law do not, and as such represents the divine on Earth. This, many believe, is simply how religions and religious laws work. Religion is often thought to be a highly theological enterprise, and religious activity is thought to always be a statement about God. God presumably sent religion as a moral code, and following this moral code will place people upon justice. Whether that code is found in historical laws or in a standard of critique, the law is always presumed to lead to Divine Justice. Therefore, all religious activity must be conducted according to religious laws if justice is to be served in this world and the next. In this way of thinking, obeying religious laws will lead

3 See for example, Majid Khadduri, *The Islamic Conception of Justice* (Baltimore: The Johns Hopkins University Press, 1984); Christina Jones-Pauly, *Women Under Islam: Justice and the Politics of Islamic Law* (London: I.B. Tauris, 2011); Farhad Malekian, *Principles of Islamic International Criminal Law: A Comparative Search* (Leiden: Brill, 2011); Ahmed Souaiaia, *Contesting Justice: Women, Islam, Law, and Society* (Albany: SUNY Press, 2008).

to justice in this life and felicity in the next, and ignoring the law will lead to perdition in this life and damnation in the next.

This is the way that religious laws tend to be presented, and that is doubly true with respect to Muslims and Islamic law. Muslims are presumed to hold Islamic law to be of great importance, and to demand that Islamic law be established in all areas of life. One way of obeying that law would be to slavishly adhere to its contents. Another way would be to critique historical laws based on rigorous religious principles and adapt them to changing circumstances. Either way, Muslims are thought to be obsessed with the law as key to worldly justice and otherworldly salvation, with some scholars of Islam going so far as to say that Islamic law is 'the very corn and kernel of Islam itself.'[4]

While this is one way to conceive of Islam, Islamic law, justice, and Muslim practice, it is certainly not the only way, or even the most popular one. Muslims throughout history have had many and varied conceptions of Islamic law's role in the world, its relationship to justice, and its importance to religious practice.[5] For some Muslims, law is an integral part of religion; for others it is entirely unnecessary. Some Muslims see their religion as merely an identity-marker, whereas for others religion informs everything that they do. Some Muslims have a tenuous relationship with law yet consider themselves good Muslims; other Muslims try to follow the law to the letter yet consider themselves bad Muslims. There are wide varieties of Muslim religious experiences and conceptions of Islamic law, and taking each of them seriously will challenge the way we think about Islamic legal justice.

Given the diversity of Muslim religious experiences, it should be no surprise that Muslim scholars throughout history put forward many different ideas about Islamic law's relationship to justice. Some argued that, indeed, Islamic legal justice is found either in submission or critique, but there is a large and illustrious history of Muslim legal thought that cannot be reduced to either of those two approaches to law. There is, for example, a long line of Sufi saints who held that

---

4 Joseph Schacht, *Islam* (Oxford: Oxford University Press, 1974), 392. See also Gotthelf Bergsträsser, *Grundzüge des islamischen Rechts* (Leipzig: De Gruyter, 1935), 1.

5 See for instance Iza Hussin, *The Politics of Islamic Law: Local Elites, Colonial Authority, and the Making of the Muslim State* (Chicago: University of Chicago Press, 2016), 7 ff; Scott Kugle, 'Framed, Blamed and Renamed: The Recasting of Islamic Jurisprudence in Colonial South Asia', *Modern Asian Studies* 35, no. 2 (2001); Judith Tucker, *In the House of the Law: Gender and Islamic Law in Ottoman Syria and Palestine* (Berkeley: University of California Press, 1998), 181 ff. To see how recent scholarship has re-conceived Muslim relationships to law, see Rumee Ahmed, 'Theology and Islamic Law', in *The Oxford Handbook of Islamic Law*, ed. A. Emon and R. Ahmed (Oxford: Oxford University Press, 2017).

laws could provide justice, but only up to a limit. After that limit, laws are no longer helpful, and a deeper knowledge must guide a learned person, or else laws will result in injustice.[6] Laws themselves, in this conception, are neither just nor unjust; rather, they are only relatively just based on the spiritual state of the practitioner, and thus are always suspect and only partially helpful in achieving both worldly justice and salvation.

This kind of nuanced relationship to law and justice is not confined to Sufis or mystical practice. There is a long history of non-Sufi jurists who held that the law is not a just moral code at all, and that following Islamic law does not lead to salvation. In this paper, I will discuss one such group of scholars, the early Ḥanafī school of Islamic law, which promoted a notion of Islamic legal justice that is different from the ones to which we are used. For these Muslim jurists, Islamic law does not have a metaphysical component, and though early Ḥanafīs thought laws to be important, they did not think them central to salvation. Importantly, while early Ḥanafīs believed that individual laws might be more or less just depending on circumstance, they did not believe that justice itself was to be found in laws. Thus, neither following the laws slavishly nor adapting them to changing mores would result in justice in this world nor felicity in the life hereafter. Understanding how and why will require closer study, and will give us new insights into how broadly justice can be conceived with respect to Islamic law.

Early Ḥanafīs

Formed in the 8th century, the Ḥanafi school quickly became the largest legal school in terms of adherents, and it remains so to this day. The Ḥanafī school boasted a pantheon of famously diverse scholars, and though some early Ḥanafīs believed that law was of the utmost importance, most thought that laws did not embody justice and morality, and had little or nothing to do with salvation. These Ḥanafī scholars nevertheless deeply revered law as an avenue of study and as a social good.

In the 10th century, the Ḥanafī school developed rival factions with major offshoots promoting different conceptions of law.[7] Up until that point, though, Ḥanafīs were largely agreed about the role of law in Islamic piety and daily practice. Their beliefs are thought to have stemmed directly from the patriarch of

6 For example, see Jalāl al-Dīn Rūmī, *The Mathnawi* (Cambridge: E.J.W. Gibb Memorial, 1990), ed. and trans. Reynold Nicholson, Introduction to Book 5, 3.

7 Rumee Ahmed, 'The Ethics of Prophetic Disobedience: Qur'an 8:67 at the Crossroads of the Islamic Sciences', *Journal of Religious Ethics* 39, no. 3 (2011), 449 ff.

the Ḥanafī school, Abū Ḥanīfa (d. 150/767). His ideas are captured in a couple of treatises likely written by his own hand,[8] but most of his thoughts reach us by way of his students and admirers. Giants of the early Ḥanafī school, like Muhammad al-Shaybānī (d. 189/805), Abū Muṭīʿ al-Balkhī (d. 199/814), Abū Manṣūr al-Māturīdī (d. 333/944), and Abū al-Layth al-Samarqandī (d. 373/983) provide us with a clear and uniform idea of Abū Ḥanīfa's thinking. The sense they give is that, for Abū Ḥanīfa and the early Ḥanafīs, law was considered tremendously important to personal practice and social success, yet largely separate from justice and salvation.

This early Ḥanafī conception of law was itself embedded in a sophisticated theology. By examining this theological system, we will be able to understand the place of law amongst early Ḥanafīs, and its relation to justice and salvation. There are three main theological issues that we will need to examine to fully appreciate the Ḥanafī approach to law, and they are: 1) God's rationality; 2) God's speech; and 3) the relationship between faith and actions. We will examine each, and together they will give us an idea of just how different the early Ḥanafī conception of Islamic legal justice was from the currently dominant presumptions about Islamic law recounted above.

God's Rationality

The cornerstone of early Ḥanafi legal theory, crucial for understanding their conception of justice, is that there exists a radical disconnect between the mind of God and the minds of humans. Early Ḥanafīs believed that God is privy to algorithms that humans cannot possibly understand, and thus humans can never comprehend God's wisdom. God, for example, can understand paradox, or make exceptions to the law of the excluded middle, whereas humans cannot. In God's mind, something might be existent and non-existent at the same time; God can comprehend timelessness and infinity; God can allow for freewill and pre-destination at the same time. These are ideas that humans can never hope to grasp.

In the face of this insurmountable handicap, humans are left to simply trust that God acts according to some divine wisdom, and must accept that they will never understand it. This is central to the early Ḥanafī notion of divine justice, because the incomprehensible nature of divine wisdom means that humans

8 Ulrich Rudolph, *al-Māturīdī and Development of Sunnī Theology in Samarqand* (Leiden: Brill, 2015), 28–30, 42–44.

are forever denied knowing the reasons behind God's actions.[9] Any attempt to understand why God acts one way or another, early Ḥanafīs believed, is an exercise in futility.

Ḥanafīs reasoned that humans should not try to figure out the divine wisdom behind God's actions, and that they are not expected to do so, since God does not task humans with what is beyond their ability, as per Q. 2:286. Humans should leave off wondering why, for instance, God created the universe, or sent down laws for people to follow.[10] In the Ḥanafī conception, humans can never really know the answers to these questions. Since they cannot know God's reasoning, and are not tasked with doing what is beyond their ability, humans must simply *believe* that God acts according to some divine wisdom and according to some divine standard of justice that transcends human reason.[11] For whatever reason God created the universe, humans should believe that it was done with justice.[12] They will never understand that justice, but can trust that it is there.

The Ḥanafī approach to divine justice runs counter to some popular ideas about the enchantedness of the world in Islamic thought. Many now argue that God acts and creates according to a beautiful, discernible logic, and that understanding that logic leads to enlightenment and salvation. With respect to creation, for instance, contemporary Muslims and non-Muslims alike are quick to provide definitive reasons for God's creative action, like that God created the universe to test human beings, or to be known, or to be worshipped.[13] Indeed, Q. 51:56 states, 'I did not create *jinns* and humans except that they worship me.' That sounds like a clear reason for why God created the universe: so that God would be worshipped. The early Ḥanafīs, however, read this verse quite differently, and maintained that God's rationale for creating the world is unknowable.

Early Ḥanafīs argued that Q. 51:56 should be read as God passively narrating the process of creation, rather than providing a rationale for creation itself. That is, the verse should, in their opinion, be read, 'I created [humans and *jinns*]

---

9 Abū Muṭīʿ al-Balkhī, 'al-Fiqh al-absaṭ', in *al-ʿAqīda wa ʿilm al-kalām*, ed. M. Zāhid al-Kawtharī (Beirut: Dār al-kutub al-ʿilmiyya, 2004), 610–612.

10 Felicitas Opwis, *Maṣlaḥa and the Purposes of the Law: Islamic Legal Discourse on Legal Change from the 4th/10th to 8th/14th Century* (Leiden: Brill, 2010), 41.

11 Abū Muṭīʿ al-Balkhī, 'al-Fiqh al-absaṭ', 613.

12 Abū Manṣūr al-Māturīdī, *Kitāb al-Tawḥīd* (Beirut: Dār Ṣādir, 2010), 164–165.

13 See for example Karen Armstrong, *A History of God: The 4,000 Year Quest of Judaism, Christianity and Islam* (New York: Ballantine, 1993), 182; Fethullah Gülen, *Essentials of the Islamic Faith* (Somerset, NJ: The Light, 2006), 111; Harun Yahya, *The Creation of the Universe* (Toronto: Al-Attique, 2000), 171–72.

knowing that I would command them to worship me and acknowledge the unity of my being.'[14] In that reading, humans have no idea why they were created, just that God knew, at the moment of creation, that humans would be commanded to worship God and accept monotheism. The reason behind God's act of creation itself is unknowable and irrelevant.

If God's actions are beyond any human rationality, then they are also above any human ideas about justice and fairness. If God wishes to create a seemingly evil action, or send a decent person to hell, that is God's prerogative, and that action will certainly be just, even if humans do not understand how. God's actions, therefore, define justice, and humans are not expected to understand how, but only to acknowledge that God's actions are, indeed, just. This early Ḥanafī belief is not, on its own, that controversial. Many Muslims believe that God's conception of justice is beyond human rationality. Many also add that humans must therefore adhere to revealed laws, whether they understand them or not. Some argue that just as one cannot fully understand how God's actions are just, one also cannot understand how God's revelation and laws are just. In that way of thinking, believers must have faith that the laws contained in the Quran are just, and they must enact them whether the laws make sense or not. Early Ḥanafīs, however, did not follow that line of reasoning. They had a more complex understanding of revelation, which made it difficult to say that God's justice can be found in adhering to the injunctions found therein.

God's Speech

Muslims have had many furious debates about the nature of God's Speech and its relation to the Quran, including a famous one about whether the Quran is the created or uncreated Speech of God. That debate is subtle and has far-reaching consequences, but there is one, distinctly Ḥanafī take on the issue that I will focus on here. For Ḥanafīs, the Quran is indeed the uncreated Speech of God, meaning that it exists beyond time and space, and beyond everything created and contingent. The Quran was uncreated when time began, uncreated when it was revealed to Muhammad, and it is uncreated whenever humans recite it with their mouths. But Ḥanafīs insisted that the uncreated Quran does not 'inhere' in any physical form, and that the act of reciting the uncreated Quran is

---

14 Abū al-Layth al-Samarqandī, *Tafsīr al-Samarqandī* (Beirut: Dār al-kutub al-ʿilmiyya, 1993), 3:280; see also Abū Manṣūr al-Māturīdī, *Sharḥ al-Fiqh al-akbar* (Beirut: al-Maktaba al-ʿaṣriyya, 1983), 10 – 11.

disconnected from the individual words and sounds that are being recited. The uncreated Speech of God, they said, is found in the act of recitation, but not in the words that comprise recitation. The actual words that are recited are themselves based on the Arabic language, and languages are created. So, once the Quran is recited and an audience hears it in the Arabic language, it is no longer the uncreated Speech of God.[15]

Thus, when the Quran is read by eyes and heard by ears it is only an earthly reflection of that uncreated Speech of God.[16] When humans try to understand the uncreated Speech of God through their human language, they necessarily have to use their limited human brains to decipher that Speech. Once they do so, they immediately lose access to the uncreated Speech of God. Since the human mind cannot possibly fathom the uncreated Speech of God, which is itself beyond time and space, the human mind can never fathom the true content of revelation.

What this means is that any interpretation of the Quran is a fallible, human attempt to approximate meaning, and almost certainly fails to reflect God's exact message. When one interprets the Quran to derive law, then, one is never certain of having arrived upon the Divine Truth (*ḥaqq*). Of course, there are things that have an extremely high degree of certainty, like that God commands humans to believe in monotheism, to worship God, and to abstain from behavior like lying and stealing. Those commands and prohibitions are such highly probable reflections of God's Will that they do not admit reasonable doubt. But most everything else is open to interpretation and debate.[17] Ḥanafīs therefore felt comfortable reading the text in multiple ways, as in the above example of Quran 51:56. Since no one can definitively say which interpretation corresponds to the Divine Truth, different and competing interpretations can only ever claim relative authority.

This view of the Quran as open to interpretation was captured in the Ḥanafī distinction between *tafsīr*, by which Ḥanafīs meant something close to 'translation', and *ta'wīl*, by which they meant 'speculative interpretation'. Early Ḥanafīs were uncomfortable with *tafsīr*,[18] since translation implies that one knows the

15 Abū Ḥanīfa, 'Waṣiyyat al-imām Abī Ḥanīfa fī al-tawḥid', in al-Kawtharī (ed.), *al-ʿAqīda wa ʿilm al-kalām*, 636.

16 Al-Māturīdī, *Sharḥ al-Fiqh al-akbar*, 35.

17 Al-Māturīdī, *Kitāb al-Tawḥīd*, 273–274.

18 Abū Zayd al-Dabūsī, *Taqwīm al-adilla* (Beirut: Dār al-kutub al-ʿilmiyya, 2001), 169; Abū Muqātil al-Samarqandī, 'Kitāb al-ʿĀlim wa al-mutaʿallim', in al-Kawtharī (ed.), *al-ʿAqīda wa ʿilm al-kalām*, 574, 577; Abū Manṣūr al-Māturīdī, *Ta'wilāt ahl al-sunna* (Beirut: Muʿassasat al-risāla, 2004), 1:1.

meaning of an original text so well that one can translate it into another language, but were quite comfortable with *ta'wīl*, in which explanations of the Quran are recognised as fallible interpretations.

Early Ḥanafīs embraced the radical indeterminacy of Quranic laws, and indeed embraced indeterminacy as a hallmark of their legal school. Their approach to law is characterised by disagreement, multiple opinions, and conflicting interpretations. The school may be named after the scholar Abū Ḥanīfa, but his views comprise only one part of the Ḥanafī legacy. The school is actually grounded in the thought of five patriarchs, of whom Abū Ḥanīfa was one, and the patriarchs regularly debated and disagreed with one another about Islamic laws. Their individual approaches to law were quite different, and the laws that they promoted were similarly different, but their differences were condoned and celebrated because humans are not expected to figure out which laws accord to the Divine Truth. Rather, it was assumed that since humans can never know the Divine Truth, they are bound to disagree about their human, and therefore irremediably fallible, legal interpretations.

The early Ḥanafī approach to both God's Rationality and God's Speech leaves us wondering about the point of Islamic law. If there are multiple laws, all of which might have value and none of which can be independently verified, then how does one know which laws lead to justice? If one can never know which laws are correct, then how can law determine correct behavior? If laws cannot definitively point toward justice and morality, then what is the point of religious law?

One might answer that religious laws are not meant to lead to justice in this world, but in the next. Perhaps following laws, however flawed they might be, is primarily about achieving salvation. In that case, justice in this life is irrelevant, and perhaps impossible. But by claiming to have *tried* to determine and follow the correct law, believers can argue that they deserve to be saved from the consequences of their erroneous actions on the Day of Judgment. Early Ḥanafīs, however, rejected the idea that following Islamic law leads to salvation in the hereafter. They maintained a doctrine that kept people's actions separate from their beliefs, effectively ensuring that religious laws would have neither metaphysical nor salvific content. Appreciating why and how they thought this will help us better understand both their distinctive answers to the questions posed in the previous paragraph and their unique approach to Islamic legal justice.

Belief and Action

Since God's Rationality and God's Speech are irremediably beyond the human imagination, neither human speech nor human action will ever truly capture Divine Justice. So, trying to get the exact right interpretation or act in exactly the right way is a fool's errand, an impossible mission. If a task is beyond human capacity, the Ḥanafīs argued, then humans are not responsible for fulfilling it. Thus, humans are tasked neither with coming up with correct interpretations nor engaging in correct actions. Rather, they are tasked with the one thing they are capable of: belief (*īmān*).

'Belief', for the early Ḥanafīs, is the defining characteristic of a Muslim. Believers, by definition, believe in God's unity and Muhammad's prophethood, and disbelievers do not. For the early Ḥanafīs, 'belief' does not denote a personal predilection, but signifies a state one achieves after having completed a certain action.[19] That action is a verbal testament; namely, speaking the words of the *shahāda:* 'There is no deity other than God, and Muḥammad is the messenger of God.' Having spoken this phrase, one must then truly believe its contents in one's heart to be a true 'believer',[20] though of course there is no way to externally validate whether one has done that or not.

Just as one becomes a believer by speaking the *shahāda* with the tongue and believing it in the heart, one does not become a disbeliever except by both denouncing the *shahāda* with the tongue and rejecting it within the heart.[21] Thus, one is considered to be a believer until and unless she both states that she disbelieves and also truly disbelieves in her heart. Since disbelief in the heart is not verifiable, the only way to determine disbelief is by a verbal statement to that effect.[22] 'Disbelief' is therefore contingent on a verbal attestation, just as 'belief' is contingent on a verbal attestation. For all intents and purposes, 'belief' is simply an identity-marker for those who have verbalised the *shahāda* as opposed to those who have not.

---

19 Abū Muqātil al-Samarqandī, 'Kitāb al-ʿĀlim wa al-mutaʿallim', in al-Kawtharī (ed.), *al-ʿAqīda wa ʿilm al-kalām*, 575. Similarly, disbelief is an active state, wherein one repudiates God and Muhammad knowingly. The same applies to 'disbelief in God's blessings' (*kufr al-niʿam*), in which someone fails to recognize God's bounty. The Ḥanafīs believed that this was a type of disbelief, but only when a person knows full well that, say, night and day were created by God, yet refuses to believe it; ibid., 593.

20 Ibid., 575–577.

21 Abū Ḥanīfa, 'Risālat Abī Ḥanīfa ilā 'Uthmān al-Battī', in al-Kawtharī (ed.), *al-ʿAqīda wa ʿilm al-kalām*, 631.

22 Abū Muqātil al-Samarqandī, 'Kitāb al-ʿĀlim wa al-mutaʿallim', in al-Kawtharī (ed.), *al-ʿAqīda wa ʿilm al-kalām*, 583–584.

In this conception, 'belief' is digital; one either believes or does not. 'Belief' does not rise or fall over time,[23] and speaking of 'weak belief' makes no sense. Abū Ḥanīfa famously compared the faith of humans to that of the angels;[24] in the Islamic tradition, angels are considered to believe wholeheartedly in God, and one does not speak about the relative strength of angelic faith. In the same way, early Ḥanafīs held that those who verbalise the *shahāda* — that is, Muslims — believe perfectly and completely.

Since belief does not rise nor fall, evil actions have no deleterious impact on belief, and, conversely, righteous actions do not increase belief.[25] Belief and action, therefore, are completely separate. This, Ḥanafīs argue, is of necessity; since one can never truly know when their actions accord with the Divine Truth, it would be unfair for humans to only gain in belief when they act correctly, or to lose belief when they act incorrectly. Humans can only be held accountable for following commands that they know to be in accordance with the Divine Truth. The only command that humans know for sure is the very command to believe in God and the Prophet.

The main task for humans, then, is to verbalise the *shahāda* and thereby become believers.[26] Once they fulfill that task, then God will forgive their sins and evil deeds, and enter them into paradise. Salvation is thus a matter of having belief, not a matter of performing righteous actions. The early Ḥanafīs were adamant on this point, and interpreted both sacred texts and Islamic law in that light. Take Abū al-Layth al-Samarqandī's (d. 370) interpretation of the following verse,

> 'You are the best nation (*umma*) raised from amongst humankind, you command what is good, and you prohibit what is evil, and you believe in God.' (3:110)

This verse appears to say that commanding good and prohibiting evil is an essential characteristic of the Muslim *umma*. Al-Samarqandī, however, interpreted

---

23 Abū Ḥanīfa, 'Waṣiyyat al-imām Abī Ḥanīfa fī al-tawḥid', in al-Kawtharī (ed.), *al-ʿAqīda wa ʿilm al-kalām*, 635. To those who might cite verses like Q. 8:2, "And when [God's] verses are recited to [believers], they increase in faith", al-Māturīdī says that this is referring to the fact that the Quran was revealed in stages. This verse was a promise for those who believed during the life of Muhammad that they would be receiving more revelation to believe in, al-Māturīdī, *Sharḥ al-Fiqh al-akbar*, 12.

24 Abū Ḥanīfa, 'al-Fiqh al-akbar', in al-Kawtharī (ed.), *al-ʿAqīda wa ʿilm al-kalām*, 622.

25 Balkhī, 'al-Fiqh al-absaṭ', 601.

26 See also Abū al-Layth al-Samarqandī's *tafsīr* of Q. 4:135 in which he says that the phrase "stand firm for justice" should be understood as "justly bear witness to God", Samarqandī, *Tafsīr al-Samarqandī*, 1:396.

the verse such that commanding good and prohibiting evil was primarily about ensuring that people have correct belief. He wrote,

The phrase 'You are' in this verse... refers to the Companions of Muhammad, as if saying to them 'You all are the best nation'. That is in line with Muhammad's statement; 'the best generation is that of my companions and those who succeed them'. God then describes [the Companions] saying, 'You command what is good' – meaning monotheism (*tawhīd*) and Islam – 'and prohibit what is evil' – meaning polytheism (*shirk*).'

Here, al-Samarqandī isolates the Companions of Muhammad as the verse's addressees, and then clarifies that their commanding good and prohibiting evil has only to do with belief, not with performing deeds. Al-Māturīdī was even clearer in his interpretation of the verse and extended it apply to all Muslims, and not just the Companions:

'"Command what is good" means command belief (*īmān*), and "prohibit what is evil" means prohibit disbelief (*kufr*). The proof of this is that the verse [continues to say] "and you believe in God." [So the people being described in this verse] themselves believe, they command others to believe, and they prohibit [others] from disbelief.'[27]

Since 'belief' hinges only on a verbal testament, commanding good and prohibiting evil is about the simple act of encouraging others to verbalise the *shahāda*, and discouraging others from refusing to verbalise it. In this interpretation of Q. 3:110, it is easy to count oneself part of the 'best *umma*'.

Of course, if good and evil are primarily about encouraging belief, and belief is achieved by a mere verbal attestation, then religious law seems superfluous. What is the point of a religious law that does nothing to increase one's belief or prospects in the afterlife? Why would anyone feel compelled to obey religious laws if they only need to believe in the Lawgiver to be saved? When belief and action are connected, it is easy to see why someone would obey the law; in that case obeying religious laws would lead to an increase in belief and would save one in the hereafter. In the Ḥanafī conception, however, disobeying the law does not affect one's belief in the least, just as strictly obeying religious laws does not result in increased belief, and, besides, God does not necessarily demand obedience to the law in order to be saved. If obeying or disobeying law does not result in belief increasing or decreasing, or even in salvation, then why obey laws at all?

To this, early Ḥanafīs had two answers, one religious and one social. The religious answer was: one does good deeds because they are good, and they might

---

27 Abū Manṣūr al-Māturīdī, *Tafsīr al-Māturīdī* (Beirut: Dār al-kutub al-ʿilmiyya, 2005), 2:451.

bring one closer to God. One avoids evil actions based on the same logic. God might decide to punish someone who commits evil deeds with a stint in hell[28] – God can do whatever God pleases – but Ḥanafīs held that God would most likely forgive believers and enter them into paradise.[29] One can never be sure about God's ultimate decision to punish or not, but worrying about the hereafter misses the point of religiosity and obeying the law. One should strive to be a good person out of love for God, and Islamic law contains rules for being good.

For instance, the law that commands drinking water with the right hand is not to be obeyed because drinking with the left hand will send one to hell. Rather, Ḥanafīs believed that drinking with the right hand was part of being a good person, much as we think that rules of etiquette make one a good citizen. One lane of the road is for driving slowly, the other is for overtaking; we say 'please' when asking for something, and 'thank you' when receiving it; these are not hard and fast laws, but are rules for good conduct. Similarly, saying 'Praise be to God' after sneezing will not enter one into paradise, just as omitting it will not lead one to hell, but it does represent good conduct and fidelity to God.

When viewed this way, many Islamic laws can be seen as instructions about etiquette. Proposed procedures for prayer, fasting, giving charity, and performing the *ḥajj* pilgrimage – rules of worship that comprise the bulk of most legal manuals – are, in this conception, exhortations for ethical conduct rather than what we might call 'religious laws'. They do not determine salvation, following them does not increase one's belief, and they do not accurately represent the Divine Truth.

Early Ḥanafīs saw their approach to law as especially virtuous, claiming that they followed the law merely out of a desire to embody good conduct and out of love for God. They chided others who linked belief and actions, denouncing them as deeply cynical for assuming that people only follow laws to increase in belief, attain heaven, or avoid hell.[30] By contrast, Ḥanafīs saw themselves as submitting out of pure devotion.

The second reason that early Ḥanafīs gave for obeying Islamic law had to do with social cohesion. This was predicated on their belief that the only thing that

---

28 Al-Balkhī, 'al-Fiqh al-absaṭ', 605.

29 Al-Māturīdī, *Sharḥ al-Fiqh al-akbar*, 235. Abū Ḥanīfa made an important distinction between 'belief' and 'worship' (*ʿibāda*) here. Whereas believers might have faith in God's forgiveness, true worshippers are those who also fear God's wrath. That level of fear is not necessary for belief, but it is necessary for proper worship; Abū Muqātil al-Samarqandī, 'Kitāb al-ʿĀlim wa al-mutaʿallim', in al-Kawtharī (ed.), *al-ʿAqīda wa ʿilm al-kalām*, 589.

30 Al-Māturīdī, *Kitāb al-Tawḥīd*, 166–167.

separates believers from disbelievers is a verbalised *shahāda*. Thus, being a believer, aside from entering one into paradise, was a statement about identity, and a desire to align oneself with others who profess faith.[31] When verbalizing the *shahāda*, one is claiming a shared identity with a group of individuals who live in a society that has shared social practices and is governed by a shared set of rules and laws. Verbalizing the *shahāda*, then, is an implicit agreement to align oneself with the Muslim community, and to follow Muslim laws and practices when living amongst Muslims.[32] These laws are termed 'Islamic laws' not because they are somehow divine, but because they describe a social contract that Muslims agree to abide by when living with one another. They are Islamic only in the sense that they are rooted in Muslim traditions and pertain to those who identify as Muslim, not because they are revealed or accord to the Divine Truth.

This is essential to the early Ḥanafī approach to law and justice. When Islamic law has no metaphysical or salvific content, it moves away from spiritual law, and moves toward civil law. These are laws that guide the community, not because they will lead to salvation, but because they order Muslim practice. That does not make the laws irreligious, it just means that we need to shift our notion of 'religion' a little, such that religion describes a community of practice rather than a disembodied set of beliefs. If Islam and 'belief' are primarily identity-markers, then 'Islamic law' is the law that governs those who identify themselves as Muslim when they are living within a Muslim community. This law functions only within political, communal boundaries, and does not make much sense outside of them.

In a nutshell, early Ḥanafīs believed that Islamic laws describe the social contract to which Muslims agree to abide while residing within the political boundaries of Muslim society (*dār al-Islām*).[33] This social contract serves as a backdrop for laws related to both religious rituals (*ʿibādāt*) and interpersonal relations (*muʿāmalāt*). In the realm of religious rituals, Ḥanafīs believed that there are some religious rituals that are so unanimously agreed upon – namely, prayer, fasting in Ramadan, giving the prescribed charity, and performing *ḥajj* – that to deny them would be tantamount to renouncing one's membership in the Muslim community. Only God may legislate these rituals in the first place, but believers are free to enact them in many different ways – or, indeed, not to enact them

31 Ibid., 475.

32 Ibid., 495–499.

33 Al-Māturīdī points out that it is called *dār al-Islam* as opposed to *dār al-imān* precisely because it is describing a polity, not a state of the heart; ibid., 493.

at all – so long as they recognise that these actions define the boundaries of citizenship within the community.[34]

Laws related to interpersonal relations are likewise subject to continual community interpretation; there can be no interpersonal law that is universally or inherently just and thus enforced in perpetuity. If the community decides to follow new or modified laws, then those laws would become Islamic law. That is true even for laws that appear deeply entrenched in Islamic legal texts and traditions. Early Ḥanafīs were resolute on this point, and said that even when a specific law is stipulated in the Quran, that does not make the law inherently just or universally applicable.[35]

To understand exactly how they saw Quranic laws as only relatively just, we can take the example of corporal punishments. The Quran prescribes corporal punishment for acts like theft, adultery, and brigandage. For theft, the Quran prescribes amputation, for adultery flogging, and for brigandage both cutting off opposing limbs and crucifixion. If we were to presume that laws have some connection to the Divine, then we might think that these corporal punishments are the embodiment of Divine Justice. Early Ḥanafīs, however, did not make such a connection, and indeed they did not think that these laws were inherently just. We can see exactly how and why by taking a closer look at one prominent early Ḥanafī, Abū Manṣūr al-Māturīdī, and his views on corporal punishment.

Al-Māturīdī on Corporal Punishment

Al-Māturīdī acknowledged that the Quran prescribes corporal punishments, but insisted that those punishments were not about justice. He reasoned that they could not possibly be, since punishments are only just if they fit the crime. Quranically-prescribed corporal punishments, said al-Māturīdī, do not fit their related crimes. In the case of theft, for instance, he said that amputation has nothing to do with the crime itself. He felt that justice would be better served if the thief were to give the victim restitution. Cutting off the hand of a thief might deliver personal satisfaction, but it does not restore the victim her property, nor make up for the time she lost with her property, nor alleviate the trauma of being a victim of theft.[36]

34 Al-Māturīdī, *Taʾwīlāt ahl al-sunna*, 2:582.

35 See for instance al-Māturīdī's equivocation on the need to divide inheritance according to the exact specifications outlined in Q. 4:10–11; ibid., 1:372–373.

36 Ibid., 2:36.

Al-Māturīdī conceded that amputating a thief's hand might prevent repeat offences, but said that imprisonment would just as easily serve that purpose, as would public humiliation. There is nothing special about amputating the hands of a thief that is more just or more fitting than those other modes of punishment. Besides, he said, if deterrence and justice are best achieved by amputating an appendage related to a crime, why not amputate the genitalia of convicted adulterers?[37] Why does whipping adulterers stop adultery whereas amputation stops theft? Why not amputate adulterers and whip thieves? For that matter, why corporally punish convicted criminals at all?

To those who would argue that society runs well when thieves and adulterers are corporally punished, al-Māturīdī answered that, in fact, the exact opposite would be true. He said that the Quran commands believers to treat one another with kindness,[38] and so Muslims should strive to create a community wherein criminals are pardoned and treated well, rather than stigmatised and punished.[39] With respect to punishing murder, for example, the Quran affirms the right for the victim's family to either exact retribution or forgive the offender (Q. 2:178), and counsels forgiveness as the best option (Q. 16:126). Why doesn't that same logic apply to the lesser crimes of theft and adultery?

Some of al-Māturīdī's detractors offered a spiritual answer, claiming that punishment in this life alleviates punishment in the afterlife. The thinking here is that if someone is whipped for adultery during their lifetime, they might be spared God's wrath in the afterlife. For al-Māturīdī, this was a dubious proposition. Recall that in the Ḥanafī framework, sin does not lessen someone's faith, and so long as sinning believers repent their crimes, they are forgiven and are blameless in the sight of God. Corporal punishment, then, would have no otherworldly benefit if convicted criminals showed remorse and repented, because they would have already been forgiven.[40] Thus, for al-Māturīdī, corporal punishment promotes neither societal nor spiritual justice. In fact, since believers are forgiven their sins by simply repenting, and believers should strive to create a culture of compassion amongst themselves, society would benefit most if

37 Ibid., 2:35–37.

38 Al-Māturīdī was particularly fond of citing Q. 48:29, "And those who are with [Muḥammad] are harsh with the disbelievers, but merciful amongst themselves."

39 Al-Māturīdī said that if a thief repents any time before having punishment handed down, the punishment of amputation should not be exacted; ibid., 2:33.

40 Note that Ḥanafīs believed that punishment in worldly life did, indeed, mitigate punishment in the hereafter, but only when the believer does not repent; Abū Muqātil al-Samarqandī, 'Kitāb al-ʿĀlim wa al-mutaʿallim', in al-Kawtharī (ed.), *al-ʿAqīda wa ʿilm al-kalām*, 591.

criminals were encouraged to repent, and forgiveness were the order of the day. What, then, is the point of corporal punishment?

The answer for early Ḥanafīs was: we don't know. All that is known is that God included corporal punishment in the Quran as one method for maintaining social order. Given this, al-Māturīdī suggested a way of thinking about corporal punishment that is not about justice *per se*, but rather about sentencing limits. Al-Māturīdī pointed out that corporal punishments are referred to in the scriptures as *ḥudūd*, literally 'limits', as in Q. 2:229, 'these are the limits (*ḥudūd*) of God, so do not exceed them'. Al-Māturīdī argued that corporal punishments mentioned in the Quran are the outer limits of the kinds of sentences that believing judges can hand down to convicted criminals.[41] Rather than being prescriptions that must be obeyed in all cases, the *ḥudūd* are limits that should not be exceeded. A thief, for example, cannot be killed, because the outermost limit for punishing theft is amputation. Should the community decide on a lesser punishment than amputation – such as imprisonment or a fine – that would be perfectly acceptable, so long as the severity of the punishment decided upon by the community does not exceed amputation.

The community and its leaders, then, have to decide on appropriate punishments within the limits prescribed in the Quran. And so, if leaders determine that adulterers should be imprisoned, or banished, or pardoned, that is their prerogative, so long as they do not exceed the limit of whipping, or, according to some, stoning.[42] The particular punishment that is decided upon is irrelevant with respect to Divine Justice; rather, justice is found in devising laws for the Muslim community, and then abiding by them, whatever they are. Again, we see that early Ḥanafīs conceived of Islamic law as a social contract according to which *dār al-Islām* functions, and not a metaphysical law that is inherently just and leads one to paradise.

Islamic Law as Muslim Law

The early Ḥanafī approach to law opens the door to a complete re-conception of religious law and Islamic legal justice. Normally when we think of religious law, we assume that it is imbued with morality and metaphysical import: following the law will result in establishing transcendent justice and attaining paradise,

41 Al-Māturīdī, *Ta'wīlāt ahl al-sunna*, 3:428.

42 Al-Māturīdī believed that stoning was actually a pre-Islamic punishment, and that the Quran instituted an outer limit of lashing convicted adulterers; ibid., 2:44.

and flouting it will result in moral decay and damnation. However, the early Ḥanafī approach treats law as a social force more than a moral one. Believers do not know why God commands one law or another – though they trust that there is some reason –, or even which laws God commands at all. They are not expected to follow laws to the letter; rather, they are supposed to determine which laws are right for the community within boundaries determined through expansive readings of foundational sources. Religious law, therefore, has more to do with religious identity within political boundaries than it does morality and salvation.

This leads to the intriguing question, what if the political boundaries of the Muslim community ceased to exist? Do Islamic laws need to be followed if there is no structure in place to enforce them? To take the question further, if Muslims do not live in a place with a social contract that permits certain actions and disallows others, are they still bound by Islamic law? For a concrete example, let's look at the law of drunkenness. Most Muslim jurists, including Ḥanafīs, agreed that public drunkenness was a crime that could be punished by lashing. In the Ḥanafī framework, lashing is only the outermost limit for punishing drunkenness, and a local *imām* may choose to pardon a convicted drunkard instead without any metaphysical consequences. The crime itself is only considered punishable because it violates a social contract agreed upon by Muslims, and, likewise, the Muslim community determines the punishment. But what if the drunkard committed his crime in a land without that social contract and without a Muslim community? Is it really a crime in that case, and should it warrant punishment? The answer to both questions for many early Ḥanafīs was: 'no'.

Early Ḥanafīs were adamant that Islamic law only functions within a clearly demarcated jurisdiction, and does not apply outside of that. We can see this at work in an exchange between Abū Ḥanīfa and Muḥammad al-Shaybānī concerning *ribā*, a commercial transaction in which either similar items are exchanged for one another or in which debt increases over time, often likened to a common interest-bearing loan. *Ribā* is unambiguously forbidden in the Quran and *ḥadīth*, with the Quran going so far as to say, 'if you do not [desist from engaging in *ribā*], take notice of war from God and God's Messenger' (Q. 2:279). Early Ḥanafīs agreed that *ribā* should be prohibited, and thus engaging in *ribā* would violate the social contract that Muslims agreed upon. Again, it is not prohibited because *ribā* is an unjust practice, but because it is a practice that Muslims disallow. If Muslims decided at some point to, say, discourage *ribā* without prohibiting it, then engaging in *ribā* would not be a punishable offense.

Interestingly, Ḥanafīs believed that the social contract that either proscribes or permits *ribā* is only relevant within the confines of a Muslim political milieu in which Muslims agree to abide by Islamic law. This political milieu is known as *dār al-Islām*. Since law needs a social contract to be binding, Islamic law makes no sense outside of the confines of *dār al-Islām*. So, in lands outside *dār al-Islam*, known as *dār al-ḥarb*, Islamic law ceases to apply to both believers and non-believers. The following discussion between Abū Ḥanīfa and his student Muḥammad al-Shaybānī captures the importance of jurisdiction with respect to *ribā:*

> [Muḥammad al-Shaybānī] asked: If a Muslim entered into a transaction with a resident of *dār al-ḥarb* involving *ribā*, wine, or corpses, do you think such a transaction would be rejected as null and void?
>
> [Abū Ḥanīfa] replied: Yes, if it took place in *dar al-Islām*. If it were in *dār al-ḥarb*, it should not be regarded as null and void.
>
> I asked: Why? Are you saying that if a Muslim enters *dar al-ḥarb*, it would be permissible for him to sell corpses and take 2 dirhams in exchange for 1?
>
> He replied: Yes, it would be quite all right to do so in their land, but not in *dār al-Islām*, where Muslim rulings are binding on them and where it is only lawful to do that which is lawful amongst Muslims. If the Muslim were in *dār al-ḥarb* under safe passage, it would be lawful for him to acquire property from them in accordance [with their law], since Muslim rulings would not be binding on them there.[43]

Muslim rulings, it would seem, only apply in a society in which there is a social contract that upholds Muslim rulings. Restrictions and permissions cease to exist wherever the social contract does not apply. It appears that residency determines whether or not Muslims have to abide by Islamic law. If individuals reside within *dār al-Islām*, then Islamic law applies, and if they live outside of *dār al-Islam*, then foreign laws apply. That is because Islamic law is not a metaphysical or salvific law in the Ḥanafī conception; rather, it is a mutually agreed upon and highly negotiable social contract.

In a similar vein, al-Shaybānī asked Abū Ḥanīfa about a rather specific scenario in which a Muslim army battalion is routed by a disbelieving army and is forced to escape to an area within *dār al-ḥarb*[44] under the protection (*amān*) of some resident disbelievers. Al-Shaybānī's question was whether the routed Muslims could regroup within *dār al-ḥarb*, join up with some of its sympathetic residents, and launch an attack on their enemy from inside *dār al-ḥarb*. Abū Ḥanīfa answered in the negative; since the routed Muslims would be residing in the land of their enemy, they would be bound by the enemy's law, which presumably does

---

43 Muḥammad al-Shaybānī, *al-Aṣl li imām Muḥammad ibn al-Ḥasan al-Shaybānī* (Beirut: Dār Ibn Hazm, 2012), 7/479–80; translation adapted from Majid Khadduri, *The Islamic Law of Nations: Shaybani's Siyar* (Baltimore: The Johns Hopkins University Press, 1966), 173. Note that this was the opinion of Abū Ḥanīfa and Muḥammad al-Shaybānī, but that Abū Yūsuf disagreed.
44 Technically, al-Shaybānī described it here as '*dār al-shirk*'.

not allow its residents, Muslim or not, to rise up against them.[45] In essence, Abū Ḥanīfa argued that Muslims are bound by the laws of the land in which they reside, whatever they might be and for whatever reason Muslims find themselves in those lands in the first place.

To drive that point home, we have the following exchange regarding the application of *ḥudūd* penalties for crimes committed outside of *dār al-Islam:*

> [Muḥammad al-Shaybānī asked:] If [in *dār al-ḥarb*] either a Muslim had become indebted to [a disbeliever] or [a disbeliever] had become indebted to [a Muslim], or [a Muslim] had usurped [a disbeliever's] property or [a disbeliever] had usurped [a Muslim's] property do you think that we should concern ourselves with any such matters?
>
> [Abū Ḥanifa] replied: I hold that we should not concern ourselves with such matters and that we should not pass judgment on them.
>
> I asked: Would the same be true of any acts of murder or wounds committed in *dār al-ḥarb?*
>
> He replied: Yes. All such things would be regarded as null and void.
>
> I asked: Why?
>
> He replied: Because they were committed [in a territory] where Muslim rulings are not applicable to them.[46]

Islamic law, it would seem, has borders. The issue of jurisdiction comes up often in early Ḥanafī legal texts, and it concerns where and when Muslims are expected to abide by Islamic law. Here we see that actions that are normally considered crimes – *ribā*, murder, personal injury – are actually only crimes when they are committed in a land in which there is a social contract forbidding those actions.[47] In absence of that contract, there is no crime to prosecute. Nor is there any concept of rendition; a crime committed outside of *dār al-Islām* will never be prosecuted within *dār al-Islām.*

Citizens of a state agree to abide by the rulings of the state; that is what makes for good citizenship and for a flourishing society. The early Ḥanafī emphasis on good citizenship suggests that they believed that social rules are enacted not because they are divinely-inspired, but because they reflect normative social practice and create social order. This pragmatic focus of the law shifts our attention away from transcendent morality and toward a desired legal ethic. It is not so much 'Islamic' law as it is 'Muslim' law. That is, Islamic law is a law that Muslims develop with reference to Islamic foundational texts and historical

45 Shaybānī, *al-Aṣl li imām Muḥammad ibn al-Ḥasan al-Shaybānī*, 7:521.

46 Ibid., 7:478–479; translation adapted from Khadduri, *The Islamic Law of Nations*, 171–172.

47 The one exception that sometimes appears in Ḥanafī texts is when the Caliph accompanies the army and is present to carry out punishment; Muḥammad b. Aḥmad al-Sarakhsī, *Sharḥ Kitāb al-siyar al-kabīr* (Beirut: Dār al-kutub al-ʿilmiyya, 1997), 5:108–109.

Muslim practice so that the Muslim community might maintain order and cohesion. It is contingent on the community's evolving interpretations and social mores and does not apply to those who live outside the political boundaries of the community.

This attitude toward jurisdiction and citizenship pervades early Ḥanafī scholarship. Take the following exchange wherein al-Shaybānī asks Abū Ḥanīfa about a non-resident alien (*musta'min*) who visits *dār al-Islam* under an order of protection (*amān*):

> I asked: If [a *musta'min*] commits fornication or theft in *dār al-Islām*, do you think that we should apply the *ḥudūd* penalties to him?
>
> [Abū Ḥanīfa] replied: No.
>
> I asked: Why?
>
> He replied: Because *musta'mins* have made neither a peace treaty [with us] nor had they become *dhimmīs* (resident non-Muslims). Thus, Muslim rulings would not apply to them.[48]

Musta'mins are only passing through *dār al-Islam*; they have no intention of residence, they are not citizens of any sort, and they normally abide by some other social contract in the land from which they came. Thus, the rules of the Muslim community do not apply to them. Surely, they might be convicted of a crime committed in *dār al-Islām* and punished, but there is no set penalty prescribed for them. The law applied to them is undoubtedly secular, and has nothing to do with what we traditionally call 'Islamic law'.

It is important to note here that the distinction between those to whom the law applies and those who are beyond the law has to do with residency and citizenship, not necessarily with religion. In the above passage and elsewhere, early Ḥanafīs made clear that *dhimmīs*, who are not Muslim, are subject to Muslim laws, not by dint of their religious affiliation, but because they accepted a social contract as a condition of residency.

This conception of law and jurisdiction flows directly from the theological precepts of the early Ḥanafīs.[49] To review, Ḥanafīs believed that God is utterly beyond human comprehension, and that humans can never really know the content of God's Speech or how to act according to God's will. That is not a problem, because God's primary command to humans is to believe in God's unity and in Muḥammad's prophethood. Once someone believes, they are free to interpret the

---

48 Shaybānī, *al-Aṣl li imām Muḥammad ibn al-Ḥasan al-Shaybānī*, 7:479; translation adapted from Khadduri, *The Islamic Law of Nations*, 172.

49 In fact, al-Māturīdī links the Ḥanafī idea of social cohesion to 'belief' in a lengthy discourse; see al-Māturīdī, *Kitāb al-Tawḥīd*, 471.

texts and act without worrying that their missteps will negatively impact their belief. So long as believers repent their sins, they will be entered into paradise. If they do not repent, they might have a stopover in hell before eventually being admitted into heaven. But they would just as easily, and in fact more likely, be admitted directly into paradise. Given this theological framework, Islamic law cannot be about creating moral agents whose adherence to the law determines their success in the life hereafter. Rather, it can only be a fallible attempt by Muslims to maintain social order while demonstrating fidelity to God.

Conclusion

This way of looking at Islamic law leaves us with many questions. Why did God make the world in this way? What is the point of creation? For early Ḥanafīs, there is no way to know the answers to these questions; one must trust that whatever the reasons, they are just. The main task for humans is to believe in God and God's unknowable justice, everything else is secondary. So long as a person believes in God and believes that God ought to be obeyed, she is free to interpret God's dictates however she likes. Getting the right interpretation and behaving in the right way are impossible, and therefore irrelevant, since no one can ever know the Divine Intention. So, all that is left is to believe. Believers can then fashion laws to govern themselves based upon their own fallible interpretations of scriptural sources, but those laws will never accurately reflect the Divine Intention.

Ḥanafī Islamic law, then, is utterly mundane. It concerns the practice of everyday communal life, religious rituals, personal conduct, and boundaries for interpersonal interaction. Islamic law, in this conception, only makes sense in the context of a community and some governing structure. Outside that structure, laws no longer function, nor do they make any sense. Far from being universal rules for achieving transcendental justice, Islamic law in this way of thinking becomes a way of ordering society and both personal and communal life according to identity and citizenship.

This does not sound like Islamic law as we tend to hear about it. In fact, most scholarship assumes that Islamic law is thoroughly imbued with metaphysical and salvific import, and that it strives to embody justice, either in its substantive content or in its principles. An oft-repeated phrase is, 'Islam is a total way of life', meaning that Islamic law, whether in its dictates or its principles, applies uniformly regardless of time, place, or context to produce worldly and otherworldly justice. However, such claims about Islam and Islamic law are by no means universal, and, given the popularity of the Ḥanafī school, might not even represent the majoritarian view. Why, then, are those claims so prevalent in modern discourse, and why it is that the early Ḥanafī conception of Islamic law sounds so alien?

There are many reasons for this, including the rise of Sunnī internationalism, manuscript availability, and colonialism, but a lot has to do with the fact that when we approach Islamic law, we tend to find what we are looking for. That is, we are looking for a religious system that is spiritual, totalizing, and always concerned with obedience and salvation. Islamic legal writings are likely being read with the pre-conception that, in Islam, the spiritual and the mundane are always bound together, and any discussion of the mundane is automatically a discussion of the spiritual. Thus, pre-colonial accounts of Islamic law, from Ḥanafīs or others, are expected to discuss Islamic law in those terms.

However, as seen above, there is no reason to presume that Muslims always thought about Islamic law in this way, or even that they do so now.[50] There is ample evidence that Muslims did not and do not always see the mundane as infused with spiritual and theological import. As I have demonstrated above, early Ḥanafīs institutionalised a separation between Islamic law and transcendental, metaphysical justice. For such Ḥanafīs, many of whom are still prominent today, it does not make sense to ask whether Islamic law is inherently just or unjust, because justice is itself an unattainable and incomprehensible concept that can only be understood and enacted by God. Believers are not tasked with establishing justice on Earth, nor are they capable of doing so. Islamic law, then, is what Muslims agree to do, nothing more and nothing less. It is contingent on the needs and desires of the community, changes with time, and serves practical, rather than metaphysical purposes.

The early Ḥanafīs were abundantly clear about this, and their writings left little ambiguity on the subject. Yet, modern scholarship is slow to accept their claims at face value, likely because they challenge popular, modern notions about 'true' Islam and Muslims, and about the uniquely spiritual nature of Islamic law. Taking early Ḥanafī legal thought seriously opens up the discussion around Islam and justice, and brings us closer to the simple notion that Islamic legal justice might mean different things to the many different Muslims around the world.

50 See Rumee Ahmed and Aryeh Cohen, 'Assuming Power: Judges, Imagined Authority, and the Quotidian', in *Islamic and Jewish Legal Reasoning*, ed. A. Emon (Oxford: Oneworld, 2016).

Bibliography

Abū Ḥanīfa. 'al-Fiqh al-akbar'. In *al-ʿAqīda wa ʿilm al-kalām*. Edited by M. al-Kawtharī, 617–627. Beirut: Dār al-kutub al-ʿilmiyya, 2004.

—. 'Risālat Abī Ḥanīfa ilā ʿUthmān al-Battī'. In *al-ʿAqīda wa ʿilm al-kalām*. Edited by M. al-Kawtharī, 627–632. Beirut: Dār al-kutub al-ʿilmiyya, 2004.

—. 'Waṣiyyat al-imām Abī Ḥanīfa fī al-tawḥid'. In *al-ʿAqīda wa ʿilm al-kalām*. Edited by M. al-Kawtharī, 633–638. Beirut: Dār al-kutub al-ʿilmiyya, 2004.

Ahmed, Rumee. 'The Ethics of Prophetic Disobedience: Qurʾan 8:67 at the Crossroads of the Islamic Sciences'. *Journal of Religious Ethics* 39, no. 3 (2011): 440–457.

—. 'Theology and Islamic Law'. In *The Oxford Handbook of Islamic Law*. Edited by A. Emon and R. Ahmed. Oxford: Oxford University Press, 2018 (DOI: 10.1093/oxfordhb/9780199679010.013.58).

Ahmed, Rumee, and Aryeh Cohen. 'Assuming Power: Judges, Imagined Authority, and the Quotidian'. In *Islamic and Jewish Legal Reasoning*. Edited by A. Emon, 3–24. Oxford: Oneworld, 2016.

Armstrong, Karen. *A History of God: The 4,000 Year Quest of Judaism, Christianity and Islam*. New York: Ballantine, 1993.

Balkhī, Abū Muṭīʿ al-. 'Al-Fiqh al-absaṭ'. In *al-ʿAqīda wa ʿilm al-kalām*. Edited by M. al-Kawtharī, 599–615. Beirut: Dār al-kutub al-ʿilmiyya, 2004.

Bassiouni, M. Cherif. *The Sharīʿa and Islamic Criminal Justice in Time of War and Peace*. Cambridge: Cambridge University Press, 2014.

Bergsträsser, Gotthelf. *Grundzüge des islamischen Rechts*. Leipzig: De Gruyter, 1935.

Cornell, Drucilla. *At the Heart of Freedom: Feminism, Sex, and Equality*. Princeton: Princeton University Press, 1998.

Dabūsī, Abū Zayd al-. *Taqwīm al-adilla*. Edited by Khalīl Mays. Beirut: Dār al-kutub al-ʿilmiyya, 2001.

Dammer, Harry, and Jay Albanese. *Comparative Criminal Justice Systems*. Belmont, CA: Wadsworth, 2014.

Gülen, Fethullah. *Essentials of the Islamic Faith*. Somerset, NJ: The Light, 2006.

Hussin, Iza. *The Politics of Islamic Law: Local Elites, Colonial Authority, and the Making of the Muslim State*. Chicago: University of Chicago Press, 2016.

Jones-Pauly, Christina. *Women Under Islam: Justice and the Politics of Islamic Law*. London: I.B. Tauris, 2011.

Kawtharī, M. Zāhid al., ed. al-ʿAqīda wa ʿilm al-kalām. Beirut: Dār al-kutub al-ʿilmiyya, 2004.

Khadduri, Majid. *The Islamic Law of Nations: Shaybani's Siyar*. Baltimore: The Johns Hopkins University Press, 1966.

—. *The Islamic Conception of Justice*. Baltimore: The Johns Hopkins University Press, 1984.

Kugle, Scott. 'Framed, Blamed and Renamed: The Recasting of Islamic Jurisprudence in Colonial South Asia'. *Modern Asian Studies* 35, no. 2 (2001): 257–313.

MacIntyre, Alasdair. *Whose Justice? Which Rationality*. Notre Dame, IN: University of Notre Dame Press, 1988.

Malekian, Farhad. *Principles of Islamic International Criminal Law: A Comparative Search*. Leiden: Brill, 2011.

Māturīdī, Abū Manṣūr al-. *Sharḥ al-Fiqh al-akbar*. Beirut: al-Maktaba al-ʿaṣriyya, 1983.

—. *Taʾwīlāt ahl al-sunna*. Edited by Fāṭima Yūsuf al-Khiyamī. Beirut: Muʿassasat al-risāla, 2004.

—. *Tafsīr al-Māturīdī.* Edited by Majdī Bāsallūm. Beirut: Dār al-kutub al-ʿilmiyya, 2005.
—. *Kitāb al-Tawḥīd.* Edited by Bekir Topaloglu and Muhammad Aruçi Beirut: Dār Ṣādir, 2010.
Opwis, Felicitas. *Maṣlaḥa and the Purposes of the Law: Islamic Legal Discourse on Legal Change from the 4th/10th to 8th/14th Century.* Leiden: Brill, 2010.
Ramadan, Hisham, ed. *Understanding Islamic Law: From Classical to Contemporary.* Lanham, MD: AltaMira, 2006.
Rawls, John. *A Theory of Justice.* Cambridge, MA: Harvard University Press, 1998.
Rudolph, Ulrich. *al-Māturīdī and Development of Sunnī Theology in Samarqand.* Leiden: Brill, 2015.
Rūmī, Jalāl al-Dīn. *The Mathnawi.* Cambridge: E.J.W. Gibb Memorial, 1990. Edited and translated by Reynold Nicholson.
Samarqandī, Abū al-Layth al-. *Tafsīr al-Samarqandī.* Edited by ʿAlī Muḥammad Muʿawwaḍ. Beirut: Dār al-kutub al-ʿilmiyya, 1993.
Samarqandī, Abū Muqātil al-. 'Kitāb al-ʿĀlim wa al-mutaʿallim'. In *al-ʿAqīda wa ʿilm al-kalām.* Edited by M. al-Kawtharī, 579–593.
Sarakhsī, Muḥammad b. Aḥmad al-. *Sharḥ Kitāb al-siyar al-kabīr.* Edited by Abū ʿAbd Allāh Ismāʿīl al-Shāfiʿī. Beirut: Dār al-kutub al-ʿilmiyya, 1997.
Schacht, Joseph. *Islam.* Oxford: Oxford University Press, 1974.
—. 'Law and Justice in Islam'. In *The Cambridge History of Islam, volume 2B: Islamic Society and Civilization.* Edited by P. M. Hold, Ann Lambton and Bernard Lewis, 539–68. Cambridge: Cambridge University Press, 2008.
Sen, Amrtya. *The Idea of Justice.* Cambridge, MA: Harvard University Press, 2009.
Shaybānī, Muḥammad al-. *al-Aṣl li imām Muḥammad ibn al-Ḥasan al-Shaybānī.* Edited by Mehmet Boynukalin. Beirut: Dār Ibn Hazm, 2012.
Souaiaia, Ahmed. *Contesting Justice: Women, Islam, Law, and Society.* Albany: SUNY Press, 2008.
Tucker, Judith. *In the House of the Law: Gender and Islamic Law in Ottoman Syria and Palestine.* Berkeley: University of California Press, 1998.
Yahya, Harun. *The Creation of the Universe.* Toronto: Al-Attique, 2000.

Abbas Poya

Conditions for a Good World

The Concept of Comprehensive Justice by Abū al-Ḥasan al-Māwardī (972–1058)

> Were the course of the stars weighed in justice,
> the state of the stars would be wholly disinterested.
> If the course of all things in the firmament were just and due,
> when would the temperament of the judicious be aggrieved?
> *Omar Khayyam*

Introduction

The apparent pessimism emanating from theses verses of Omar Khayyam points to a fundamentally human, cross-cultural yearning for justice.[1] Within an Islamic context, this yearning is expressed in numerous discourses surrounding different conceptions of justice, extending back to the formative years of the religion, all the way into the present. Although modern Islamic debates concerning justice enjoy more popularity today than they have done for several centuries,[2] it is important to look also to the pre-modern Islamic discourse concerning justice. For pre-modern ideas of justice have played a decisive role in the theological, legal, and socio-political conflicts of Muslims.

Fundamental questions of grave theological concern, pertaining to matters such as freedom of will and theodicy,[3] were answered in different ways early on. Two broad schools of thought emerged from this process, the Muʿtazila[4]

1 On justice as a human yearning or demand, see Otfried Höffe, *Gerechtigkeit: Eine philosophische Einführung* (Munich: Beck, 2010), 9.

2 Birgit Krawietz, 'Gerechtigkeit als Leitidee islamischen Rechts', in *Islam und Rechtsstaat: Zwischen Scharia und Säkularisierung*, ed. Birgit Krawietz and Helmut Reifeld (Berlin: Konrad-Adenauer-Stiftung e.V., 2008), specifically 37.

3 For discussions on both these themes in early Islamic times, see Josef van Ess, *Theologie und Gesellschaft im 2. und 3. Jahrhundert Hidschra: Eine Geschichte des religiösen Denkens im frühen Islam*, 6 vols. (Berlin: De Gruyter, 1991), 4/489–512.

4 These are the so-called rationalist theologians. The formative period of this thought was between the ninth and eleventh centuries. They affirmed human free will while presupposing the justness of God. According to their line of thought, it would be unjust to hold humans accountable for predetermined actions. The principle of justice took on a central role in their doctrine, becoming a basis for belief. For more on this school of thought and its understanding of justice,

https://doi.org/10.1515/9783110574593-003

and the Ash'ariyya/ Māturīdiyya.[5] This theological differentiation, going back to fundamentally different conceptions of justice, is still maintained today. Within this scheme, Shiites tend to adhere more to the Mu'tazila school of thought, while the majority of Sunnis usually designate themselves as adherents of Ash'ariyya/Māturīdiyya.

Different conceptions of justice have been debated even within the field of jurisprudence. Thus, witnesses were not the only people expected to prove themselves just. This was also expected of persons practicing certain professions, such as medical men, scholars of jurisprudence, or prayer-leaders.[6] Furthermore, procedural justice was a central theme in classical Islamic jurisprudence.[7] There are numerous scholars, past and present, who perceive a fundamental connection between justice and Islamic norms. In Ibn Taymiyya's (1263–1328) works, for example, we read that the sharī'a is justice and that justice is the sharī'a; whosoever judges in a just manner, judges in accordance with the sharī'a.[8] The modern Iranian scholar Murtaḍā Muṭahharī (1919–1979) writes that justice is the principle by which religious dictates are to be judged.[9]

On a socio-political level the importance of justice and the different conceptions of the term are most directly attested to by an extensive history of revolt. The long history of rebellion throughout different periods of Islamic rule is composed of different groups that more often than not framed their opposition to the ruling establishment in terms of unjust rule, or unjust social conditions. In early

---

see Anja Middelbeck-Varwick, 'Über göttliche Gerechtigkeit und menschliche Erkenntnis bei 'Abd al-Ğabbār (gest. 1024): Dialog mit einer mu'tazilitischen Rechtfertigung Gottes', in *Heil in Christentum und Islam, Erlösung oder Rechtleitung? Theologisches Forum Christentum – Islam*, ed. Hansjörg Schmid, Andreas Renz and Jutta Sperber (Stuttgart: Akademie der Diözese Rottenburg-Stuttgart, 2004).

5 The term Ash'arī refers to the name of the Iraqi scholar Abū al-Ḥasan al-Ash'arī (873–935), while the term Māturīdī refers back to the central Asian theologian Abū Manṣūr al-Māturīdī (853–944). Both scholars represent the same basic doctrine, placing great emphasis on the omnipotence of God. Human reason and the perception of God's justice are subordinated to God's omnipotence. Thus, according to this doctrine, all actions of God are necessarily just, even if humans do not perceive them to be so. On the Ash'ariyya, see George Makdisi, 'Ash'ari and Ash'arites in Islamic religious history', in *Islamic Philosophy and Theology: Critical Concepts in Islamic Thought*, ed. Ian R. Netton (London: Routledge, 2007); on the Māturīdiyya, see Ulrich Rudolph, *Al-Māturīdī und die sunnitische Theologie in Samarkand* (Leiden: Brill, 1996).

6 Krawietz, 'Gerechtigkeit als Leitidee islamischen Rechts', 42–43.

7 Ibid., 43.

8 Aḥmad Ibn Taymiyya, *Majmū' fatāwā shaykh al-islām Aḥmad ibn Taymiyya*, ed. 'Abd ar-Raḥmān Ibn Muḥammad ibn Qāsim and Muḥammad Ibn 'Abd al-Raḥmān ibn Qāsim (Riyadh, Mecca, n.d. [1962–7]), 35/366.

9 Murtaḍā Muṭahharī, *Barrasī-yi ijmālī-yi mabānī-yi iqtiṣād-i islāmī* (Qom, 1990), 14.

Islamic texts, the word *ʿadl* (justice) usually refers to worldly and social dimensions of justice. Whether used by Khārijīs, Shiites, or even Muʿtazilites, the term functioned as an expression of discontent towards what was perceived as unjust rule. In the same vein, the ideal and expected ruler (Messiah), was described as the Mahdī (the justly guided one) who will fill the earth with justice.[10]

In all these debates, however, justice was conceived in one of two ways. Either, it was a metaphysical characteristic (holy justice), or it was a human virtue one should aspire to (in cases of legal and political conflict).[11] Muslim scholars considered rarely justice as a normative and social conception. A notable exception, however, is the work of the jurist and political philosopher Abū al-Ḥasan al-Māwardī (972–1058). He does not discuss justice within the standard theological or juridical frameworks, but as a worldly (*dunyawī*) and comprehensive (*shāmil*) matter that is essential for the functioning of society. This paper will present to the reader his concept of comprehensive justice, as introduced by himself in his ethical work, *Adab al-dunyā wa al-dīn* (The Ethics of Religion and of this World).

The State of the Field

Most publications on the theme of justice in Islam are concerned with its theological dimension.[12] They generally address both modern debates,[13] as well as conceptualizations of justice within Islamic scripture: Quran and *ḥadīth*.[14] Other works have analysed the political dimensions of justice in Islam[15] and the role of justice in inter-religious dialogue.[16] Several studies have also dis-

---

10 Van Ess, *Theologie und Gesellschaft im 2. und 3. Jahrhundert Hidschra*, 4/507–508.

11 In many of the relevant works pertaining to discussions of justice, this same assumption is made for Judaism and Christianity. See, e.g., Höffe, *Gerechtigkeit* 31 and 33.

12 Jameleddine Ben Abdeljelil, 'Die Frage der Theodizee im Islam: Mensch Gott Gerechtigkeit', *Wiener Zeitschrift für die Kunde des Morgenlandes* 97 (2007); Middelbeck-Varwick, 'Über göttliche Gerechtigkeit und menschliche Erkenntnis bei ʿAbd al-Ğabbār (gest. 1024),' 167–184.

13 Ibrahim M. Abu-Rabiʿ, ed., *Theodicy and Justice in Modern Islamic Thought: The Case of Said Nursi* (Edmonton: Ashgate, 2010).

14 Ryad Alabied, *Die Gerechtigkeit im Islam: Unter besonderer Berücksichtigung des Koran* (Aachen: Verlag Mainz, 2001); Nasr Hamid Abu Zayd, 'Der Begriff "Gerechtigkeit" nach dem Koran', accessed August 1, 2017, https://them.polylog.org/3/fan-de.htm; Abdoldjavad Falaturi, 'Gerechtigkeit im Islam', accessed August 1, 2017, http://www.ahlebeyt.ch/de/index.php/bibliothek/122-gerechtigkeit-im-islam.

15 See his contribution in the current issue, 'Justice as Political Principle in Islam'.

16 Adel T. Khoury, 'Für eine größere Gerechtigkeit in den Beziehungen zwischen Christen und Muslimen', in *Gerechtigkeit in den internationalen und interreligiösen Beziehungen in islamischer*

cussed justice within the context of modern, legal, and social concerns.[17] What is lacking however, is research on justice as a central and socially decisive concept within Muslim communities of the Middle Ages, with a specific focus on al-Māwardī.

Numerous works about al-Māwardī and his thought have been published. Their focus, however, is usually on his main work concerning constitutionality,[18] *al-Aḥkām al-sulṭāniyya* (The Ordinances of Government). The principal themes in these publications are his political thought,[19] his political activities under the

---

und christlicher Perspektive: 1. Iranisch-Österreichische Konferenz, Teheran, 25. bis 28. Februar 1996, Referate – Anfragen – Gesprächsbeiträge, ed. Andreas Bsteh and Seyed A. Mirdamadi (Mödling: St. Gabriel, 1997); Andreas Bsteh and Seyed A. Mirdamadi, eds., *Gerechtigkeit in den internationalen und interreligiösen Beziehungen in islamischer und christlicher Perspektive: 1. Iranisch-Österreichische Konferenz, Teheran, 25. bis 28. Februar 1996, Referate – Anfragen – Gesprächsbeiträge* (Mödling: St. Gabriel, 1997).

17 Fazlur Rahman Malik, 'Islam and the Problem of Economic Justice', *Journal of Islamic Economics* 1 (1995); Baber Johansen, 'The Constitution and the principles of Islamic normativity against the rules of fiqh: A judgment of the Supreme Constitutional Court of Egypt', in *Dispensing Justice in Islam: Qadis and their Judgments*, ed. Muhammad Khalid Masud, Rudolph Peters and David S. Powers (Leiden, Boston: Brill, 2006); Ziba Mir-Hosseini, 'Justice and Equality and Muslim Family Laws: New Ideas, New Prospects', in this issue; Lawrence Rosen, *The Anthropology of Justice: Law as Culture in Islamic Society* (Cambridge: Cambridge University Press, 1989); Lawrence Rosen, *The Justice of Islam: Comparative Perspectives on Islamic Law and Society* (Oxford: Oxford University Press, 2000); Klaus Timm, 'Der moderne Islām über Privateigentum, soziale Gerechtigkeit und Nationalisierung', *Wissenschaftliche Zeitschrift der Humboldt Universität zu Berlin* 21 (1972); Amina Wadud, 'American Muslim identity: Race and ethnicity in progressive Islam', in *Progressive Muslims: On Justice, Gender and Pluralism*, ed. Omid Safi (Oxford: Oneworld, 2003).

18 The description is from Irene Schneider, 'Vernunft oder Tradition: Abū al-Ḥasan ʿAlī al-Māwardīs (d. 49/1058) Hermeneutik des Korans im Spiegel seiner Zeit', *Zeitschrift der Deutschen Morgenländischen Gesellschaft* 156 (2006), especially 59.

19 Norman Calder, 'Friday prayer and the juristic theory of government: Sarakhsī, Shīrāzī, Māwardī', *Bulletin of the School of the Oriental and African Studies* 49 (1986); Patricia Crone, *Medieval Islamic Political Thought* (Edinburgh: Edinburgh University Press, 2004), 259–285; Hamilton A.R. Gibb, 'Al-Mawardī's Theory of the Caliphate', in *Studies on the Civilization of Islam*, ed. Hamilton A.R. Gibb (Boston: Beacon Press, 1962); Eltigani Abdulqadir Hamid, 'Al-Mawardi's theory of state: Some ignored dimensions', *American Journal of Islamic Social Sciences* 18, no. 4 (2001); Hanna Mikhail, *Politics and Revelation: Māwardī and After* (Edinburgh: Edinburgh University Press, 1995); Henri Laoust, 'La pensée et l'action politiques d'al-Mawardi (364–450/974–1058)', *Revue des études islamiques* 36 (1968); Erwin Rosenthal, *Political Thought in Medieval Islam: An Introduction Outline* (Cambridge: Cambridge University Press, 1958), 27–37; and Maria G. Stasolla, 'Some considerations on the second chapter of the Kitāb al-Aḥkām al-sulṭāniyyah. Research Prospective', in *Studies in Arabic and Islam: Proceedings of the 19th congress,*

Abbasids,[20] his theological insights,[21] his method of Quranic exegesis,[22] his activities as a legal scholar, and his thoughts on particular juridical bodies.[23] There is no publication, however, that specifically addresses al-Māwardī's conceptualization of justice in his work *Adab al-dunyā wa al-dīn.*

Biography

The name al-Māwardī is derived from the profession of the scholar's ancestors, who most probably worked in the production and trade of rosewater.[24] Māward is an elision of *mā' al-ward*, rosewater. Needless to say, the suffix -ī is used in this case, to form a name from a job title; māward becomes al-Māwardī, i.e., he who is employed in the production and/or trade of rosewater.

Al-Māwardī was born in Basra in 972 into relatively comfortable living conditions. He studied Islamic jurisprudence (*fiqh*) in both Basra and Baghdad, at a time when these cities were important centres of learning for Mu'tazilite ('rationalistic') thought.[25] His contemporaries gave praise to him and demonstrated their appreciation for his numerous abilities as a well-respected jurist, a skilled diplomat, an excellent rhetorician, and a reliable *ḥadīth*-narrator.[26] Biographical writings describe him as friendly, a man of moderation and virtue.[27]

In terms of legal theory and affiliation, he was a follower of the Shāfi'ī school of thought that has been, in theological terms, categorised as being of Ash'arī orientation. Much of his learning however, was under scholars of strong Mu'tazilite tendencies, and as will be shown later, his arguments contain numer-

Union Européenne des Arabisants et Islamisants, Halle 1998, ed. H. Kilpatrick, B. Martel-Thoumian and H. Schönig (Leuven: Peeters, 2002).

20 Louise Marlow, *Hierarchy and Egalitarianism in Islamic Thought* (Cambridge: Cambridge University Press, 1997).

21 Mohammed Arkoun, 'L'éthique musulmane d'après Mâwardî', *Revue des études islamiques* 31 (1963).

22 Schneider, 'Vernunft oder Tradition'.

23 Henry F. Amedroz, 'The office of Kadi in the Ahkam Sultaniyya of Mawardi', *Journal of the Royal Asiatic Society*, 1910; and idem., 'The Hisba jurisdiction in the Ahkam Sultaniyya of Mawardi', in *Journal of the Royal Asiatic Society* (1916), 77–130.

24 'Abd al-Karīm b. Muḥammad al-Sam'ānī, *Kitāb al-Ansāb*, ed. David S. Margoliouth (Leiden: Brill, 1912), 504.

25 Carl Brockelmann, 'al-Māwardī', in *Encyclopaedia of Islam: Second Edition*, ed. C. Bosworth et al. (Leiden: Brill, 1991).

26 Al-Khaṭīb al-Baghdādī, *Tārīkh madīnāt al-salām*, 17 vols., ed. Bashshār 'Awwād Ma'rūf (Beirut: Dār al-gharb al-islāmī, 2001), 13/587.

27 Brockelmann, 'al-Māwardī'.

ous strong rationalistic strands. Within the judiciary, he rose to the highest ranks when he was appointed supreme judge in Baghdad.[28] He advocated strong central rule, reasoning that this was the only way to guarantee the implementation of rights and justice. He supported a unified confessional authority that was represented, at the time, by the Abbasid caliphs al-Qādir (r. 991–1031) and al-Qā'im (r. 1031–1074). He opposed the increasing power of the Būyids who sought to secede nominally from the central government in Baghdad and establish an independent government. Thus, when the Būyid Jalāl al-Dawla pressured the Abbāsid caliph al-Qā'im to confer upon him the title of *shāhanshāh* ('King of Kings'), al-Māwardī condemned this action and considered that 'such a title was befitting only to God and could not be applied to a worldly ruler.'[29] And yet, even as a general supporter of the interests of the central authority in Baghdad, he was valued by the rival Būyids as a trusted mediator.[30]

Just as other great scholars before him, al-Māwardī did not commit himself to any particular tradition in his political and theological thought, but cultivated his own methodologies and approaches. Many of his contemporaries were irritated by what they perceived as irregularities, leading some to designate him a Muʿtazilite while others classified him as an Ashʿarite.[31] Others still, saw him as a Shāfiʿī in the field of practical-legal matters, and as a rationalist Muʿtazilite in theological-speculative concerns.[32] Clearly, he was not a dogmatic follower of any field. Rather, he was a creative academic who stood for his views, even though they were often contested. His rulings on inheritance rights are an illustrative example. Although it is one of the few themes, discussed at length in the Quran, al-Māwardī opposed the widely held opinion on the matter by not differentiating between close and distant relatives of the deceased. On one occasion he was reproached for this and told to adhere to tradition and avoid innovation. He responded that he held an independent opinion and was no mere imitator.[33]

His religious integrity is emphasised and affirmed by numerous, albeit not verifiable, anecdotes. One such story concerns his piety; it is said that he hid his works in an undisclosed location and refused, during his entire life, to confide their whereabouts. He did this out of fear that he might have considered appeasing interests other than God's while compiling these works. It was only on

28 Brockelmann, 'al-Māwardī'.
29 Mikhail, *Politics and Revelation*, 63.
30 Yāqūt al-Ḥamawī, *Muʿjam al-udabā': Irshād al-arīb ilā maʿrifat al-adīb,* 7 vols. in 1, ed. Iḥsān ʿAbbās (Beirut: Dār al-gharb al-islāmī, 1993), 1955.
31 Mikhail, *Politics and Revelation*, xxxi.
32 Ḥamawī, *Muʿjam al-udabā'*, 1955.
33 Ibid., 1956–1957.

his deathbed that he revealed their location to a trusted friend. He gave him clear instructions: he asked him to hold his hand through death and stated that, if his hand remained closed after his last breath, this would be an indicator that his works were not to the satisfaction of God and that they were to be thrown into the Tigris. If, on the other hand, he opened his closed hand after death, this would mean that his work was satisfactory to God and that it might be made available to others.[34] The authenticity of this kind of anecdote is of course hagiographic in nature;[35] but regardless of its veracity it points to the perception of al-Māwardī as a reputable and faithful scholar.

His epic work in the legal sciences is *Kitāb al-Ḥāwī al-kabīr fī al-furūʿ*. It largely falls within the Shāfiʿī school of thought and has been published in various editions, covering varying scopes of material.[36] In his Quranic exegesis, *Kitāb al-Nukat wa al-ʿuyūn*,[37] he selectively, though not consistently, supports Muʿtazilite views. His best-known work is that in which he discusses his political theories: *al-Aḥkām al-sulṭāniyya wa al-wilāyāt al-dīniyya*,[38] or in short form, *al-Aḥkām al-sulṭāniyya*. More than any other, it was this work that introduced al-Māwardī into Western academia, prompting scholars to designate him the first Muslim thinker to whom was attributed a comprehensive illustration of the Islamic polity.[39]

His most important ethical work, and the work at the centre of this author's contribution about his writings, is *Adab al-dunyā wa al-dīn* (The Ethics of Religion and of this World). The work's original title was, *Al-Bughya al-ʿulyā fī adab al-dīn wa al-dunyā* (The Greatest Ambition in relation to the Ethics of the World and Religion). Over time and due to editorial encroachment the title was changed. The work was translated into German by Oskar Rescher at the be-

---

34 Ibn Khalikān, *Wafayāt al-aʿyān wa anbāʾ abnāʾ al-zamān*, ed. Iḥsān ʿAbbās (Beirut: Dār Ṣādir, 1970), 3/282–283.

35 Ibn Khalikān retells this story with some clear doubts of his own as to its veracity. He uses the weakest form for the narration of an anonymous report by stating 'it has been said' (*qīla*). Gibb also relativizes the claim, and writes in reference to al-Māwardī's *Aḥkām as-sulṭāniyya:* 'it can hardly be true of a work written to the commend and for the use of the caliph.' Gibb, 'Al-Mawardī's Theory of the Caliphate', especially 153.

36 Abū al-Ḥasan al-Māwardī, *Kitāb al-Ḥāwī al-kabīr*, 18 vols., ed. ʿAlī Muḥammad Muʿawwad (Beirut: Dār al-kutub al-ʿilmiyya, 1994).

37 Abū al-Ḥasan al-Māwardī, *Kitāb al-Nukat wa al-ʿuyūn*, 6 vols., ed. al-Sayyid b. ʿAbd al-Maqṣūd b. ʿAbd al-Raḥīm (Beirut: Dār al-kutub al-ʿilmiyya, 1992).

38 Abū al-Ḥasan al-Māwardī, *al-Aḥkām al-sulṭāniyya wa al-wilāyāt al-dīniyya*, ed. Aḥmad Mubārak al-Baghdādī (Kuwait: Dār Ibn Qutayba, 1989).

39 Tilman Nagel, *Staat und Glaubensgemeinschaft im Islam: Geschichte der politischen Ordnungsvorstellungen der Muslime*, 2 vols. (Zurich, Munich: Artemis & Winkler, 1981), 1/394.

ginning of the 20th century, and a new edition has since been made available.[40] Rescher denies the book any claim to originality, and instead sees the main value of the work in the wealth of material it provides on Quranic exegesis, on *ḥadīth* (although a large part of it is suspect, that is, apocryphal), its poetics, literary strength (*adab*), ethics, dictum, etc.[41] This contribution will, to the extent possible, support Rescher's findings concerning the wealth of valuable material found in this book. Additionally, however, this study seeks to provide proof of the originality of the work's content, at least in relation to the theme of justice.

Al-Māwardī's Approach to the Topic

In contrast to other influential thinkers in his age, such as the Muʿtazilite theologian Qāḍī ʿAbd al-Jabbār (932–1025) or the philosopher Abū ʿAlī ibn Sīnā (980–1037), al-Māwardī did not conceive of justice as a matter of theological or philosophical concern. According to ʿAbd al-Jabbār, justice is a central characteristic of God, that can be ascertained by human reason and that affirms free will.[42] Ibn Sīnā discussed justice within the neo-Platonic tradition as a virtue that sustains the natural/holy order of things, both in society and within the family.[43]

Unlike these scholars, al-Māwardī sees justice as a wholly worldly matter that is absolutely central to the functioning of all aspects of society. In his work, *Adab al-dunyā wa al-dīn*, he lists five main themes: virtues of reason

40 Oskar Rescher, *Gesammelte Werke: Eine Sammlung der wichtigsten Schriften Oskar Reschers, teilweise mit Ergänzungen und Verbesserungen aus dem handschriftlichen Nachlaß; in V Abt.: 2,3. Abt. II, Schriften zur Adab-Literatur; Bd. 3. ĞBḥiẓ, Abū-ʿUṯmān ʿAmr Ibu-Baḥr al-: Das Kitāb al-maḥāsin wa"l-masāwī. Das Kitāb adab ad-dunyā wa"d-dīn / Qāḍī abū"l-Ḥasan ʿAlī b. Muḥammad al-Māwardī. Aus d. Arab. übers. von O. Rescher*, ed. Necati Lugal (Osnabrück: Biblio-Verlag, Nachdr. 1984).

41 Ibid.

42 On the views of Qādī ʿAbd al-Jabbār concerning the theme of justice, see al-Qāḍī ʿAbd al-Jabbār, *Sharḥ uṣūl al-khamsa*, ed. ʿAbd al-Karīm ʿUthmān (Cairo: Maktabat al-Wahba, 1965), 299–608; and al-Qāḍī ʿAbd al-Jabbār, *al-Mughnī fī abwāb al-tawḥīd wa al-ʿal-*, 14 vols. in 16, ed. Ibrāhim Madhkūr et al. (Cairo: Wizārat al-Thaqāfa wa al-irshād al-qawmī, 1960), vol. 6.

43 At different points in the text, Ibn Sīnā discusses his ideas concerning social and family relations. These passages are indicative of his conceptualization of justice. This is most visible in the thematic area *ilāhiyyāt* ('metaphysics') towards the end of his work, *al-Shifāʾ* (namely, in the chapters *fī ʿaqd al-madīna wa ʿaqd al-bayt, wa huwa al-nikāḥ wa al-sunan al-kulliyya fī dhālik*, 447–451, and, und *fā al-khalīfa wa al-imām wa wujūb ṭāʿatihimā, wa al-ishāra ilā al-siyāsāt wa al-muʿāmalāt wa al-akhlāq*, 451–455); Abū ʿAlī Ibn Sīnā, *al-Shifāʾ*, *ilāhiyyāt*, ed. al-Ab al-Qanawātī and Saʿīd Zāyid (Cairo: al-Hayʾa al-ʿāmma li shuʾūn al-maṭābiʿ al-amīriyya, 1960).

(*faḍl al-ʿaql*), ethics of knowledge (*adab al-ʿilm*), ethics of the soul (*adab al-nafs*), ethics of religion (*adab al-dīn*) and worldly ethics (*adab al-dunyā*). It is within the last chapter about how to conduct oneself in the world, that al-Māwardī discusses his thoughts concerning justice and demonstrates how it represents a comprehensive concept that should govern all social relations.

We find a similar formulation at a later period of the Middle Ages in the work of the distinguished Doctor of the Church Thomas Aquinas (1225–1274). With regard to the conceptualizsation of justice in antiquity, and with reference to Plato and Aristotle, he spoke of general or universal justice. He meant by this an understanding that is relevant for all basic relations within society. He set up two opposite conceptualizations of justice, however: general justice was separate from special or particular justice, which ordered the relationship between one human and another or within a small group.[44]

Although al-Māwardī differentiates between different spheres of relations within society, he does not find it necessary to differentiate between general and particular forms of justice. For he believes there is no possibility of just relations existing in one realm, if relations are unjust in another. He discerns three conceivable sets of relations within a polity and emphasises how justice must preside within each of these in order for society to function. There is the relationship between ruler and ruled (or in modern terminology the relationship of the state to its citizens); the relationship of ruled to ruler (or the relationship of citizen to the state), and lastly, the relationships of the subjects amongst themselves (relationships between citizens). He finds that justice is not conceivable if the relationships in all three spheres are not just.

The Concept of Comprehensive Justice

Al-Māwardī's concept begins with a basic premise, namely, that in order for the world to be a good[45] world, six criteria must be met: a religion that is followed

44 Stefan Lippert, *Recht und Gerechtigkeit bei Thomas von Aquin: Eine rationale Rekonstruktion im Kontext der Summa Theologiae* (Marburg: Elwert, 2000), 83–85.

45 Under this adjective good, I intend to group together in a very general way the following three characteristics: well, ordered, harmonious. These are the words with which al-Māwardī describes the world that he considers desirable, and for which just conditions are a precondition. It is also in this unspecific manner that the Duden dictionary of the German language uses the gradation of good to describe relationships and conditions that are pleasant and enjoyable. Duden-Redaktion, *Duden: Das große Wörterbuch der deutschen Sprache,* 10 vols. (Mannheim: Duden-Verlag, 1999), 4/1620. The use of the concept of the good in the history of philosophy

(*dīn muttabaʿ*), a firm ruler (*sulṭān qāhir*), comprehensive justice (*ʿadl shāmil*), public security (*amn ʿāmm*), lasting fecundity (*khiṣb dāʾim*) of the land, and the broad hope (*amal fasīḥ*) of the people.[46]

In the following I shall explain these points in more detail:

Religion: although al-Māwardī considers religion essential to his conception of a good world, his understanding of religion is rationalistic. Adherence to religious guidance is not important simply because it is commanded, or for fear of punishment from God, but rather, because it impedes the overstepping of moral boundaries and contributes to a well-adjusted life.[47] He differentiates between the terms *sharʿ* (in this case, synonymous with religion) and *ʿaql* (reason), and he explains that in his opinion, religion follows on from reason, i.e., religion appears to the human who is already equipped with reason. According to him, reason leads humans to recognise the necessity of religious guidance.[48] Interestingly, he differentiates between the spheres of religion and politics. Both are connected to justice, however, and both ensure healthy rule and the prospering of countries.

He reinforces the separation of religion and politics in the next part of his argument, in which he states that it is important to follow religious as well as political guidelines. He reasons that if one does not follow religious obligations, one harms oneself; but if one brings ruin to other countries, one is inflicting harm on others.[49] Thus, for him, the religious sphere concerns individual, personal space, while political prescriptions affect society as a whole.

Firm ruler: the second condition for a good world, according to al-Māwardī, is to have a strong ruler. This is not an end in itself, however, but a means of guaranteeing justice.

As an experienced judge and effective emissary, al-Māwardī had no illusions about the difficulty inherent in achieving the type of comprehensive justice that

---

has generally been ascribed to the pre-modern age, when the good was conceived as existing independently of the individual and the world. On the historical-philosophical development of the term, see Robert Spaemann, 'Gut, höchstes', in *Historisches Wörterbuch der Philosophie*, vol. 3, ed. Joachim Ritter et al., 13 vols. (Basel: Schwabe, 1971–2007), 3. In al-Māwardī's thought, however, the connection of the good world with humans and their actions is very clear.

46 Abū al-Ḥasan al-Māwardī, *Adab al-dunyā wa al-dīn*, ed. Muṣṭafā al-Saqqā (Cairo: Maktabat al-Wahba, 1973), 135–136.

47 Ibid., 136.

48 Ibid.

49 Ibid.

is so central to his conception of a good world. He endorsed the need for a strong ruler in order to fight potential abuses of power, rivalries, to contain outbreaks of violence, and to combat injustice.[50] And although he concedes that it is possible to confront injustice through one's own reason and spiritual conviction, both reason and religion are still susceptible to weakness and liable to be abused; they may be put to personal use by being interpreted in favour of self-serving interests. Only strong rule then, can reliably stave off injustice.[51] His thoughts on this theme are very far-reaching. Translated into modern terminology, he is basically making the case that rational or religious arguments, compelling as they might be, are insufficient to guarantee justice; to this end, one needs strong institutions that are able to act in a decisive manner. He does not, however, discuss the question of what to do when the institutions or political leadership no longer act in a just manner. As will become clear, he hopes that he can trust in the ruler's common sense and ego, as he considers that unjust action will not serve a ruler's interests either.

It is not essential for al-Māwardī whether the necessity of a strong ruler is justified in religious or in rational terms. He is more concerned with a different argument, namely that systems of parallel rule are not permissible on religious or on rational grounds.[52] This is also borne out by his stance vis-à-vis the Būyid power struggle against the caliphate in Baghdad; he was at pains to convince the Būyids to submit to the caliph.[53]

He lists the duties of a ruler as follows: a) the safeguarding of religion against falsification and the fostering of compliance with religious prescriptions; b) the defence of central authority, the protection of society in the face of enemies of religion and dangers to the lives and property of the citizens; c) the construction of cities and streets; d) the sound management of finances; e) the fight against injustice and the provision of just conditions; f) the execution of the law in an even-handed manner, without dilution or exaggeration; and g) the consideration of competence and reliability when it comes to official authorities.[54]

Al-Māwardī concludes that if a ruler manages to accomplish all of these, then he has acted justly towards God and deserves the loyalty and sympathy of his subjects.[55]

---

50 Ibid., 136–137.
51 Ibid., 137.
52 Ibid., 138.
53 Brockelmann, 'al-Māwardī', 869.
54 Al-Māwardī, *Adab al-dunyā wa al-dīn*, 139.
55 Ibid.

Comprehensive justice: the third condition for a good world that al-Māwardī lists is that of comprehensive justice (*al-ʿadl al-shāmil*). If this criterion is fulfilled, it will foster mutual trust, encourage citizens to be law-abiding, promote the flourishing of communities, the increase of wealth and of the children, and overall heightened security.[56] He warns, however:

> nothing destroys the earth and the hearts of humans more swiftly than injustice; for injustice knows no limits and obeys no boundaries. Every one of its manifestations (*kull juzʾ minhu*) shares in the ruin, until it is omnipresent.[57]

Al-Māwardī clearly believes that legislation is insufficient to guarantee justice. He emphasises, in a somewhat didactic manner, that it is equally important for an individual to be convinced of justice and its general advantages. To demonstrate this point more clearly, he makes recourse to an anecdote, as is the case in many of his works. During the conquest of India, Alexander the Great is said to have encountered some local scholars; in mild bewilderment, he asked them why there were so few laws governing societies in the region. They are said to have answered, because everyone respects the rights of others and the rulers act justly.[58] While it is impossible to ascertain the veracity of the encounter, the point here is rather to consider the function of anecdotes and proverbs in al-Māwardī's work. In this case, he makes use of the anecdote to suggest that the execution of existing laws is more effective than constantly passing new ones.

Early on in his thoughts on justice, al-Māwardī established a differentiation between the individual and the social sides of justice. He discusses on the one hand what it means to act in a just manner towards oneself (*ʿadl al-insān fī nafsihi*), and on the other, what justice means in relation to others (*ʿadluhu fī ghayrihi*).[59] He does not have much to say about the individual side of it, save that to be just towards oneself is to turn to what is good and to distance oneself from vice. This also means to know oneself, one's habits and weaknesses, in order to remain centred along the continuum of excess and neglect. For there is injustice in both, excess and neglect; if you are unjust toward yourself, you are more likely to be unjust unto others, and if you do yourself an injustice, then you are committing a larger injustice towards others.[60]

56 Ibid.
57 Ibid.
58 Ibid.
59 Ibid.
60 Ibid.

Al-Māwardī's exposition on the social aspects of justice is both more elaborate and more remarkable. He establishes different relational spheres within society, illustrates the ways in which they are connected, and gives each of them equal importance in the conceptualization of comprehensive justice. His is a remarkable thought process and very much ahead of his time. This becomes clearer, however, when his ideas are translated into modern terminology, as will be shown below.

Al-Māwardī distinguishes three spheres of relationships within society: there is the top-down relationship (*ʿadl al-insān fī man dūnahu*), there is the bottom-up relational sphere, (*ʿadl al-insān maʿa man fawqahu*), and then there is the realm of 'horizontal relations' (*ʿadl al-insān maʿa akfāʾihi*).[61] Al-Māwardī makes conscious use of vague expressions of top and bottom, above, below, high, and low, by which he indicates social hierarchies. The top rungs include the individuals who occupy higher positions within the social structure, such as the ruler, a judge, an employer, or simply anyone in a superior position.[62] These are distinguished from the subjects, the citizens, who are at a lower level within the social hierarchic structure.[63] The horizontal sphere is the mutual relationship of the subjects/citizens. The three dimensions are illustrated below.

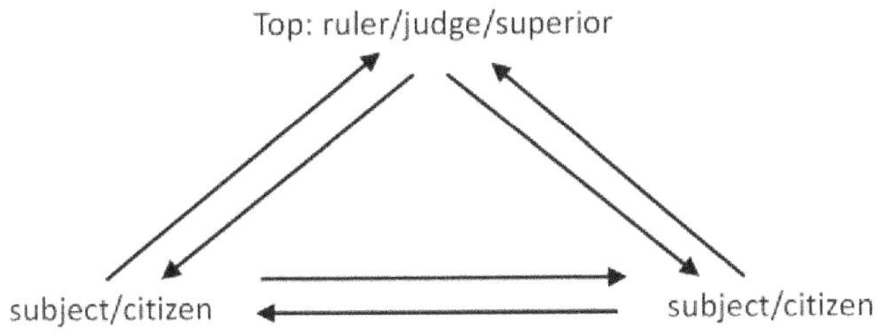

Al-Māwardī considers the hierarchic structure of society to be rational. He warns, however, that the sustainability of contentedness within society is only achieved if and when those at the top rule over their subjects in a just manner. According to him, this means: a) asking of their subjects only what is within reason (*maysūr*); b) omitting that which is not within reason (*maʿsūr*); c) not attempting to solidify their rule through acts of violence; and d) striving to be

61 Ibid., 142.
62 Ibid.
63 Ibid.

just in all their actions.[64] Al-Māwardī backs these claims up by saying that following what is reasonable to ask of people is sustainable in the long-run, avoiding demanding what is not feasible provides for safety, refraining from violence builds up sympathy, and just behaviour secures a strong support base.[65]

Conversely, when considering the behaviour of those below towards those above, justice is served when citizens can wholeheartedly follow the commands of those above them, fully support them, and be honest in their loyalty towards them. For a loyal following leads to solidarity; devotion and support are the best defences against weakness, and honest loyalty does away with distrust.[66] Al-Māwardī is very much aware of the consequences of a distrustful relationship between the state and its citizens. He warns against betrayal, stating that the subjects will, in the end, have to be fearful of the very entity of which they seek protection.[67]

He then discusses the third sphere, the relationship of citizens with one another. Their relations are just if every citizen treats the other as an equal, is not arrogant, and inflicts no harm. Treating each other as equals fosters harmony, avoiding arrogance promotes mutual understanding, and avoiding harm supports justice.[68] If citizens neglect these points, al-Māwardī continues, there will be constant enmity between them that will eventually lead everyone into destruction.[69]

In his explications, al-Māwardī consistently reasons on deontological and more so on teleological grounds. This reasoning occurs already in his discussion of how top-down relations in society can be considered just. By always referring back to the Quran or *ḥadīth*, he simultaneously reinforces the notion that just behaviour is a religious and moral imperative. He is more concerned, however, with explaining how acting in a just manner is advantageous to all parties involved. Throughout the work he formulates his arguments with reference to relevant aphorisms or verses of poetry. He refers to sayings such as: rule can be maintained by deceit, but not by injustice; or, the unjust will never have a neighbor / friend, nor a home; or, if a sovereign turns his back on justice, his subjects will turn their backs on him; or, lastly, injustice destroys wealth and engenders rage.[70] He further maintains his teleological form of argumentation in a para-

64 Ibid.
65 Ibid.
66 Ibid.
67 Ibid.
68 Ibid., 143.
69 Ibid.
70 Ibid., 142.

graph concerning the relationships of subjects amongst each other. At the end of it, he concludes: in this respect, there is nothing more beneficial than justice and nothing more detrimental than injustice.[71]

Public security: without public security, there is no comprehensive justice and the good world al-Māwardī imagines remains unattainable. There can be just conditions only in a society in which one does not need to fear for one's life, one's family, or one's wealth. Where there is fear, there is no possibility of caring for oneself, or of pursuing one's rights, let alone of tending to the needs of others.[72] At the same time, however, he warns that one should not become too accustomed to general safety or take it for granted. For the real value of security is realised only when it is not there and one must fear everything. In the same vein, a healthy individual will only appreciate the value of health when he is afflicted by illness.[73] To reinforce his point, al-Māwardī makes use of another proverb: the value of a comfort is only recognised when one is forced to struggle with its opposite.[74]

Lasting fecundity: the fifth condition for a good world listed by al-Māwardī is the lasting fecundity (*khiṣb dāʾim*) of the land for this guarantees the well-being of the individual. He emphasises that all members of society, rich and poor, must be equal participants in maintaining the fertility of the land.[75] This way, he believes, there will be hardly any room for jealousy or hate. The fertility of the land makes more offspring possible, leads to mutual support, and general social cohesion.[76] This will strengthen efforts towards well-being and order in the world; for a fertile land will lead to prosperity, and prosperity in turn to security and munificence.[77] Here also al-Māwardī considered both sides of the coin: the general availability of sufficient goods has a positive effect on the public, just as a scarcity of resources affects all as well. Hence, the fertility of the land is to be seen as one of the conditions of a good world.[78] Al-Māwardī does not deny that agricultural yields also depend on factors outside human control

71 Ibid., 144.
72 Ibid., 144.
73 Ibid., 145; Rescher, *Gesammelte Werke*, 2/29.
74 Al-Māwardī, *Adab al-dunyā wa al-dīn*, 145.
75 Ibid., 145.
76 Ibid.
77 Ibid.
78 Ibid., 146.

(precipitation, sunshine, etc.), but emphasises that their effectiveness is strongly connected to justice.[79]

Broad hope: in order for the well-being of the good world and all its other advantages to extend into the next generation, humans should consider and plan for the long-term sustainability of their actions and think about their consequences beyond their own lifetimes. This way of life that is oriented toward the future is expressed in al-Māwardī's writing as far-reaching, broad hope (*amal fasīḥ*):[80]

> Concerning the sixth precondition, it consists of an expansive hope, that drives the acquisition [production] of things, for whose attainment and ascertainment this life is too short.[81]

It would be anachronistic to project onto al-Māwardī's broad hope the modern conception of generational justice. His formulation does, nonetheless, call for gainful occupation, be it agricultural or artisanal, for as long and as well as possible, so that the next generations may also gain something from it:

> Were it not that the descendant benefits from the work of his predecessor, then the people of each generation would have to begin anew which would involve a great deal of hardship. Hence, may humans be blessed with expansive hope. If people cultivate only short-term hopes, then the individual will not overcome/surpass the needs of each day, and will tend only to his immediate needs. But then the world would but be passed in a wholly decayed state from one generation to the next.[82]

In this manner, al-Māwardī devises a good world, that requires adherence to religion, but in the centre of which stands the concept of justice that cannot be guaranteed without state force, that is not realizable without security and a sufficient amount of material well-being, and that, in the absence of expansive hope, will not bear fruit for future generations.

At the end of his explications, al-Māwardī anticipates the question that logically arises after this conceptualization, namely: what to do when the conditions of this good world/society have been met? Is this not then the end of social processes? Will the good world not fall into stagnation from this point onwards? How can the members of this good world motivate themselves further?

79 Ibid.
80 Ibid.
81 Ibid.
82 Ibid., 146, the English rendering here is very close to the German translation by Rescher, *Gesammelte Werke*, 2/32–33.

Without actually formulating these questions, al-Māwardī points out, in an almost deconstructivist manner, that there can be no moment of perfection or completion in a world that is constantly in flux. And thus, the striving for a good/*just* world will never cease. In his words:

> These six conditions provide for the well-being and fidelity of the world. If they are all met, the world will be perfect. It is unlikely, however, for man to have a completely perfect world. The world is created as something that is alterable and ephemeral. As one man once lamented that God was always transforming the world, a sage responded, then the world is in order, insofar as it is ever-changing.[83]

Conclusion

In his ethical book *Adab al-dunyā wa al-dīn*, al-Māwardī discusses a concept of 'comprehensive Justice' that seems to me to be innovative. He does not focus on the concept as a metaphysical characteristic (holy justice), which is the subject of theological differences (e.g. between the Muʿtazila and the Ashʿariyya). He also does not regard the term as an human virtue, which is the focus of the questions related to the law. Rather, he views justice as a profane question and as a socially relevant concept, which is decisive for the regulation of social conditions and thus for the functioning of a social system. It is also striking that he argues for the justifying of the necessity of just behavior in an experience-oriented and pragmatic manner. His basic argument in this context is that a just behavior is indispensable for the functioning of the community and therefore advantageous for all members of the community.

Bibliography

ʿAbd al-Jabbār, al-Qāḍī. *Al-Mughnī fī abwāb al-tawḥīd wa al-ʿadl.* Edited by Ibrāhim Madhkūr et al. 14 vols. in 16. Cairo: Wizārat al-Thaqāfa wa al-irshād al-qawmī, 1960.

—. *Sharḥ uṣūl al-khamsa.* Edited by ʿAbd al-Karīm ʿUthmān. Cairo: Maktabat al-Wahba, 1965.

Abu Zayd, Nasr Hamid. 'Der Begriff "Gerechtigkeit" nach dem Koran'. Accessed August 1, 2017. https://them.polylog.org/3/fan-de.htm.

Abu-Rabiʿ, Ibrahim M., ed. *Theodicy and Justice in Modern Islamic Thought: The Case of Said Nursi.* Edmonton: Ashgate, 2010.

Alabied, Ryad. *Die Gerechtigkeit im Islam: Unter besonderer Berücksichtigung des Koran.* Aachen: Verlag Mainz, 2001.

---

83 Al-Māwardī, *Adab al-dunyā wa al-dīn*, 147.

Amedroz, Henry Frederick. 'The office of Kadi in the Ahkam Sultaniyya of Mawardi'. *Journal of the Royal Asiatic Society*, 1910, 635–674.

Arkoun, Mohammed. 'L'éthique musulmane d'après Mâwardî'. *Revue des études islamiques* 31 (1963): 1–31.

Baghdādī, al-Khaṭīb al-. *Tārīkh madīnāt al-salām*. Edited by Bashshār 'Awwād Ma'rūf. 17 vols. Beirut: Dār al-gharb al-islāmī, 2001.

Ben Abdeljelil, Jameleddine. 'Die Frage der Theodizee im Islam: Mensch Gott Gerechtigkeit'. *Wiener Zeitschrift für die Kunde des Morgenlandes* 97 (2007): 15–20.

Brockelmann, Carl. 'al-Māwardī'. In *Encyclopaedia of Islam: Second Edition*. Edited by C. Bosworth et al., 869. Leiden: Brill, 1991.

Bsteh, Andreas and Seyed A. Mirdamadi, eds. *Gerechtigkeit in den internationalen und interreligiösen Beziehungen in islamischer und christlicher Perspektive: 1. Iranisch-Österreichische Konferenz, Teheran, 25. bis 28. Februar 1996, Referate – Anfragen – Gesprächsbeiträge*. Mödling: St. Gabriel, 1997.

Calder, Norman. 'Friday prayer and the juristic theory of government: Sarakhsī, Shīrāzī, Māwardī'. *Bulletin of the School of the Oriental and African Studies* 49 (1986): 35–47.

Crone, Patricia. *Medieval Islamic Political Thought*. Edinburgh: Edinburgh University Press, 2004.

Duden-Redaktion. *Duden: Das große Wörterbuch der deutschen Sprache*. 10 vols. Mannheim: Duden-Verlag, 1999.

Ess, Josef van. *Theologie und Gesellschaft im 2. und 3. Jahrhundert Hidschra: Eine Geschichte des religiösen Denkens im frühen Islam*. 6 vols. Berlin: De Gruyter, 1991.

Falaturi, Abdoldjavad. 'Gerechtigkeit im Islam'. Accessed August 1, 2017. http://www.ahlebeyt.ch/de/index.php/bibliothek/122-gerechtigkeit-im-islam.

Gibb, Hamilton A.R. 'Al-Mawardī's Theory of the Caliphate'. In *Studies on the Civilization of Islam*. Edited by Hamilton A.R. Gibb, 151–165. Boston: Beacon Press, 1962.

Ḥamawī, Yāqūt al-. *Mu'jam al-udabā': Irshād al-arīb ilā ma'rifat al-adīb*. Edited by Iḥsān 'Abbās. 7 vols. in 1. Beirut: Dār al-gharb al-islāmī, 1993.

Hamid, Eltigani Abdulqadir. 'Al-Mawardi's theory of state: Some ignored dimensions'. *American Journal of Islamic Social Sciences* 18, no. 4 (2001): 1–18.

Höffe, Otfried. *Gerechtigkeit: Eine philosophische Einführung*. Munich: Beck, 2010.

Ibn Khalikān. *Wafayāt al-a'yān wa anbā' abnā' al-zamān*. Edited by Iḥsān 'Abbās. Beirut: Dār Ṣādir, 1970.

Ibn Sīnā, Abū 'Alī. *Al-Shifā', ilāhiyyāt*. Edited by al-Ab al-Qanawātī and Sa'īd Zāyid. Cairo: al-Hay'a al-'āmma li shu'ūn al-maṭābi' al-amīriyya, 1960.

Ibn Taymiyya, Aḥmad. *Majmū' al-fatāwā shaykh al-islām Aḥmad ibn Taymiyya*. Edited by 'Abd ar-Raḥmān Ibn Muḥammad ibn Qāsim and Muḥammad Ibn 'Abd al-Raḥmān ibn Qāsim. Riyadh, Mecca, n.d. [1962–7].

Johansen, Baber. 'The Constitution and the principles of Islamic normativity against the rules of fiqh: A judgment of the Supreme Constitutional Court of Egypt'. In *Dispensing Justice in Islam: Qadis and their Judgments*. Edited by Muhammad Khalid Masud, Rudolph Peters and David S. Powers, 169–93. Leiden, Boston: Brill, 2006.

Khoury, Adel Theodor. 'Für eine größere Gerechtigkeit in den Beziehungen zwischen Christen und Muslimen'. In *Gerechtigkeit in den internationalen und interreligiösen Beziehungen in islamischer und christlicher Perspektive: 1. Iranisch-Österreichische Konferenz,*

Teheran, 25. bis 28. Februar 1996, Referate – Anfragen – Gesprächsbeiträge. Edited by Andreas Bsteh and Seyed A. Mirdamadi, 351–75. Mödling: St. Gabriel, 1997.
Krawietz, Birgit. 'Gerechtigkeit als Leitidee islamischen Rechts'. In *Islam und Rechtsstaat: Zwischen Scharia und Säkularisierung*. Edited by Birgit Krawietz and Helmut Reifeld, 37–52. Berlin: Konrad-Adenauer-Stiftung e.V., 2008.
Laoust, Henri. 'La pensée et l'action politiques d'al-Mawardi (364–450/974–1058)'. *Revue des études islamiques* 36 (1968): 11–92.
Lippert, Stefan. *Recht und Gerechtigkeit bei Thomas von Aquin: Eine rationale Rekonstruktion im Kontext der Summa Theologiae*. Marburg: Elwert, 2000.
Makdisi, George. 'Ashʿari and Ashʿarites in Islamic religious history'. In *Islamic Philosophy and Theology: Critical Concepts in Islamic Thought*. Edited by Ian R. Netton, 255–302. London: Routledge, 2007.
Malik, Fazlur Rahman. 'Islam and the Problem of Economic Justice'. *Journal of Islamic Economics* 1 (1995): 14–58.
Marlow, Louise. *Hierarchy and Egalitarianism in Islamic Thought*. Cambridge: Cambridge University Press, 1997.
Māwardī, Abū al-Ḥasan al-. *Adab al-dunyā wa al-dīn*. Edited by Muṣṭafā al-Saqqā. Cairo: Maktabat al-Wahba, 1973.
—. *Al-Aḥkām al-sulṭāniyya wa al-wilāyāt al-dīniyya*. Edited by Aḥmad Mubārak al-Baghdādī. Kuwait: Dār Ibn Qutayba, 1989.
—. *Kitāb al-Nukat wa al-ʿuyūn*. Edited by al-Sayyid b. ʿAbd al-Maqṣūd b. ʿAbd al-Raḥīm. 6 vols. Beirut: Dār al-kutub al-ʿilmiyya, 1992.
—. *Kitāb al-Ḥāwī al-kabīr*. Edited by ʿAlī Muḥammad Muʿawwad. 18 vols. Beirut: Dār al-kutub al-ʿilmiyya, 1994.
Middelbeck-Varwick, Anja. 'Über göttliche Gerechtigkeit und menschliche Erkenntnis bei ʿAbd al-Ǧabbār (gest. 1024): Dialog mit einer mu'tazilitischen Rechtfertigung Gottes'. In *Heil in Christentum und Islam, Erlösung oder Rechtleitung? Theologisches Forum Christentum – Islam*. Edited by Hansjörg Schmid, Andreas Renz and Jutta Sperber, 167–84. Stuttgart: Akademie der Diözese Rottenburg-Stuttgart, 2004.
Mikhail, Hanna. *Politics and Revelation: Māwardī and After*. Edinburgh: Edinburgh University Press, 1995.
Muṭahharī, Murtaḍā. *Barrasī-yi ijmālī-yi mabānī-yi iqtiṣād-i islāmī*. Qom, 1990.
Nagel, Tilman. *Staat und Glaubensgemeinschaft im Islam: Geschichte der politischen Ordnungsvorstellungen der Muslime*. 2 vols. Zurich, Munich: Artemis & Winkler, 1981.
Rescher, Oskar. *Gesammelte Werke: Eine Sammlung der wichtigsten Schriften Oskar Reschers, teilweise mit Ergänzungen und Verbesserungen aus dem handschriftlichen Nachlaß; in V Abt.: 2,3. Abt. II, Schriften zur Adab-Literatur; Bd. 3. Ǧaḥiẓ, Abū-ʿUṯmān ʿAmr Ibu-Baḥr al-: Das Kitāb al-maḥāsin wa'l-masāwī. Das Kitāb adab ad-dunyā wa'd-dīn / Qāḍī abū'l-Ḥasan ʿAlī b. Muḥammad al-Māwardī. Aus d. Arab. übers. von O. Rescher*. Edited by Necati Lugal. Osnabrück: Biblio-Verlag, Nachdr. 1984.
Rosen, Lawrence. *The Anthropology of Justice: Law as Culture in Islamic Society*. Cambridge: Cambridge University Press, 1989.
—. *The Justice of Islam: Comparative Perspectives on Islamic Law and Society*. Oxford: Oxford University Press, 2000.
Rosenthal, Erwin. *Political Thought in Medieval Islam: An Introduction Outline*. Cambridge: Cambridge University Press, 1958.

Rudolph, Ulrich. *Al-Māturīdī und die sunnitische Theologie in Samarkand.* Leiden: Brill, 1996.
Samʿānī, ʿAbd al-Karīm b. Muḥammad al-. *Kitāb al-Ansāb.* Edited by David S. Margoliouth. Leiden: Brill, 1912.
Schneider, Irene. 'Vernunft oder Tradition: Abū al-Ḥasan ʿAlī al-Māwardīs (d. 49/1058) Hermeneutik des Korans im Spiegel seiner Zeit'. *Zeitschrift der Deutschen Morgenländischen Gesellschaft* 156 (2006): 57–80.
Spaemann, Robert. 'Gut, höchstes'. In *Historisches Wörterbuch der Philosophie.* Vol. 3. Edited by Joachim Ritter et al. 13 vols., 974–76. Basel: Schwabe, 1971–2007.
Stasolla, Maria Giovanna. 'Some considerations on the second chapter of the Kitāb al-Aḥkām al-sulṭāniyyah. Research Prospective'. In *Studies in Arabic and Islam: Proceedings of the 19th congress, Union Européenne des Arabisants et Islamisants, Halle 1998.* Edited by H. Kilpatrick, B. Martel-Thoumian and H. Schönig, 523–30. Leuven: Peeters, 2002.
Timm, Klaus. 'Der moderne Islām über Privateigentum, soziale Gerechtigkeit und Nationalisierung'. *Wissenschaftliche Zeitschrift der Humboldt Universität zu Berlin* 21 (1972): 201–219.
Wadud, Amina. 'American Muslim identity: Race and ethnicity in progressive Islam'. In *Progressive Muslims: On Justice, Gender and Pluralism.* Edited by Omid Safi, 270–285. Oxford: Oneworld, 2003.

Werner Ende

Justice as a Political Principle in Islam

Any detailed description of a particular set of facts of the religion and civilisation of Islam should be prefaced with introductory comments specifying its frame of reference. If this is not done, any statements made about, for example, the situation of women, children, farmers, craftsmen, traders, court officials or rulers 'in Islam' is apt to be misleading. (Basically, the same holds true for any statements about corresponding phenomena in Christianity and/or in Christendom as well as in other religions, but this is not our subject.) What needs to be clarified at the outset is to what a particular description and analysis refers. In other words, is it, as some Muslim intellectuals demand, exclusively about statements made in the Quran, the pure word of God as Muslims firmly believe? Or should it also concern itself with the sayings and doings of the prophet Muhammad (d. 632 CE), the so-called Hadith, which are regarded as normative, as well as with his religious, political and social practices, or Sunna? If so, what is the importance of the decisions and actions of his companions, particularly the first successors to the leadership of the early Muslim community, the four so-called 'rightly- guided caliphs' who reigned from 632 to 661?

It is the statements of the Quran and the traditions of the early age of Islam on which the Sharia rests, a code that was developed essentially during the first three centuries. The Sharia is a monumental system of rules on ritual, social, ethical and legal questions, which is however rent by denominational disputes and partly ossified. How important is the Sharia for any general statements about conditions in Islam? Or, to put it differently: What is the current and former status of its detailed regulations *vis-à-vis* the legal and social realities past and present in a territory that ranges from Morocco to Chinese Turkistan? Moreover: When we make statements about 'Islam as such', are we talking only about the religious and legal norms that were developed by jurists or also about the discourses written down in Arabic or any other language of the Islamic culture by Muslim theologians, philosophers, historians, geographers or poets? What value do we accord to observations by Muslim and non-Muslim travellers, ethnographers and other observers regarding the diversity of ideas and religious practices followed by certain groups in the 'Islamic reality' of the present? What is the scientific import of the content and manifestations of what is called 'popular Islam'? Does it really have nothing to do with 'true Islam', as today's fundamentalists and their followers would have us believe? Is it admissible in the first place to include in a consideration of the essence of Islam the partially syncretistic ideas of heterodox communities? And when it comes to the some-

https://doi.org/10.1515/9783110574593-004

times discriminatory judgements to be found in traditional entertainment literature, to what extent may or should these be considered in describing certain phenomena, such as the way the various human ethnicities are regarded? Is it not enough merely to say that neither the Quran nor the Hadith contains statements that might be interpreted as justifying racial discrimination on religious grounds? And if so, what about the fact that racism was and is present in the thoughts and actions of Muslims?

The above shows how very problematic it is to make generalised statements about 'Islam as such', for any statement necessarily relates to a limited field of observation. Many Muslims believe it is their right and/or their duty to speak as apologists. (Most followers of other religions or secularist world views do not behave much differently where their convictions are concerned.)

Be that as it may: Both Muslims and non-Muslims should steer clear of any undifferentiated (or, to use a modern buzzword, essentialist) statements when talking about Islam or any other religion. In our case, this refers to generalised statements like 'Islam as such is tolerant/intolerant'. Those who make such generalised judgements pretend that there is a single subject named Islam that is capable of talking and acting. They dispense with comprehensively addressing all the different things that can be subsumed under Islam, things that are regarded as Islamic in the narrower or broader meaning of the word by many Muslims as well as many outsiders. To quote one example: The followers of Sufism and Wahhabism widely differ on essential points of their own religious interpretation and practice. From their respective points of view, many of the convictions and phenomena that characterise the religious life of the other side are nothing but false doctrines from the fringes or even from outside true Islam. At the same time, any holistic representation of Islamic civilisation that strives to be objective will never be complete without including these two manifestations of Islam, once again differentiated by space and time. Of course, it is not necessary for such considerations to be free from criticism.

What I have said so far is intended to provide a historical and geographical context for the following, necessarily sketchy remarks about concepts of 'justice in Islam'. There can be no serious doubt that such concepts do exist and that they have played an eminent role in the thinking of many Muslims since the dawn of Islam.

After the dispute that arose over who should succeed Muhammad as leader of the community after his death (632 CE), the debate centred on questions related to finding and confirming a ruler, the conditions under which he should exercise power and his personal justice. Even in the early age of Islam, the comments of the religious and political opposition parties revolved around such issues. While they may have lost some of their divisiveness in the later course of Islam's intellectual history, they were never forgotten, and the discourse of today's Muslim fundamentalists has revived them to a degree that is partially astonishing and threatening. The fact that, both within the Sharia and beyond, justice is one of the key ideas of the Islamic concept of order in no way implies that Muslims regard the course of their civilisation's history as a triumphant progress of law and justice. Moreover, most of those who think about such things at all believe that the actual history of their religion and/or the societies characterised by it feature/s a number of tragically misdirected developments from the very beginning. In their opinion, these manifested themselves in those numerous cases in which power was usurped, the people were oppressed and Islamic law (i.e. the will of God) was infringed in other ways. This view explains why, even in the early age of Islam, there was an idea that God would send a messiah some time before the end of the world who would conquer evil and create a realm of justice. The Quran does not mention the eschatological figure of this redeemer, called in Arabic the *mahdi* (literally: 'he who is guided to the right' or, in a secondary meaning, 'he who rightly guides'), but some of its verses are interpreted as referring to him. Even in the early centuries of Islam, there were many Muslims who regarded the way certain rulers or even entire dynasties exercised their power as unlawful, tyrannical and exploitative. This is why *mahdi*s kept appearing who promised redemption by divine order. Both Sunni and Shiite Islam have a history of such persons and their followings that reaches to the present. In Europe, the most generally known *mahdi* is the one who appeared in the Sudan in the 19th century. (The specificity and current political importance of the Mahdist belief in Shiite Islam will be discussed below.)

The idea that misdirected developments began early naturally begs the question of who should be blamed for the wide spread of injustice. Marking the beginnings of denominational rifts in early Islam, the divergent answers to this question are passionately debated even today, albeit occasionally intermingled with nationalist views. Even the Hadith contains utterances of the Prophet that are interpreted as assigning blame, for instance his prediction that the (true) caliphate (see below) would endure for no more than 30 years after his death, to be followed by nothing more than *mulk*, meaning the rule of kings (*muluk*, singular *malik*), who would be devoid of true justice as well as other properties. Quite obviously, this prophecy (construed subsequently) primarily refers to the assumption of power by the Umayyads after 661 CE, i.e. the rule of a Meccan family that, having formed the backbone of pagan resistance against Islam until 630 CE, usurped the caliphate a few decades later. The same tendency to regard the *mulk* as inferior to a caliphate with its religious legitimation, lawful rule and obligation to justice emerges from a purported exchange between the second of the 'rightly-guided' (*rashidun*) caliphs, 'Umar, and a companion of the Prophet, Salman. When 'Umar asked, 'Am I a king (*malik*) or a caliph (*khalifa*) in thine eyes?' Salman is said to have responded, 'If thou hast taken no more than a single Dirham – or more or less – from a Muslim and used it unlawfully, thou art a *king* and not a caliph.' Upon which, so tradition has it, 'Umar broke into tears'.

This is literary fiction, to be sure, but it is nevertheless impressive, for in (Sunni) tradition, 'Umar is seen as an unbending man of strict beliefs and great integrity. Now, if even such a person cannot be sure that everything within his responsibility has been handled properly, and if he begins to cry at the thought, this highlights the discrepancy between ideal and reality that, according to a widespread conviction, appeared very early in the history of Islam. (By and large, the term king (*malik*) began to be used in the Islamic world to describe a monarch in a positive vein only in the 20th century, mainly because of endeavours to appear on an equal footing on the international stage.)

The Quran and the religious literature that is based on it contain quite a number of other terms that (more or less precisely) mean 'just' and/or 'justice' or their opposites, i.e. 'injustice', etc. Thus, the Quran uses the term *qist* in chapter 57, verse 25 to describe the notion of justice. The text reads as follows: 'We have (in the course of time) sent our apostles (to mankind) with veritable signs and through them have brought down scriptures and the scales of justice, so than men might conduct themselves with fairness.'

As Muslims generally understand the Quran, it is the ruler more than anybody else who is called upon by Allah to act with moderation and justice. Thus, chapter 38:26 says: 'David, we have made you master in the land. Rule with justice among men and do not yield to lust, lest it turn you away from God's path!' In the Muslim exegesis of the Quran, truth (*ḥaqq*), the principle by which King David (one of God's emissaries) is to rule as a successor (*khalifa*, hence the word caliph) by the order of God, implies nothing but justice in the exercise of power combined with the control of personal inclinations. In Islamic legal literature, this Quranic verse has been cited – together with others – again and again as a condition of legitimate good governance. In that context, observing the Sharia and defending it against usurpers, violent warlords and alien 'infidel' conquerors became the crucial criterion by which the justice expected of a ruler was assessed. Moreover, there are words of the Prophet to point the way. Thus, he is said to have proclaimed once, 'One hour of justice is worth more than sixty years of divine service.'

In addition to the numerous religious law treatises about the caliphate that were written, enlarged and commented on over the centuries (often in the service and interest of a particular dynasty), there are certain literary genres that describe the rights and duties of a ruler and the conditions of successful governance. In some of these works, there are passages that criticise the misdemeanours of certain rulers and their confidants relatively openly. Most notable among them are writings that resemble the 'mirrors for princes' that were popular in the Occident. Some of these writings go back to pre-Islamic, i.e. ancient Greek or Iranian models. Although they are not necessarily free from near-Machiavellian ideas relating to the preservation of power pure and simple, quite a few of these often-copied and often-quoted works are the product of an earnest endeavour to instruct rulers in acting ethically and justly, not least in their own interest and that of the stability of their dynasty. A similar genre is that of the 'political testaments' that were made by certain rulers or that are ascribed to them. Some of their directives have undergone a surprising revival in the discourses of the present. The religious and political instructions given by the fourth caliph (and first imam of the Shia), 'Ali, to his chosen governor of Egypt, Malik al-Ashtar, are a case in point. These instructions, which mainly deal with how to administer the country so as to maintain justice and peace, played a role anything but minor in the discussions about the constitution of the Islamic Republic of Iran in 1979.

Concerning the content of the term justice, the Sharia – with the support of the Quran, the Hadith and the practice of the early caliphs – addresses a society in which, to name but a few examples, slavery and strict corporal punishment prevailed, capital interest was banned and the deposition of one man in court could be outweighed only by that of two women. Female judges were unknown, and no Muslima was allowed to marry a non-Muslim man. These and many other regulations are entirely 'just' within the meaning of the Sharia, a code that essentially dates back to the period from the 7th to the 9th century CE. Some present-day Muslim apologists maintain that these regulations are not as strict as they might appear at first glance. Many of them point out that Muslim jurists did and still do give consideration to certain exemptions, mitigating circumstances, etc. in their rulings and/or legal opinions (sing. *fatwa*), although this was and is not done uniformly across all fields covered by the Sharia. By differentiating their interpretations from one case to the next, jurists wanted to adhere to justice without endangering the validity of the system. One often-quoted example of a practice that is flexible and reflects social reality is the way the implementation of punishment for theft (severing the right hand) is circumscribed by conditions. And indeed, the number of cases in which this punishment was actually carried out in the history of most Muslim societies is, by and large, much lower than one might suppose, given the theoretical background and the social conditions described by historians and other authors. (For the contemporary debate about this question, see below.) In saying anything definite about actual legal practice, therefore, it is necessary to differentiate, as mentioned above, on the basis of historical developments and regional peculiarities. While some of the latter spring from pre- or non-Islamic traditions, others are the result of separate developments based on denominational features. Especially the unceasing complaints and polemical comments of 'orthodox' Muslim scholars reveal that, almost everywhere, cases abounded in which the provisions of the Sharia were not implemented consistently. Though nominally Muslim, some groups of the population – nomads, for instance – hardly knew them at all. In many ways, these provisions were (and sometimes still are today) pervaded by elements of customary law that had nothing to do with the Sharia. Such local codes appeared and still appear 'just' to the members of the group in question, serving, for example, to justify so-called honour killings.

One aspect that cannot be discussed in greater detail in this paper is the justice of *God*. This was quite a controversial question in the formative phase of Islamic theology. Complicated disputes arose about the characteristics of God to which the Quran bears witness (compassionate and merciful as well as wrathful and threatening), about man's free will as a prerequisite for being punished or rewarded and about similar points. The view that ultimately gained acceptance after a prolonged struggle was that God is absolutely just, even though mankind may be unable to perceive his justice every time and everywhere. In the religious and political programs of present-day Islamic and/or Islamist movements, this dogma manifests itself in an avowal of the 'justice of God in creation and legislation', as in Article 2 of the constitution of the Islamic Republic of Iran.

As mentioned above, disputes about the religious and legal legitimacy of Islamic rule arose very early on. The denominational groups (some of them short-lived) that emerged in Islam in the course of these confrontations largely justified their ambitions by the claim that injustices committed by usurpers had to be atoned for and that the righteous and religiously mandated cause of their party had to be helped to victory. In the process, each of these groups developed its own specific view of the events in the early age of Islam, ranging from the lifetime of the Prophet to the bloody upheavals of the internal Islamic 'civil war', the death of the fourth caliph, 'Ali, and the assumption of power by the Umayyads, the first hereditary monarchy in Islam (661 CE). These views inform not only the theories these groups hold about governance, but also their ideas about justice in government and society. Together with other events that occurred later, Islam's first internal 'civil war' (656–661 CE in the narrower definition), in which companions of the Prophet, all persons of great merit, fought on both sides, induced large segments of the population to adopt a quietist attitude. While revolutionary religious movements, some of them extremely militant, did manage to gather a following every now and then, the bloody events associated with revolts motivated many true believers to bow to the bitter insight that 'a century of tyranny is better than a single day of civil war'. This insight turned into a kind of conventional wisdom that is evoked to this very day whenever the occasion arises. Not a few Muslim (especially Sunni) jurists and theologians endeavoured to turn this into an argument for recognising, at least superficially, rulers who are illegitimate and, therefore, unjust. Ultimately, it is all about choosing the lesser evil. Thus, the great theologian and legal scholar al-Ghazāli (d. 1111) drew a parallel between submitting to a tyrant and the emergency of a man who has to eat carrion (banned under Sharia law) to avoid dying of hunger. In this sense, al-Ghazāli demands allegiance even to an unjust ruler.

The Shiites in general and particularly the community that is most powerful among them today, the so-called Twelver Shia, tend to take a critical and even polemical view of Islam's early history. According to them, a number of companions of the Prophet had plotted against him (and implicitly, against the will of God) in order to keep the Prophet's blood relations away from power. They already did this while Muhammad was still alive. They succeeded in doing so over centuries, not entirely but largely, and the consequences for true Islam and the Muslims were catastrophic. Since the death of the Prophet, therefore, justice has been largely absent from the world of Islam, which is why any rule that is or ever was could only be conditionally legitimate at best. According to Shiite scholars this does not rule out the possibility that there may be rulers who prove sufficiently just for people to submit to them and even enter into their service. What is more, this may apply to rulers who do not follow the Shiite or even the Muslim faith, provided they offer a certain degree of protection to the Shiites.

Shiites accept the fact that they are in a minority almost everywhere in the Islamic world. Living in an environment that is basically hostile and dangerous, the best course for a Shiite is to remain quiet and merge with the background even to the extent of denying his own convictions. This principle of dissimulation (*taqiya*) is not only admissible for members of the Twelver Shia, but even regarded as highly meritorious, because it serves to protect one's own life and to defend, albeit indirectly, one's brothers in faith. Ultimately, however, it can be understood only as a stratagem employed in a world that is threatening and unjust. The only source of hope is the prospect of a messiah, a *mahdi*, who will appear one day to 'establish a realm that is as just as it was filled with injustice before'. While this formula has cropped up also among the Sunni ideas about a *mahdi* ever since the early age of Islam (see above), its spread and formative influence among the Twelver Shiites is extraordinary. The reason for this lies in a close association between the figure of the *mahdi* and the concept of the Imamate. The idea is that throughout history, Allah has provided his true followers, the Shiites, with a leader (Imam) endowed with superhuman abilities, a manifestation of his goodness and justice towards mankind. Twelver Shiites firmly believe that the twelfth of these Imams was removed to a mysterious place of secrecy in 874 CE, that he is alive today, and that he will reappear some day in the future. Millions of Shiites profess their hope for this event, a hope embodied, for example, in Article 5 of the 1979 constitution of the Islamic Republic of Iran. In the language of agitation that was used during the upheavals in Iran, the expected reappearance of the messiah was called a 'revolution'. While this was in keeping with the spirit of the times, it also tied in with the centuries-old legends about the *mahdi* who was to come: his appearance in Mecca, his progress to Iraq via Medina, his fight against the Antichrist in which he is supported by Jesus Christ and the apocalyptic events that will lead up to his ultimate victory. Describing all this in great and sometimes gruesome detail, the voluminous Shiite literature on the subject revolves around the idea of taking revenge on the enemies of the Shiites (especially those who were responsible for the deaths of its Imams). To break the ground for the realm of justice that will be established by the *mahdi*, therefore, all evildoers past and present must be punished without mercy. This includes taking retrospective revenge even on those companions of the Prophet who are revered by the Sunnis but, according to the conviction of the Shiites, once sinned against the will of God. We are here looking at the downside of the cult of mourning that surrounds the twelve Imams of the Shiites who, it is said, all died as martyrs, except for the twelfth. For their sake, people whip themselves or at least shed floods of tears in the month of Muharram each year. This cult may be one of the reasons why Shiite believers become politically paralysed and passive in the face of blatant injustice. Indeed, this was so for a long time. In certain circumstances, however, the mood may change, so that masses rise in readiness to take up arms to fight for justice and sacrifice themselves. This is exactly what the world has witnessed in the last few decades in Iran, Lebanon and elsewhere. Everywhere, the language of words and images used by the political Shiite movements is fraught with references to religious metaphors and symbols. Thus, for instance, the Quranic term used to describe an unjust ruler is *taghut* (meaning approximately 'idol' and by extension, 'tyrant', 'despot', etc.). During and after the Iranian Revolution of 1978/79, the term *nezam-e taghuti* (meaning 'the pagan tyrannical system') was commonly used to describe the overthrown regime of the Shah.

Not only in the Shiite but also in the Sunni world, has the revival of the concept of justice and its exploitation for political purposes assumed yet another dimension, that of a call for social justice as one of the key concerns of Islam. Already since the 19th century, Muslim thinkers and politicians tried to launch social and political reforms in a modern sense. This they did with reference to the precepts of the Quran and the practices of the Prophet. To gain acceptance, the theoretical justification of these reforms in a modern sense must create the impression that the changes envisaged could be reconciled with Islam without difficulty. Many of these reforms aim to adapt Western institutions that are regarded as successful to the needs of an Islamic society. Thus, the system of parliamentary democracy may be made to appear harmless and even worthy of imitation by evoking the principle of mutual consultation (*shura*), which the Quran commends. Some modernist politicians and writers regard the so-called statutes with which the Prophet tried to regulate conditions in Medina as the precursor of a constitution and a few even call it 'the first written constitution in the history of the world'. One remarkable example that illustrates the general trend to forge links between the political values of Western modernity (the French Revolution in this case) and the heritage of Islam is that of Rafiq al-'Azm, a politician and journalist from Syria who campaigned for reforms in Turkey from his Egyptian exile in the early 20th century. In the preface to his book, which appeared in Cairo in 1903, about famous personages in Islam he spoke of Muhammad as the prophet 'who established the Sharia on the pillars of freedom, justice and fraternity'. It is probably not by chance that the author (a member of a notable Syrian family) named justice instead of equality, which one might normally expect to be included in this triad.

When the concept of development was introduced to intra-Islamic discourse, it was possible to put certain legal constructs of the Sharia in their historical perspective and to mitigate them indirectly. By the same token, it became possible to reinterpret related social institutions as well as norms and behaviour patterns that had been regarded as legitimate and just for centuries. In the case of slavery, for instance, the argument ran as follows: While early Islamic society had accepted slavery as a social fact, based in part on statements in the Quran, Islam had improved the slaves' situation considerably compared to older and contemporary societal orders, demanding that they should be treated justly. The manumission of slaves had always been seen as an act that was pleasing to God. While the Prophet had been unable to abolish slavery entirely and immediately, all sorts of former justifications for it have become obsolete by now. Together with developments in international law, a progressive interpretation of Islam demanded that the slave hunts that were conducted in Black Africa well into the 19th century should be rejected and, consequently, suppressed by the governments of Islamic countries.

Muslim modernists in the late 19th and throughout the 20th centuries used a similar rationale to justify a demand for improving the social status of Muslim women, up to and including equality. In a highly condensed form, the train of thought ran as follows: In its early age, Islam had brought about enormous improvements in the legal status of women compared to pre-Islamic times, but the process had been neglected later on over a long period. Thus, the claim to education for women that was embedded in Islam had not been realised in general. Currency had even been given to a false Hadith that was supposed to prove that the Prophet himself had recommended teaching girls and women neither reading nor writing, but only how to use a spinning wheel and how to recite a certain chapter of the Quran, the 24th. According to the modernists, present-day Muslims are called upon to join in helping to victory the original intention of Islam, which is to promote justice for women in education as well as in other respects.

Referring to episodes in early Islamic history (whose veracity we are not discussing at the moment) may also serve to mitigate the severity of punishments under Sharia law. Thus, tradition has it that the previously mentioned Caliph ‘Umar, in a year of famine, had suspended amputation as a punishment for theft. Now, seeing that large parts of the population are currently suffering from want to an extent that is always bitter and sometimes life-threatening, we might conclude that this punishment for theft should not apply today. It would be unjust in view of the fact that most Muslims presently are not living in a truly Islamic society. While this would not imply the permanent abolition of this punishment, its modern interpretation obliges judges to impose retaliatory punishments only in recognition of the prevailing circumstances.

The process of re-Islamization that has been taking place for some decades in quite a number of countries has considerably hampered and sometimes totally perverted these attempts to adapt the Sharia and render it more flexible. Radical Islamic fundamentalists accord little or no value to instruments like the Human Rights Charter (HRC) of the United Nations that are widely recognised (although not always consistently observed) on the international level. To their minds, the introduction of legal regimes and constructions that began to be imported from Western culture in the 19th century is nothing but a consequence of European colonialism. Since the latter was entirely pernicious, being unjust in the eyes of Islam, all traces of it in legislation and jurisdiction have to be obliterated. However, even the fundamentalists’ thoughts revolve around justice of a kind, although the way they interpret its content differs not only from the HRC but also from the understanding of the Muslim modernists and even more from that of the secularists. What the Ayatollah Khomeini is alleged to have said about punishment by whipping and/or stoning is characteristic in this respect. Expressing himself unequivocally in favour of these punishments, he nevertheless demanded moderation, saying that not a single stroke of the whip should be administered beyond the number prescribed in Islamic law. He also said it was forbidden to humiliate the guilty. According to Khomeini, the role model in this case was the Imam ‘Ali, who was in the habit of treating with benevolence and sensitivity those who had lost a hand in punishment by his order, thus winning their hearts afterwards. On the other hand, he is said to have been quite capable of drawing his sword and hacking incorrigible criminals to pieces. 'Such was the way of his justice,' Khomeini concluded.

Yet current developments in Iran do not necessarily follow the direction that might be implied in Khomeini's statements. There as well as elsewhere, the dispute about how Islamic justice should be rightly interpreted is not resolved yet. To the Taliban in Afghanistan, the apartheid of the sexes that they proclaimed and largely implemented in their territory is entirely just in the context of 'true' Islam. Conversely, they regard the equality demanded by modernists for Muslim women as well as their appearance in public as the work of the devil. However, it is anything but certain that this policy will help the Taliban to win over the majority of the population.

The examples cited above are situated on a plane of discussion where the arguments employed are 'Islamic' in the narrower or broader meaning of the word. However, we should not overlook that, in the 20th century, the Islamic countries were influenced by ideologies whose foundations were non-Islamic and whose proponents even adopted attitudes that were more or less hostile towards Islam. These include Kemalism in Turkey (with a grain of salt), the communist parties that temporarily gained considerable influence in Iran, Iraq, Indonesia and elsewhere and – with certain limitations – the Baath Party. The reasons why some of these movements had so much success with some parts of the population are many and varied. One of them is that they may have succeeded, at least to a certain extent, in tying their propaganda in with the wish for more social and political justice, albeit with 'Islamic' connotations. The term *'adāla*, meaning justice and derived from *'adl* (see above), turns up in the name of Iran's first communist party, the *Hezb-e 'Adalat* which was founded shortly after the First World War. Non-Marxist socialist regimes, parties and movements in the Islamic world made similar or even more forceful attempts to underpin their programmes with eclectic references to the Islamic heritage, including the Quran. The Egyptian president Nasser's 'National Charter' of 1961, together with the relevant official commentaries, quotes 'Islamic' reasons for the need to establish social justice. However, on the subject of parties and their self-chosen names, those more or less 'moderate' Islamist parties whose name includes the word justice (surely not by accident) are more important at present. One such party exists in Morocco, for example – the *Hizb al-'Adala wal-Tanmiya* (*Parti de la Justice et du Développement)*. Another party that is considerably better known in the West is the Turkish AKP, which attained governmental powers under Recep Tayyip Erdogan: The letter A in the acronym stands for '*Adalet*'.

Prompted by the success attained by some left-wing (or pseudo-left-wing) parties, movements and regimes in certain Islamic countries in the 1950s and 1960s, Muslim scholars tried to counter the ideologies of their opponents, which, in their opinion, were alien to Islam, by establishing an economic theory that was modern, just and conformable with the Sharia. While the theoretical quality of their writings is not always impressive in the judgement of experts, there is no mistaking the earnestness of their endeavours to find an Islamic rationale for reforms. Whereas the practicability of a 'truly Islamic' system (including interest-free banking, etc.) may be regarded with scepticism, the wealth of ideas developed by the proponents of these experiments appears considerable.

At a rather lower but highly practical level, attempts are being undertaken to establish Islamic welfare organisations in order to mitigate social distress at least in part, thus establishing justice of a kind. By way of justification, their initiators may refer directly to the demands for charity (especially towards widows, orphans and other socially deprived persons) that are to be found both in the Quran and the Hadith. Throughout the last few years and decades, Islamist organisations especially distinguished themselves by founding and (relatively) successfully operating welfare institutions, such as hospitals, orphanages, kindergartens, schools (often directly connected to a mosque) and other facilities, which also helps them to gain political influence. In this, they are succeeding not least in those suburbs where farmers and workers from the rural regions gather and settle together with other destitute persons.

These welfare institutions, whose names show Islamic connotations almost without exception, are funded mainly by donations, voluntary gifts and 'pious endowments' (*awqaf*). Governmental control of many of these institutions is either non-existent or limited. Potentially, the resultant autonomous networks may engage in far-flung international activities that in some instances have little to do with the original purpose of the welfare organisations from which they originated.

The idea that Islam aims at a just society that Muslims entirely or partially failed to establish so far was and is widespread among Muslims. As history teaches us, this idea may engender a fundamentally pessimistic attitude towards any chance of improvement in the present situation or, in other words, it may lead to passivity. On the other hand, there are certain circumstances in which it may help to mobilise certain parts of the population in support of religious and political objectives. At the moment, the Islamic world is undergoing a phase in which many are inspired by the desire for revenge for injustice suffered (purportedly or actually), by thoughts of revolt and by utopian hopes.

Bibliography

Black, Anthony. *The History of Islamic Political Thought: From the Prophet to the Present.* Edinburgh: Edinburgh University Press, 2001.

Crone, Patricia. *Medieval Islamic Political Thought.* Edinburgh: Edinburgh University Press, 2004.

Gudrun, Krämer. *Gottes Staat als Republik: Reflexionen zeitgenossischer Muslime zu Islam, Menschenrechten und Demokratie.* Baden-Baden: Nomos, 1999.

Lewis, Bernard. *The Political Language of Islam.* Chicago, London: The University of Chicago Press, 1988.

Nagel, Tilman. *Staat und Glaubensgemeinschaft im Islam: Geschichte der politischen Ordnungsvorstellungen der Muslime.* 2 vols. Zurich, Munich: Artemis & Winkler, 1981.

Reissner, Johannes. 'Die innerislamische Diskussion zur modernen Wirtschafts- und Sozialordnung'. In *Der Islam in der Gegenwart.* Edited by Werner Ende and Udo Steinbach. 5th ed., 151–62. München: Beck, 2005.

Sachedina, Abdulaziz. *The Just Ruler in Shiite Islam.* Oxford: Oxford University Press.

Ziba Mir-Hosseini

Justice and Equality and Muslim Family Laws: New Ideas, New Prospects*

Contemporary notions of justice, informed by the ideals of human rights, equality and personal freedom, depart substantially from those that underpin rulings in classical *fiqh* (Islamic jurisprudence) and established understandings of the Shari'a. This disjunction is a central problem that permeates debates and struggles for an egalitarian family law in Muslim contexts.

For instance, take the following two statements:

> The fundamentals of the *Shari'a* are rooted in wisdom and promotion of the welfare of human beings in this life and the Hereafter. *Shari'a* embraces Justice, Kindness, the Common Good and Wisdom. Any rule that departs from justice to injustice, from kindness to harshness, from the common good to harm, or from rationality to absurdity cannot be part of *Shari'a*.[1]
>
> The wife is her husband's prisoner, a prisoner being akin to a slave. The Prophet directed men to support their wives by feeding them with their own food and clothing them with their own clothes; he said the same about maintaining a slave.[2]

Both statements are by Ibn Qayyim al-Jawziyya (1292–1350 CE), a 14th-century jurist and one of the great reformers of his time.[3] The first statement speaks to all contemporary Muslims, and both advocates of gender equality and their opponents often use it as an epigraph.[4] But the second statement, which reflects classical *fiqh* conceptions of marriage, goes against the very grain of what many con-

---

* I would like thank Cassandra Balchin for her extensive and perceptive comments; and Richard Tapper, as always, for help with thinking through the argument and editing. Any remaining faults are mine. This article has already appeared in Ziba Mir-Hosseini, Lena Larsen, Christian Moe, and Kari Vogt (eds), *Gender and Equality in Muslim Family Laws: Justice and Ethics in the Islamic Legal Tradition* (London: IB Tauris, 2013).

1 Ibn Qayyim al-Jawziyya, *I'lām al-muwaqqi'īn 'an rabb al-'ālamīn* (Beirut: Dār al-fikr al-'arabī, 1956), 3/1.

2 Quoted in Yossef Rapoport, *Marriage, Money and Divorce in Medieval Islamic Society* (Cambridge: Cambridge University Press, 2005), 52.

3 He is also an inspiration for Islamist movements in Sunni contexts. For his thought and scholarship, see Caterina Bori and Livnat Holtzman, eds., *A Scholar in the Shadow: Essays on the Legal and Theological Thought of Ibn Qayyim al-Ǧawziyyah* (Rome: Istituto per l'Oriente; Herder, 2010).

4 For example, by Muhammad Khalid Masud, *Shatibi's Philosophy of Islamic Law* (New Delhi: Kitab Bhavan, 1997); the statement also features on the *Musawah* website (www.musawah.org), as well as on those of many conservative and reactionary Muslim organizations.

https://doi.org/10.1515/9783110574593-005

temporary Muslims consider to be 'Justice, Kindness, the Common Good and Wisdom'. Consequently, Muslim legal tradition and its textual sources have come to appear hypocritical or at best contradictory. This faces those who struggle to reform Muslim family laws with a quandary and a host of questions: What is the notion of justice in Islam's sacred texts? Does it include the notion of equality for women before the law? If so, how are we to understand those elements of the primary sources of the Shari'a (Qur'an and hadith) that appear not to treat men and women as equals? Can gender equality and Shari'a-based laws go together?

These questions are central to the ongoing struggle for an egalitarian construction of family laws in Muslim contexts, and have been vigorously debated among Muslims since the late nineteenth century.[5] Some consider religion to be inherently patriarchal and that any engagement with it to be a futile and incorrect strategy;[6] others argue that, given the linkage between the religious and political dimensions of identity in Muslim contexts, the path to legal equality for women in those contexts necessarily passes through religion.[7] This chapter aims to explore these questions and address what often remains neglected in this debate: how Muslim women's struggle for equality is embedded in the intimate links between theology and politics. My central argument has two elements. First, the struggle is at once theological and political, and it is difficult and sometimes futile to decide where theology ends and politics begin. Secondly, in last two decades of the twentieth century a growing confrontation between political Islam and feminism has made the intimate links between theology, law and politics more transparent. New voices and forms of activism have emerged that no longer shy away from engagement with religion. A new discourse, which has come to be known as 'Islamic feminism', has started to challenge the patriarchal interpretations of the Shari'a from within.

After a brief examination of the notion of gender justice in classical *fiqh* texts, I sketch twentieth-century developments in the politics of religion, law

5 In recent years this debate has come to centre on the notion of 'Islamic feminism', to which I return later. For recent contributions to this debate, see articles in *Contestations: Dialogue on Women's Empowerment, http://www.contestations.net/issues/issue-1/*, and Margot Badran, 'From Islamic feminism to a Muslim Holistic Feminism', *Institute of Development Studies Bulletin* 42, no. 1 (2011); Ziba Mir-Hosseini, 'Muslim women's Quest for Equality: Between Islamic Law and Feminism', *Critical Inquiry* 32, no. 1 (2006), and Ziba Mir-Hosseini, 'Beyond "Islam" vs "Feminism"', *Institute of Development Studies Bulletin* 42, no. 1 (2011).

6 For instance, see Haideh Moghissi, *Feminism and Islamic Fundamentalism: The Limits of Post-Modern Analysis* (London: Zed Press, 1999).

7 For instance, see Mir-Hosseini, 'Muslim Women's Quest for Equality'.

and gender in Muslim contexts. This is followed by a discussion of two reform texts that negotiate and bridge the chasm, the dissonance, between contemporary notions of justice and gender rights and those informed by classical *fiqh* rulings and lay the groundwork for an egalitarian family law. These are the book *Women in the Shari'a and in Our Society* (1930) by the Tunisian religious reform thinker Tahir Haddad, and the article 'The Status of Women in Islam: A Modernist Interpretation' (1982) by the Pakistani reform thinker Fazlur Rahman. I have chosen to focus on these two texts because they belong to two key moments in the Muslim debate and struggle for defining the scope of women's rights in the twentieth-century. Haddad's book appeared in the context of early twentieth-century debates and the early phase of the codification of Muslim family law; Fazlur Rahman's article was published when political Islam was at its zenith and Islamists, trumpeting the slogan of 'return to Shari'a' were dismantling some earlier reforms. Both thinkers met with a great deal of opposition from the clerical establishments in their own countries at the time, but their ideas, which conservative clerics declared to be heretical, proved to be instrumental in shaping later discourses and developments. Tahir Haddad's ideas informed Tunisian family law, which was codified in 1956 and to this day remains the only Muslim code that bans polygamy. Fazlur Rahman developed a methodology and framework that by the end of the century facilitated the emergence of feminist scholarship in Islam. I conclude by considering the implication of this scholarship for changing the terms of reference of the debates over Muslim family law reforms.

Men's Authority over Women: *Qiwama* as a Legal Postulate

At the heart of the unequal construction of gender rights in Muslim legal tradition lies the concept of *qiwama* (guardianship), which has been commonly understood as mandating men's authority over women. The *ulema* frequently invoke Qur'an 4:34 (from which the idea is derived) as the main textual evidence in its support; it is often the only verse that ordinary Muslims know in relation to family law. It reads:

> Men are ***qawwamun*** (protectors/maintainers) in relation to women,
> according to what God has favoured some over
> others and according to what they spend from
> their wealth. Righteous women are ***qanitat*** (obedient)
> guarding the unseen according to what God
> has guarded. Those [women] whose ***nushuz***
> you fear, admonish them, and abandon them in
> bed, and ***adribuhunna*** (strike them) If they obey you, do not

> pursue a strategy against them. Indeed, God is
> Exalted, Great.[8]

Since the early twentieth century, this verse has been the focus of intense contestation and debate among Muslims, centring on the four terms I have highlighted. There is now a substantial body of literature that attempts to contest and reconstruct the meanings and connotations of these terms as understood and turned into legal rulings by classical jurists.[9] Recent contributions have been most concerned with the last part of the verse, and the issue of domestic violence.[10] Neither this concern nor the contestation over the meanings of these terms is new; they occupied the minds of classical Muslim jurists, when they inferred from the verse legal rulings regarding the rights and duties of spouses in marriage.[11] But the nature and the tone of the debates are new. Juristic disagree-

---

8 The translation is by Kecia Ali, 'Understanding a Difficult Verse, Qur'an 4:34', accessed October 14, 2017, https://www.brandeis.edu/projects/fse/muslim/diff-verse.html. Ali leaves the italicized words untranslated, pointing out that any translation is in the end an interpretation; she also provides links to three other translations of the verse; and to additional interpretations http://www.brandeis.edu/projects/fse/muslim/mus-essays/mus-ess-diffverse-intrprt.html.

9 See for instance Abulhamid A. Abusulayman, *Marital Discord: Recapturing the Full Islamic Spirit of Human Dignity,* Occasional Paper Series 11 (London, Washington: The International Institute of Islamic Thought, 2003); Aziza Al-Hibri, 'An Islamic perspective on domestic violence', *Fordham Law Journal* 27 (2003); Wadud, *Qur'an and Woman*, 70–79; idem, *Inside the Gender Jihad: Women's Reform in Islam*, (Oxford: Oneworld, 2006), 198–202. Jolana Guardi, 'Women Reading the Qur'an: Religious Discourse in Islam', *Hawwa: Journal of Women in the Middle East and the Islamic World* 2, no. 3 (2004); Shamon Dunn and Rosemary B. Kellison, 'At the Intersection of Scripture and Law: Qur'an 4:34 and Violence against Women', *Journal of Feminist Studies in Religion* 26, no. 2 (2010); Manuela Marin, 'Disciplining Wives: A Historical Reading of Qur'an 4:34', *Studia Islamica* 98 (2003); Sa'diyya Sheikh, 'Exegetical Violence: Nushuz in Quranic Gender Ideology', *Journal for Islamic Studies* 17 (1997); Hadia Mubarak, 'Breaking the Interpretive Monopoly: A re-examination of Verse 4:34', *Hawwa: Journal of Women in the Middle East and the Islamic World* 2, no. 3 (2004); Mohamed A. Mahmoud, 'To Beat or Not to Beat: On the Exegetical Dilemmas over Qur'an, 4:34', *Journal of American Oriental Society* 126, no. 4 (2006).

10 For instance, a panel at the 2006 meeting of the American Academy of Religion was devoted to discussion of the verse; the papers were published in the *Comparative Islamic Studies* 2 (2), 2006, see editorial; see also Al-Hibri, 'An Islamic Perspective on Domestic Violence'; Murad H. Elsaidi, 'Human Rights and Islamic Law: A Legal Analysis Challenging the Husband's Authority to Punish "Rebellious" Wives"', *Muslim World Journal of Human Rights* 2 (2011).

11 They remained at the level of ethical recommendations without legal force. For discussion of Shafi'i's treatment of this verse and its contradiction with the Prophet's sunnah, see Kecia Ali, *Sexual Ethics and Islam: Feminist Reflections on Qur'an, Hadith and Jurisprudence* (Oxford: Oneworld, 2006); Kecia Ali, 'The Best of You Will Not Strike', *Comparative Islamic Studies* 2, no. 2 (2006).

ments were not, as now, about the legitimacy or legality of a husband's right to beat his wife if she defies his authority; they were about the extent and harshness of the beating he should administer. In classical *fiqh* texts, the validity and inviolability of men's superiority and authority over women was a given; the verse was understood in this light, and the four key terms were used to define relations between spouses in marriage, and notions of gender justice and equity. As we shall see, all revolved around the first part of the verse and the notion that men are women's *qawwamun,* protectors and providers.

Let us call this the *qiwama* postulate,[12] which I shall argue is the lynchpin of the whole edifice of the patriarchal model of family in classical *fiqh.* We see the working of this postulate in all areas of Muslim law relating to gender rights, but its impact is most evident, as I have argued elsewhere, in the laws that classical jurists devised for the regulation of marriage.[13] They defined marriage as a contract (*nikah*), and patterned it after the contract of sale (*bay*ʿ). The contract renders sexual relations licit between a man and woman, and establishes a set of default rights and obligations for each party, some supported by legal force, others by moral sanction. Those with legal force revolve around the twin themes of sexual access and compensation and are embodied in two central legal concepts: *tamkin* (submission) and *nafaqa* (maintenance).[14] *Tamkin,* obedience or submission, specifically sexual access, is the husband's right and thus the wife's duty; whereas *nafaqa,* maintenance, specifically shelter, food and clothing, is the wife's right and the husband's duty. The wife loses her claim to maintenance if she is in a state of *nushuz* (disobedience). The husband has the unilateral and extra-judicial right to terminate the contract by *talaq* or repudiation; a wife cannot terminate the contract without her husband's consent or the permission of the Islamic judge upon producing a valid reason. There are numerous moral injunctions that could have limited men's power to terminate marriage;

---

12 I take the concept of a 'legal postulate' from Chiba, who defines it as a norm, a value system that simply exists in its own right, as an element of a specific cultural context, which is connected with a particular 'official' or 'unofficial law'. For his tripartite model of legal systems ('official law', 'unofficial law' and 'legal postulates'), see Masaji Chiba, ed., *Asian Indigenous Law in interaction with Received Law* (London, New York: KPI, 1986).

13 Ziba Mir-Hosseini, 'The Construction of Gender in Islamic Legal Thought and Strategies for Reform', *Hawwa: Journal of Women in the Middle East and the Islamic World* 1, no. 1 (2003); Ziba Mir-Hosseini, 'Towards Gender Equality: Muslim Family Law and the Shari'a', in *Wanted: Equality and Justice in Muslim Family Law,* ed. Zainah Anwar (Kuala Lumpur: Sisters in Islam, 2009), accessible at http://www.musawah.org/background_papers.asp.

14 For discussions of how early jurists conceptualised marriage, see Kecia Ali, *Marriage and Slavery in Early Islam* (Cambridge, MA: Harvard University Press, 2010); and Rapoport, *Marriage, Money and Divorce in Medieval Islamic Society.*

for instance there are sayings from the Prophet to the effect that *talaq* is among the most detested of permitted acts, and that when a man pronounces it, God's throne shakes. Yet classical *fiqh* made no attempt to restrict a man's right to *talaq*. He needs neither grounds nor the consent of his wife.

There were, of course, differences between and within the classical schools over what constituted and what defined the three interrelated concepts – *nafaqa*, *tamkin* and *nushuz* – but they all shared the same conception of marriage, and the large majority linked a woman's right to maintenance to her obedience to her husband. The reason for their disagreement, Ibn Rushd tells us, was 'whether maintenance is a counter-value for (sexual) utilization, or compensation for the fact that she is confined because of her husband, as the case of one absent or sick.'[15] And it was within the parameters of this logic – men provide and women obey – that notions of gender rights and justice acquired their meanings. Cognizant of the inherent tension in such a construction of marriage, and seeking to contain the potential abuse of a husband's authority, classical jurists narrowed the scope of this authority to the unhampered right to sexual relations with the wife, which in turn limited the scope of her duty to obey to being sexually available, and even here only when it did not interfere with her religious duties (for example, when fasting during Ramadan, or when bleeding during menses or after childbirth). Legally speaking, if we take the *fiqh* texts at face value, according to some a wife had no obligation to do housework or to care for the children, even to suckle her babies; for these, she was entitled to wages. Likewise, a man's right to discipline a wife who was in the state of *nushuz* was severely restricted; he could discipline her, but not inflict harm. For this reason, some jurists recommended that he should 'beat' his wife only with a handkerchief or a *miswak*, a twig used for cleaning teeth.[16]

Whether these rulings corresponded to actual practices of marriage and gender relations is another area of inquiry, one that recent scholarship in Islam has started to uncover.[17] What is important to note here is that the *qiwama* postulate served as a rationale for other legal disparities – such as men's rights to polygamy and unilateral repudiation, women's lesser share in inheritance, or the ban on women being judges or political leaders. That is to say, women cannot occupy

---

15 Ibn Rushd, *The Distinguished Jurist's Primer: Bidayat al-Mujtahid wa Nihayat al-Muqtasid*, trans. Imran Ahsan Khan Nyazee, 2 vols. (Reading: Garnet Publishing, 1996), 2/63.

16 See Mahmoud, 'To Beat or Not to Beat', footnote 35.

17 See, for instance, Rapoport, *Marriage, Money and Divorce in Medieval Islamic Society*; Amira El-Azhary Sonbol, ed., *Women, Family and Divorce Laws in Islamic History* (Syracuse: Syracuse University Press, 1996); Judith Tucker, *In the House of Law: Gender and Islamic Law in Ottoman Syria and Palestine* (Berkeley: University of California Press, 2000).

positions that entail the exercise of authority in society because they are under their husband's authority and thus not free agents, and they will not be able to deliver impartial justice. Similarly, since men provide for their wives, justice requires that they be entitled to a greater share in inheritance. These inequalities in rights were also rationalised and justified by other arguments, based on assumptions about innate, natural differences between the sexes: women are by nature weaker and more emotional, qualities inappropriate in a leader; they are created for child-bearing, a function that confines them to the home, which means that men must protect and provide for them.[18]

The Reform and Codification of Classical *Fiqh* Provisions of Family Law[19]

In the course of the twentieth century, as nation-states emerged among Muslim populations, classical *fiqh* conceptions of marriage and family were partially reformed, codified and grafted onto modern legal systems in many Muslim-majority countries.[20] The best-known exceptions were Turkey, which abandoned *fiqh* in all areas of law, Saudi Arabia, which preserved classical *fiqh* as fundamental law and attempted to apply it in all spheres of law, and Muslim populations that came under communist rule. In countries where classical fiqh remained the main source of family law, the impetus and extent of family law reform varied, but with the exception of Tunisia, which banned polygamy, on the whole the classical *fiqh* construction of the marital relationship was retained more or less intact. Reforms were introduced from within the framework of Muslim legal tradition, by mixing principles and rulings from different *fiqh* schools and by procedural devices, without directly challenging the patriarchal construction of marriage in *fiqh*.[21] They centred on raising the age of marriage, expanding

---

18 For the ways in which these arguments shape legal rulings, see in particular Ali, *Marriage and Slavery in Early Islam*; Hammudah 'Abd Al 'Ati, *The Family Structure in Islam* (Plainfield: American Trust Publications, 1997); Mahmoud, 'To beat or not to beat'.

19 This section repeats an argument I have published in other places, but which I feel is essential background to what follows; see Ziba Mir-Hosseini, 'Criminalizing Sexuality: Zina Laws as Violence Against Women in Muslim Contexts', Women Living Under Muslim Laws, accessed September 15, 2012, http://www.stop-stoning.org/node/882.

20 For the codification, see James Norman Anderson, *Law Reforms in the Muslim World* (London: Athlone, 1976); Tahir Mahmood, *Family Law Reforms in the Muslim World* (Bombay: N.M. Tripathi, 1976).

21 These were established *fiqh* procedures: eclectic choice (*takhayyur*) and mixing (*talfiq*) of legal opinions and rulings from different schools; the exercise of *ijithad* remained limited. For

women's access to judicial divorce, and restricting men's right to polygamy. This involved requiring the state registration of marriage and divorce, or the creation of new courts to deal with marital disputes. The state now had the power to deny legal support to those marriages that were not in compliance with official state-sanctioned procedures.

All these changes transformed relations between Muslim legal tradition, state and social practice. Codes and statute books took the place of *fiqh* manuals; family law was no longer solely a matter for private scholars – the *fuqaha* – operating within a particular *fiqh* school; rather it became the concern of the legislative assembly of a particular nation-state. Confined to the ivory tower of the seminaries, *fiqh* and its practitioners became increasingly scholastic, defensive and detached from realities on the ground. Patriarchal interpretations of the Shari'a acquired a different force; they could now be imposed through the machinery of the modern nation-state, which had neither the religious legitimacy nor the inclination to challenge them.

With the rise of Islam as both a spiritual and a political force in the latter part of the twentieth-century, Islamist political movements became closely identified with patriarchal notions of gender drawn from classical *fiqh*. Political Islam had its biggest triumph in 1979 in the popular revolution that brought clerics into power in Iran. This year also saw the dismantling of some of the reforms introduced earlier in the century by the modernist governments – for instance in Iran and Egypt – and the introduction of the Hudood Ordinances in Pakistan that extended the ambit of *fiqh* to certain aspects of criminal law. Yet this was the year when the United Nations General Assembly adopted the Convention on the Elimination of all forms of Discrimination Against Women (CEDAW), which gave gender equality a clear international legal mandate.

The decades that followed saw the concomitant expansion, globally and locally, of two powerful but seemingly opposed frames of reference. On the one hand, the human rights framework and instruments such as CEDAW gave women's rights activists what they needed most: a point of reference and a language with which to resist and challenge patriarchy. The 1980s saw the expansion of the international women's movement and the emergence of NGOs with international funds and transnational links that gave women a voice in policymaking and public debate over the law. On the other hand, Islamist forces – whether in power or in opposition – started to invoke 'Shari'a' in order to dismantle earlier efforts at reforming and/or secularizing laws and legal systems. Tapping into

a discussion, see Fazlur Rahman, 'A Survey of Modernization of Muslim Family Law', *International Journal of Middle East Studies* 11 (1980).

popular demands for social justice, they presented this dismantling as 'Islamization' and as the first step to bring about their vision of a moral and just society.

In other words, the twentieth century witnessed the widening of a chasm between notions of justice and gender rights found in Muslim legal tradition and those that were being adopted internationally. This chasm, this dissonance, as we shall see, was as much political as epistemological. I now turn to the texts of Tahir Haddad and Fazlur Rahman, which try to negotiate and bridge the chasm. They appeared at two critical moments in the twentieth-century politics of modernism: the struggle against colonial powers, and the challenges posed by political Islam. At both moments, the issue of gender rights and Muslim legal tradition became part of an ideological battle between different forces and factions.

Al-Tahir al-Haddad (1899–1935): A Lonely Reformer

Al-Tahir al-Haddad's book, *Our Women in the Shari'a and Society*,[22] is part of a considerable nationalist and reformist literature dating to the early twentieth century and the fierce debate on the 'status of women in Islam' ignited by the encounter with Western colonial powers. Two genres of texts emerged. The authors of the first more or less reiterated the classical *fiqh* positions, and confined themselves to enumerating the rights that Islam conferred on women. Texts of the second genre, the most influential of which was Qasim Amin's *The Liberation of Women* (1899), offered a critique of *fiqh* rulings and proposed reforms to realise women's rights. They called for women's education, for their participation in society, and for unveiling. One subtext in these texts was the refutation of the colonial premise that 'Islam' was inherently a 'backward' religion and denied women their rights; another was the quest for modernization and the reform of laws and legal systems as part of the project of nation building. Without women's education and their participation in society, the modern, independent and prosperous state for which they were struggling could not be achieved.[23]

22 The book was translated into English in 2007; Ronak Husni and Daniel Newman, *Muslim Women in Law and Society: Annotated Translation of al-Tahir al-Haddad's Imra'tuna fi 'l-shari'a wa l-mujtama' with an Introduction* (London: Routledge, 2007).

23 For the intellectual genealogy of Haddad's text, see ibid., 1–25; for accounts of the intellectual and social change that made women's issue central to politics, see Leila Ahmed, *Women and Gender in Islam: Historical Roots of a Modern Debate* (New Haven: Yale University Press, 1992), chapter 7; for the experience of different countries, see Nikki Keddie, *Women in the Middle East: Past and Present* (Princeton: Princeton University Press, 2007), 60–101.

Haddad's book belongs to the second genre, and is not free of the ambivalence that permeated the nationalist/modernist texts of the time, which have rightly been criticised for their patriarchal undertones.[24] But it differs from the rest in two respects. First, in his proposals for reform Haddad went much further than other twentieth-century reformers, even arguing for equality in inheritance, an issue that became a priority for Muslim women's movements only in the next century.[25] Secondly, Haddad provided a framework for rethinking *fiqh* legal concepts, and offered a definition of marriage that was premised on mutual affection and responsibility. In that sense, it is indeed a feminist text.

Haddad received only a traditional education, first at Qur'anic school and later at the Great Mosque of Zaytouna in Tunis, where he studied Islamic sciences.[26] He obtained accreditation as a notary in 1920, but opted for journalism instead of a seminary life. As a journalist he became involved in the movement for independence from France, and joined the Dustur Party that promoted a vision of a socially just, democratic and modern Tunisia. Critical of its policies, however, Haddad left the party after a short time to became active in labour movements, helping to launch the country's first independent trade union. These activities sensitised Haddad and made him deeply concerned about the situation of workers and women, and the injustices to which they were subjected, for which he held erroneous interpretations of Islam's sacred texts accountable. In 1927 he published a book on labour law and three years later his second book: *Our Women in the Shari'a and Society*, which contains his critique of the way in which women are treated in Tunisian society. The book caused immediate outrage; Haddad was denounced and declared an apostate; Zaytouna revoked his degree and notary licence. Many of his modernist and nationalist friends deserted him; they were in a politically difficult situation at the time, and an easy way out was to compromise on an issue that was sensitive and was already triggering

24 These reformist texts – as others have noted – often tended to reinforce patriarchal notions of women's traditional roles as wives, mothers and guardians of Islamic tradition; Lamia Ben Youssef Zayzafoon makes this criticism of Al-Haddad's text, see her chapter 4 of her book, Lamia Ben Youssef Zayzafoon, *The Production of the Muslim Woman: Negotiating Text, History, and Ideology* (New York: Lexington Books, 2005). For another critique of Qasim Amin, see Ahmed, *Women and Gender in Islam*, chapter 8.

25 A joint campaign by Moroccan and Tunisian women's organizations went public in 2006, with a two-volume publication, *Egalité dans l'Héritage: Pour Une Citoyenneté Pleine et Entière* (Tunis, Association des Femmes Tunisiennes pour la Recherche et le Développement).

26 For this biographical account, I have largely relied on Husni and Newman, *Muslim Women in Law and Society*, 19–25.

the anger of the religious establishment and conservative forces.[27] Haddad died in 1936 in poverty and isolation.

Haddad's Framework and Proposals for Reform

What was it in Haddad's book that provoked such a reaction from his seminary teachers and colleagues? The book has two parts. The first, 'Legislative Section: Women in Islam', contains Haddad's critique of *fiqh* rulings and his proposals for reform. In the final chapter of this part, he poses a set of questions to the scholars and jurists, including his teachers at Zaytouna, who included eminent scholars of the time such as Tahir Ibn Ashur, a former judge and a leading scholar of Maliki law. He did this 'in the hope of getting answers from them that would elucidate our position and where we stand in our reform of the judiciary which is necessary for the benefit of justice and progress for women' (p. 81).[28] This chapter – fascinating to read – reveals the distance between Haddad's vision of Shari'a and that of the *ulema* of his time. It also gives us a glimpse of why Haddad caused such outrage.

The second part, 'Social Section: How to Educate Girls to be Wives and Mothers', is his critique of the current situation and his proposals for socio-cultural change. I confine my discussion to the first part, which contains Haddad's framework for redressing gender inequalities in Muslim legal tradition. Haddad is neither apologetic nor defensive. 'I am not oblivious to the fact that Shari'a accorded lower status to women than men in certain situations,' and that the sacred texts 'make us believe that in essence [Islam] favoured men over women'. But he goes on to argue the need to go beyond the literal meanings of the two main sources of the Shari'a, the Qur'an and the Prophet's Sunna: 'if we look into their aims, we realise that they want to make woman equal to man in every aspect of life' (p. 104).

There are two related elements in Haddad's approach to Islam's textual sources. The first is the distinction between laws that are essential to Islam as a religion, and those that are contingent and time- and context-bound; in his words:

---

27 For a discussion of the political context, reactions to Haddad's book, and the politics of family law in Tunisia, see Norma Salem, 'Islam and the status of women in Tunisia', in *Muslim Women*, ed. Freda Hussain (London: Croom Helm, 1984); Marion Boulby, 'The Islamic challenge: Tunisia since Independence', *Third World Quarterly* 10, no. 2 (1988); Mounira Charrad, *States and Women's Rights: The Making of Postcolonial Tunisia, Algeria and Morocco* (Berkeley: University of California Press, 2001).

28 Quotations and references are from Husni and Newman, *Muslim Women in Law and Society.*

> We should take into consideration the great difference between what Islam brought and its aims, which will remain immortal in eternity, such as belief in monotheism, moral behaviour, and the establishment of justice, dignity and equality among people. Furthermore, we have to consider the social situation and the deep-rooted mindset that existed in Arab society in the pre-Islamic era when Islam first emerged. The prescriptions for confirming or amending previous customs remained in force as long as these practices existed. Their disappearance, however, did not harm Islam as practices such as slavery, polygamy, etc cannot be considered inherent to Islam (p. 36).

The second element in his perspective is what he calls the 'policy of gradualism' (*siyasa tadrijiyya*), which he argues governs the process of legislation in the Qur'an and Sunna. In Islam the 'highest aim is equality among all God's creatures', but it was not possible to achieve this aim in the seventh century and during the lifetime of the Prophet; 'the general conditions in the Arabian Peninsula forced the legal texts to be laid down gradually, especially those concerning women' (p. 104). 'Islam is the religion of freedom', but it tolerated 'the selling and buying of human beings as goods, and their exploitation as animals for the duration of their lives' (p. 48). This toleration was a concession to the socio-economic imperatives of the time. It was not then possible to do away with slavery all together, but the Qur'an and the Prophet encouraged the freeing of slaves, and made it crystal clear that the principle is freedom. For exactly the same reason, gender hierarchy was tolerated then, but the principle in Islam remains equality.

> Although Islam highlights a number of differences between man and woman in several verses in the Qur'an, this does not in any way affect the principle of social equality between them when the necessary conditions were [to become] present over time since Islam in essence aims for complete justice and fairness. It introduced its laws and gradually adapted them according to the capacity of people to obey them. There is no reason to believe that the gradual changes that took place in the life of the Prophet should stop after the passing away of the Prophet. The gradual changes in the Shari'a law took place at a pace that could be sustained by society and there are clear examples to testify to that (p. 48).

The Qur'an's gradual ban on drinking wine, Haddad argues, is a clear example of the 'policy of gradualism' in the formulation of legislation that unfolded during the lifetime of the Prophet. At first, drinking was tolerated; then later verses abrogated the earlier one and the ban was introduced. But he maintains that other issues, such as slavery, polygamy, men's authority over women, and unilateral divorce remained to be resolved later. Slavery was eventually abolished, when societies evolved and humans realised its evil; abolition took place first in the West, Muslim countries followed suit, and Shari'a-based laws relating to slavery all became obsolete. Now the time has come to honour 'Islam's love for equality' and to abolish unjust and discriminatory laws that have kept women backward and denied them their rights. To do so we must, first, discover the principle and the objective behind Qur'anic laws, and secondly, understand that they were means to an end; they were not meant to be eternal or rigid in form, they are just shells and can be changed when they no longer serve the social objectives of Islam, which are those of freedom, justice and equality. They were revealed to the Prophet so that he could reform and change the unjust values and practices of his time.

With respect to family law, there are again two important elements in Haddad's approach. First, he rejects the argument that women are unfit for certain activities and that their primary role is motherhood. 'Islam did not assign fixed roles to men and women... Nowhere in the Qur'an can one find any reference to any activity – no matter how elevated it may be – whether in government or society, that is forbidden to woman' (p. 39). Yes, men and women are different; women give birth and are physically and emotionally suited to care for children, but this in no way means that Islam wanted them to be confined to the home and to domestic roles. He argues for the creation of institutions to liberate women. 'Islam truly is a religion that is rooted in reality and evolves as it changes over time; herein lies the secret of its immortality. As human societies progress and evolve, new institutions emerge to liberate women, such as crèches and nurseries, as in France and other nations that have advanced' (p. 47). The problem is not with Islam but with patriarchy, with reducing women to sex objects; it is 'primarily due to the fact that we [men] regard them [women] as vessels for our penises'.[29]

Secondly he breaks away from the transactional logic of marriage in *fiqh*, and places mutual affection and cooperation at the centre of the marital relationship.

> Marriage involves affection, duties, intercourse and procreation. Islam regards affection as the foundation of marriage since it is the driving force, as witnessed by the following verse:
>
> And among His signs is this, that He created for you mates from among yourselves, that you may dwell in tranquillity with them, and He has love and mercy between your (hearts): Verily in that are signs for those who reflect.[30]

29 This phrase appears towards the end of Haddad's preface to the book; here I did not use Husni and Newman's translation, which renders the phrase as '... we regard them as an object to satisfy our desires' (p. 31).
30 Qur'an 30:21; the translation is by Yusuf Ali, p. 1012; interestingly, Yusuf Ali finds it necessary to include a footnote comment to the effect that tranquillity, love and mercy are found in the normal relations of a father and mother, and love and mercy between men and women; excluding any possible alternative reading of the text.

> As for duty, this refers to the fact that husband and wife have to work together to build a life. In this sense, duty both preserves and enhances the emotional ties that exist between them and which enable them to carry out their duty wilfully (p. 57).

Having shifted the focus from Qur'an 4:34 to 30:21, his starting point for discussing marriage becomes freedom of choice (*hurriyyat al-ikhtiyar*). Love and compassion cannot develop in a relationship that is imposed; women, like men, must have the freedom to choose their spouses and to be able to leave an unwanted marriage, and this is what Islam mandates. He then goes on to break the link between maintenance and obedience as constructed in classical *fiqh* texts.

> If we look at the origins of the Shari'a in order to understand the meaning of duty in matrimony, we would find that it is incumbent upon the man to support his wife and children financially, on the grounds that they are not able to do so themselves. With the exception of this, no duty is specified, for either the husband or the wife, to dictate how they behave within marriage or toward each other. Whatever duties the man has towards his wife, they are equal to the duties she has towards him. This is illustrated in the following verse 'Women shall have such honourable rights and obligations' (p. 59).

The verse to which Haddad refers here (2: 228) goes on to say 'but men have a degree (of advantage) over them;'[31] this part of the verse is often invoked in conjunction with Qur'an 4:34 as textual evidence of men's superiority in order to justify their authority over women. But his reading of these two verses is different from that of the classical jurists. He argues that both verses must be read in the context of marriage and divorce practices of the time, and the privileges that men enjoyed before Islam: both verses aim to restrain these privileges. This becomes clear when we read these verses in their entirety and in conjunction with those that precede and follow them. In verse 4:34, a husband is required to provide for his wife, so that 'the continued growth of the world' can be ensured; he was given the right to 'correct' his wife's behaviour in order to prevent a greater ill, divorce. According to Haddad, this verse is not speaking about the rights and duties of spouses, but about the course of action to be taken when there is marital discord, and it offers ways to resolve it. This becomes clear in the verse that follows, which reads 'if you have reason to fear that a breach might occur between a couple, appoint an arbiter from among his people and an arbiter from among her people; if they both want to set things aright, God may bring their reconciliation' (4:35). Men are addressed because they are the ones who, then as now, have the

---

31 This is from Yusuf Ali's translation, p. 92; see below for Asad's translation, which is rather different and, I find, clearer.

power to terminate marriage, and the objective was to restrain this power and give the marriage a chance. Likewise, with respect to verse 2:228, which the jurists quote to argue for men's superiority, Haddad maintains that it must be read in its entirety[32] and in connection with the preceding and following verses, which are all related to marital separation and the protection of women. The final part of the verse speaks of men's power to divorce, and this is what 'men having a degree over women' is about; divorce was in their hands.

After a lengthy discussion of various forms of divorce in *fiqh* and the acts of injustice and suffering that they entail for women, Haddad concludes that men's right to *talaq* (i.e unilateral and extrajudicial divorce) must be abolished:

> [T]here is no other way of dealing with matters relating to marriage and divorce cases, except through the courts so that everything is done in conformity with the spirit and the letter of the Shari'a (p. 72).

Asserting that 'the Qur'anic text generally sets forth means of achieving justice between man and woman' (p. 79), Haddad also argues for the abolition of polygamy, which he contends 'has no basis in Islam; it is... one of the evils of the pre-Islamic era which Islam challenged through its gradualist method' (p. 63). Polygamy is unjust, inimical to the very foundation of marriage, which is based on affection and harmony between the couple. It was one of those practices that Islam wanted to eradicate but had to tolerate and could only modify. The Qur'an limited the number of wives a man could have to four, and stipulated conditions of just equality among the wives; but made it clear that such justice is impossible to establish, however hard a man tries. Here Haddad quotes Qur'an 4:3, which says 'Marry such women as seem good to you, two, three, four; but if you fear you will not be equitable, then only one.' He also rejects the conventional argument that the Prophet himself was polygamous, and thus his practice should be followed:

> The fact that the Prophet had many wives does not mean that he legislated for this practice or wanted the Muslim community to follow this path. Indeed he had taken these wives before the limitations had been imposed. It is worth bearing in mind that the Prophet was

32 Asad's translation of the whole verse is: 'And the divorced woman shall undergo without marrying, a waiting period of three monthly courses: for it is not lawful for them to conceal what God may have created in their wombs, if they believe in God and the Last Day. And during this period their husbands are fully entitled to take them back, if they desire reconciliation; but, in accordance with justice, the rights of the wives [with regard to their husbands] are equal to [husbands'] rights with regard to them, although men have precedence over them [in this respect]. And God is almighty, wise' [Muhammad Asad, *The Message of the Qur'an* (Bristol: Foundation Books, 2003), 61].

> also a human being, and as such was subject to human tendencies as regards issues that had not been sent down to him as revelation from the heavens (p. 64).

In short, Haddad argues for legal equality for women in all areas, including in inheritance. According to him, the Qur'an's assignment of a lesser share of inheritance to women was due to the conditions of the time; it was a concession to the social order. But here again equality is the principle and when we look closely, we find that,

> Islam did not allocate a lesser share in the woman's inheritance compared to that of man as a principle applicable in all cases. It gave her the same share in the case of parents inheriting from their dead son when there is a male child and if it involves inheritance among blood siblings (p. 47).

In other instances where women were allocated lesser shares, it had to do with the context; the Arabs then would not have accepted equal shares for women, which they would have seen as unjust, as women did not participate in warfare and were under men's protection. But 'there is no reason why such a position should remain fixed in time without change.'

Haddad's ideas and proposals for reform were indeed radical for the time, which to a large extent explains the harsh reaction of the clerical establishment to his book. A year later (1931), one of the officials of Zaytouna, Saleh Ibn Murad, published a book in response, entitled *Mourning over al-Haddad's Woman or Warning off Errors, Apostasy and Innovation.* But in 1956, in a changed political context, when the nationalists/modernists had prevailed and Tunisia was an independent nation-state, many of Haddad's proposals for reform were adopted. Under the leadership of Habib Bourguiba, the modernists embarked on reform of the judiciary, and among their first acts was the codification of family law. The new code made polygamy illegal and gave women equal access to divorce and child custody; though the inheritance laws remained unchanged. All these reforms were of course introduced from above, when women were still not vocal participants in the debate.[33]

---

33 For an overview and analysis of these reforms, see Patricia Kelley, 'Finding common ground: Islamic values and gender equity in Tunisia's reformed Personal Status Code', in *Shifting Boundaries in Marriage and Divorce in Muslim Communities*, ed. Homa Hodfar (Grabels: Women Living Under Muslim Laws, 1996).

Fazlur Rahman (1919–1988): Reforming Islamic Intellectual Tradition

Fazlur Rahman was another daring twentieth-century reformer whose ideas met a great deal of opposition in his own country, Pakistan, though his situation and background were different from those of Haddad. More of a scholar than an activist, Fazlur Rahman's intellectual genealogy is through reform thinkers in the Indian sub-continent.[34] Likewise, unlike Haddad, the formation of his ideas belongs to the tail end of Western colonialism in Muslim contexts, when processes of nation building, the modernization and reform of the judiciary, and the codification of family law were well under way.[35]

Born in pre-partition India, Fazlur Rahman was instructed in traditional Islamic sciences by his father,[36] then went on to study Arabic and Islamic studies at Punjab University in Lahore, and Islamic philosophy at the University of Oxford. After graduation in 1958, he taught at universities in the United Kingdom and Canada until 1961, when he was invited by the President of Pakistan, General Ayub Khan, to help with reforming religious education in Pakistan. He became director of the Islamic Research Institute, recently created to provide intellectual backing for Ayub Khan's modernization project and to steer the path of reform in ways that would not offend the religious establishment.[37] He became entangled with the politics of modernization and reform in Pakistan, and his reformist ideas and approach to Islamic tradition from a critical perspective made him a target for Ayub Khan's influential religious and political opponents. The fiercest opposition came from religious conservatives, and was centred on the question of women's rights and the reform of family law. Rahman began to re-

---

34 Prominent among them were Syed Ahmad Khan (1871–1898) and Muhammad Iqbal (1877–1938); Iqbal delivered his reform agenda in a series of six lectures published in Lahore in 1930 (see *Reconstruction of Religious Thought in Islam*, Oxford University Press, 1934). These lectures, which did not receive much attention at the time, later became central to the formation of Muslim reform thought. For an illuminating exposition of Iqbal's lecture on the notion of *ijtihad*, see Muhammad Khalid Masud, *Iqbal's Reconstruction of Ijtihad*, 2nd ed. (Lahore: Sadat Art Press, 2003).

35 For an analysis of their impact on the rethinking of notions of gender rights in Muslim legal tradition, see Ibrahim Moosa, 'The Poetics and Politics of Law after Empire: Reading Women's Rights in the Contestations of Law', *UCLA Journal of Islamic and Near Eastern Law* 1, no. 1 (2001–2).

36 His father Mawlana Shibat al-Din was a graduate of the Deoband Seminary in India.

37 Major family law reforms in the sub-continent took place before Rahman's directorship; the 1939 Dissolution of Marriages Act, the 1961 Muslim Family Laws Ordinance. Women's groups were instrumental in pushing for these reforms.

ceive death threats, and eventually decided to return to academic life in the West. In 1968 he was appointed Professor of Islamic Thought at the University of Chicago, where he remained until his death in 1988, leaving behind an impressive body of scholarship. His work in turn has been the subject of scholarship, and played an important role in the USA in the development of Islamic studies.[38] But his vast output, all in English, remains almost unknown in the Arab world and in traditional religious circles, and his influence in his own country Pakistan is limited.

Unlike Haddad, Rahman did not write a book about women's rights, nor did he offer specific proposals for reforming Muslim family law. But his writings are permeated by a critique of patriarchal readings of Islam's sacred texts, and his framework for interpreting the ethico-legal content of the Qur'an has been crucial to feminist scholarship in Islam.[39] He considered the reform of Muslim family laws to be on the whole moving in the right direction, and he saw the weight of conservatism in Muslim contexts as the main obstacle to bringing about radical reform. In 'A survey of modernization of Muslim Family Law', an article published in the 1980s, Rahman opens the discussion by pointing to the fate of Haddad, and the harsh reaction his book and his proposals for family law reform received from the very clerics who were not perturbed by his earlier quasi-Marxist book on the rise of trade unionism and the interpretation of history.[40]

In his approach to Islam's sacred texts, Rahman shares Haddad's historicism and gradualism in revelation and legislation. The Qur'an 'is the divine response, through the Prophet's mind, to the moral-social situation of the Prophet's Arabia, particularly to the problems of commercial Meccan society of the day.' Not all these solutions are relevant or applicable to all times and all contexts. What is immutable and valid are the moral principles behind these solutions. These moral principles shows us the way, the Shari'a, how to establish a society on earth where all humans can be treated as equals as they are equal in the eyes

38 For studies on Fazlur Rahman's work, see Tamara Sonn, 'Fazlur Rahman's Islamic methodology', *The Muslim World* 81 (1991); Ibrahim Moosa's introduction to Fazlur Rahman, *Revival and Reform in Islam* (Oxford: Oneworld, 2000); Abdullah Saeed, 'Fazlur Rahman: a Framework for Interpreting the Ethico-Legal Content of the Qur'an', in Taji-Farouki, *Modern Muslim Intellectuals and the Qur'an*. For his impact on American Islamic discourse, see Waugh H. Earle and Frederic M. Denny, eds., *The Shaping of An American Islamic Discourse: A Memorial to Fazlur Rahman* (Atlanta: Scholars Press, 1998).

39 For his views on gender rights and his impact on the development of a new Islamic feminism, see Part III of ibid., in particular the chapter by Tamara Sonn, 'Fazlur Rahman and Islamic feminism'.

40 Rahman, 'A Survey of Modernization of Muslim Family Law', 451.

of God. This is at once 'the challenge and the purpose of human existence, the trust – *amana* – that humanity accepted at creation.'[41]

But Muslims betrayed this trust as, in the course of the historical development of Islam, the moral principles behind Qur'anic laws were distorted. This distortion has its roots in political developments after the Prophet's death and in the subsequent decay and stagnation of Islamic intellectualism, which predates Islam's encounter with Western colonial powers. Muslims failed to create a viable system of Qur'an-based ethics, and from the outset jurisprudence has overshadowed the science of ethics in Islam; in developing the latter, Muslim scholars relied more on Persian and Greek sources than on the Qur'an itself. The link between theology, ethics and law will remain tenuous as long as Muslims fail to make the crucial distinctions in the Qur'an and the Prophet's Sunna, between essentials and accidentals, and between prescriptive and descriptive. They mistakenly view the Qur'an as a book of law, and take its legal and quasi-legal passages to be relevant to all times and places.

To revive the Qur'an's 'élan', Rahman argues, Muslims need two things. First is a fresh engagement with the Qur'an and a critical reassessment of the entire Islamic intellectual tradition: theology, ethics, philosophy and jurisprudence. The second is a realistic assessment and understanding of the contemporary socio-political context. It is only then that Muslims can overcome centuries of decadence and backwardness and meet the challenges of modernity. The interpretative process that Rahman proposes for this revival is a 'double movement', which entails a movement 'from the present situation to Qur'anic times, then back to the present'. In the first movement 'general principles, values and long-range objectives' of the Qur'an are elicited and separated from the socio-historical context of the revelation. In the second, these principles are applied to issues at hand, taking into consideration the current context and its imperatives.[42] In his words, this:

> ... requires the careful study of the present situation and the analysis of its various component elements so we can assess the current situation and change the present to whatever extent necessary, and so we can determine priorities afresh in order to implement the Qur'anic values afresh. To the extent that we achieve both moments of this double movement successfully, the Qur'an's imperatives will become alive and effective once again. While the first task is primarily the work of the historian, in the performance of the second the instru-

41 Sonn, 'Fazlur Rahman and Islamic feminism', 128.

42 Fazlur Rahman, *Islam & Modernity: Transformation of an Intellectual Tradition* (Chicago: The University of Chicago Press, 1982), 5.

> mentality of the social scientist is obviously indispensable, but the actual 'effective orientation' and 'ethical engineering' are the work of the ethicist.[43]

In 'The status of women in Islam: a modernist interpretation',[44] Rahman suggests what 'effective orientation' and 'ethical engineering' entail when it comes to the issue of gender equality and family law. This is the only place where Rahman focuses his attention on this issue (apart from his 1980 article on family law reforms, already cited); elsewhere he mentions it only in passing. Published in 1982, the same year as his last major work (*Islam and Modernity*), this article can be seen as the application of his 'double movement' theory in the area of gender rights and family law reform. Rahman begins by identifying himself as a 'Muslim modernist', one who pursues social reform through a new interpretation of Islamic sources and 'in contradistinction to the stance taken on most social issues by Muslim conservative-traditionalist leaders'. Islamic modernism, Rahman argues, 'developed under the impetus of modern Western liberalism but contains within it tangible differences on sexual issues, but is to be sharply distinguished from secularism.'[45] He is equally critical of social reform without reference to Islam, which he calls 'secularism (à la Mustafa Kemal Ataturk)', the 'apologetic aspect' of Islamic modernism that rationalises and justifies gender inequality (p. 285).[46]

The legislation in the Qur'an on the subject of women, Rahman contends, is part of the effort to strengthen the position of the weaker segments of the community, which in pre-Islamic Arabia were the poor, orphans, women, slaves and those chronically in debt. Through reforming existing laws and practices and introducing new ones, the Qur'an aimed to put an end to their abuse and to open the way for their empowerment. Departing from the apologetic refrain on the po-

---

43 Ibid., 7.

44 In Hanna Papanek and Gail Minault, eds., *Separate Worlds: Studies of Purdah in South Asia* (Delhi: Chanakya Publications, 1982), 285–310. The article also appeared in a revised and shortened version in a later collection on women's rights in Islam: Guity Nashat, ed., *Women and Revolution in Iran* (Boulder, CO: Westview Press, 1983), 37–54.

45 Rahman does not spell out the differences here, but in a later article he gives us a clue as to what he means when he states the position of a Muslim modernist: 'While he espouses the cause of the emancipation of women, for example, he is not blind to the havoc produced in the West by its new sex ethics, not least in the dilapidation of the family institution' [Fazlur Rahman, 'Islam and political action: Politics in the service of religion', in *Cities of Gods: Faith, Politics and Pluralism in Judaism, Christianity and Islam*, ed. Nigal Biggar, Jamie Scott and William Schweiker (New York: Greenwood Press, 1986), 160].

46 References are to Fazlur Rahman, 'Status of women in the Quran', in *Women and Revolution in Iran*, ed. Guity Nashat (Boulder: Westview Press, 1983).

sition of women in pre-Islamic time, Rahman argues that the position of women was not altogether low, 'for even a slave woman could earn and own wealth, like a slave male, let alone a free woman. Khadija, the first wife of the Prophet, owned a considerable business which the Prophet managed for her sometime before their marriage, and after their marriage she helped him financially' (p. 286). But women could also be treated as property, as 'a son inherited his stepmother as part of his father's legacy and could force her to marry him or could debar her from marrying anyone else through her life, coveting her property' (p. 288). Women were also 'the central focus of the "honour" (*'irḍ*) of a man whose "manliness" (*muruwwa*) demanded that her honour remain inviolate' (p. 287). This, according to Rahman, was the distorted logic behind the practice of female infanticide, which was a way of preventing the eventual infringement of a man's honour.

What the Qur'anic reforms achieved was 'the removal of certain abuses to which women were subjected': female infanticide and window-inheritance were banned, laws of marriage, divorce and inheritance were reformed. As with slavery, however, these reforms did not go as far as abolishing patriarchy. But they expanded women's rights and brought tangible improvements in their position – though not social equality. Women retained the rights they had to property, but they were no longer treated as property; they could not be forced into marriage against their will, and they received the marriage gift (*mahr*); they also acquired better access to divorce and were allocated shares in inheritance.

The essential equality between the sexes is clearly implied in the Qur'an; both men and women are mentioned separately 'as being absolutely equal in virtue and piety with such unflinching regularity that it would be superfluous to give particular documentation' (p. 291). Those sayings attributed to the Prophet that speak of women's inferiority and require them to obey and worship their husbands, Rahman argues, are clearly 'a twisting of whatever the Qur'an has to say in matters of piety and religious merit' (p. 292) and marriage.

> The Qur'an speaks of the husband and wife relationship as that of 'love and mercy' adding that the wife is a moral support for the husband (30:21). It describes their support for each other by saying, 'they (i.e. your wives) are garments unto you and you are garments unto them' (2:187). The term 'garment' here means that which soothes and covers up one's weakness (p. 293).

Such sayings also contradict what we know of the Prophet's own conduct, thus must be rejected.

> The Prophet's wives, far from worshiping him – with all his religious authority – wanted from him the good things of life, so that the Qur'an had to say, 'O Messenger! Say to your wives: "If you want to pursue this-worldly life and its good things, then I will give you wealth, but let you go in gentleness (i.e. divorce you)"' (33:29).[47] What the Qur'an required from a woman was to be a good wife, adding, 'Good women are those who are faithful and who guard what is their husband's in his absence as God wants them to guard' (4:34) (p. 293).

The Qur'an does speak of inequality between sexes. But when it does, it gives the rationale, which has to do with socio-economic factors.

> In 2:228 we are told, 'For them (i.e. women) there are rights (against them), but men are one degree higher than women.' That is to say, in the social (as opposed to religious) sphere, while the rights and obligations of both spouses towards each other are exactly commensurate, men are, nevertheless, a degree higher. The rationale is not given in this verse which simply adds 'And God is Mighty and Wise.' The rationale is given later, in verse 4:34 (p. 294).

This verse, Rahman continues, begins by saying that men are 'managers over (i.e., are superior to) women because some of humankind excel others (in some respects) and because men expend of their wealth (for women)' and then goes on to give them the authority to discipline their wives when they do not obey them. Thus the two rationales that this gives for male superiority in socioeconomic affairs are: '(1) that man is "more excellent", and (2) that man is charged entirely with household expenditure', but not any inherent inequality between sexes. (p. 294).

> What the Qur'an appears to say, therefore, is that since men are the primary socially operative factors and bread-winners, they have been wholly charged with the responsibility of defraying household expenditure and upkeep of their womenfolk. For this reason man, because by his struggle he has gained more life-experience and practical wisdom, has become entitled to 'manage women's affairs', and, in case of their recalcitrance, admonish them, leave them alone in their beds and, lastly, to beat them without causing injury (p. 294–5).

Having given his interpretation of Verse 4:34 and the rationale behind the gender inequality in the Qur'an, Rahman then poses two questions: Are these socio-economic roles on which gender inequality is based immutable, even if women want to change them? If they are changeable, how far can they be changed? His answer to the first question is a definite no, these inequalities are not inherent in the nature of the sexes; they are the product of historical socio-economic de-

47 [sic: should be 33:28].

velopments. Once women acquire education and participate in society and economy, the 'degree' that the Qur'an says men have over women also disappears. But the answer to the second question, Rahman contends, is not that simple, and he is hesitant whether 'women should ask or be allowed to do any and all jobs that men do' – although he admits that 'if women insist on and persist in this, they can and eventually will do so' (p. 295).

But he has no doubt that law reforms must give women equality in all other spheres; classical *fiqh* rulings in marriage, divorce and inheritance can and must be reformed because 'it is the most fundamental and urgent requirement of the Qur'an in the social sector that abuses and injustices be removed' (p. 295). These inequalities are now the cause of suffering and oppression and go against the Qur'anic spirit, which is that of the equality of all human beings.

He then goes on to discuss in detail the laws of polygamy, divorce, inheritance and hijab, and reiterates the gist of his framework:

> One must completely accept our general contention that the specific legal rules of the Qur'an are conditioned by the socio-historical background of their enactment and what is eternal therein is the social objectives or moral principles explicitly stated or strongly implied in that legislation. This would, then, clear the way for further legislation in the light of those social objectives or moral principles. This argument remains only elliptically hinted at by the Modernist, who has used it in an *ad hoc* manner only for the issue of polygamy, and has to not clearly formulated it as a general principle (p. 301).

Rahman ends by stressing that legal reform can only be effective in changing the status of women in Muslim contexts when there is an adequate basis for social change. It is only then that the Qur'anic objective of social justice in general and for women in particular can be fulfilled; otherwise its success will be limited, transitory and confined to certain social groups (p. 308).

Where We Are Now: New Contexts and New Questions

Appearing at two different junctures in the twentieth-century, these pioneering texts by Tahir Haddad and Fazlur Rahman lay the ground for an egalitarian construction of family law within an Islamic framework. The issues that they raise are still with us, and relevant to current debates and struggles to reshape and redefine Muslim family laws, but two developments towards the end of the last century changed the context and tone of these debates.

The first was the ways in which the successes of political Islam and the ideological use of Shari'a transformed relations between religion, law and politics for Muslims. The slogan of 'Return to Shari'a' in practice amounted to nothing more than attempts to translate into state policy classical *fiqh* rulings on gender relations and family and some areas of penal law. In late colonial times and the immediately post-colonial middle decades of the century, activist women in Muslim contexts had increasingly come to identify Islam with patriarchy, and to fear that the removal of the latter could not be achieved under a polity and a legal regime dominated by Islam. Now, wherever Islamists gained power or influence – as in Iran, Sudan, Pakistan and Malaysia – their policies proved the validity of the activists' fears. Arguing for patriarchal rulings as 'God's Law', as the authentic 'Islamic' way of life, they tried to reverse some of the legal gains that women had acquired earlier in the century; they dismantled elements of earlier family law reforms and introduced morality laws, such as gender segregation and dress codes.

But these Islamist measures had some unintended consequences; the most important was that, in several countries, they brought classical *fiqh* texts out of the closet, and exposed them to unprecedented critical scrutiny and public debate; Muslim women now found ways to sustain a critique – from within – of patriarchal readings of the Shari'a and of the gender biases of *fiqh* texts in ways that were previously impossible. At the same time, a new wave of Muslim reform thinkers started to respond to the Islamist challenge and to take Islamic legal thought onto new ground. Building on the efforts of previous reformers, and using the conceptual tools and theories of other branches of knowledge, they have developed further interpretive-epistemological theories. Their conceptual tools, such as the distinctions between religion (*din*) and religious knowledge (*ma'rifat-e dini*), between Shari'a and *fiqh*, between essentials and accidentals in the Qur'an have stretched the limits of traditional interpretations of Islam's sacred texts. Revisiting the old theological debates, they have revived the rationalist approach that was eclipsed when legalism took over as the dominant mode and gave precedence to the form of the law over substance and spirit.[48]

48 In this respect, the works of the new wave of Muslim thinkers such as Mohammad Arkoun, Khaled Abou El Fadl, Nasr Hamid Abu Zayd, Mohammad Mojtahed Shabestari and Abdolkarim Soroush are of immense importance and relevance. For Arkoun, see Ursula Günther, 'Mohammad Arkoun: Towards a Radical Rethinking of Islamic Thought', in Taji-Farouki, *Modern Muslim Intellectuals and the Qur'an*; for Khaled Abou El Fadl, *Speaking in God's Name: Islamic Law, Authority and Women* (Oxford: Oneworld, 2001); for Abu Zayd, see Navid Kermani, 'From Revelation to Interpretation: Nasr Hamid Abu Zayd and the Literary Study of the Qur'an', in Taji-Farouki, *Modern Muslim Intellectuals and the Qur'an*; for Soroush, see Abdolkarim Soroush, *Reason, Freedom, & Democracy in Islam: Essential Writings of 'Abdolkarim Sorush*, trans. and ed. with a critical introduction by Mahmoud Sadri and Ahmed Sadri (Oxford: Oxford University Press, 2000), and the articles available on his website (http://www.drsoroush.com/English.htm), and for his ideas on gender, see Ziba Mir-Hosseini, *Islam and Gender: The Religious Debate in*

The second development was the expansion of transnational feminism and women's groups, and the emergence of NGOs, which led to the opening of a new phase in the politics of gender and law reform in Muslim contexts. In the first part of the twentieth century women were largely absent from the process of reform and codification family law and the debates that surrounded it. But by the end of the century, Muslim women were refusing to be merely objects of the law, but rather claiming the right to speak and to be active participants in the debates and in the process of law making. The changed status of women in Muslim societies and other socio-economic imperatives meant that many more women than before were educated and in employment. Women's rights were by now part of human rights discourse, and human rights treaties and documents, in particular CEDAW, gave women a new language in which to frame their demands.

The confluence of these two developments opened new space for activism and debate. Both recognised religious authorities (*fuqaha*) and those with other interpretations and agendas, not least women scholars and lay people, started engaging in debate and in criticism of the interpretations, old and new, of key concepts such as *qiwama*. There were always Muslim reformers and women who argued for an egalitarian interpretation of the Shari'a, but it was not until the 1980s that critical feminist voices and scholarship emerged from within the Muslim legal tradition, in the form of a new literature that deserves the label 'feminist', in that it is sustained and informed by an analysis that inserts gender as a category of thought into religious knowledge. Pioneers among them were the works of Aziza Al-Hibri, Riffat Hassan, Amina Wadud and Fatima Mernissi,[49] to be followed by others who are breaking new ground.[50]

Contemporary Iran (Princeton: Princeton University Press, 1999), Chapter 7; for Shabestari, see Farzin Vahdat, 'Post-Revolutionary Modernity in Iran: The Subjective Hermeneutics of Mohamad Mojtahed Shabestari', in Taji-Farouki, *Modern Muslim Intellectuals and the Qur'an*; and articles and interviews at *Qantara.de* (http://qantara.de/webcom/show_article.php/_c-575/i.html).

49 Their early works are: Aziza Al-Hibri, 'A Study of Islamic Herstory: Or How Did We Ever Get Into This mess?', *Islam and Women* 5, no. 2 (1982); Riffat Hassan, 'Equal before Allah? Woman-Man Equality in the Islamic Tradition', *Harvard Divinity Bulletin* 7, no. 2 (1987); Fatima Mernissi, *Women and Islam: An Historical and Theological Enquiry,* trans. Mary Jo Lakeland (Oxford: Blackwell, 1991); Amina Wadud, *Qur'an and Woman: Rereading the Sacred Text from a Woman's Perspective* (New York: Oxford University Press, 1999).

50 See, for instance, Kecia Ali, 'Progressive Muslims and Islamic jurisprudence: The Necessity for Critical Engagement with Marriage and Divorce Law', in *Progressive Muslims*, ed. Omid Safi (Oxford: Oneworld, 2003); Asma Barlas, *Believing Women in Islam: Unreading Patriarchal Interpretations of the Qur'an* (Austin: University of Texas Press, 2002); Sheikh, 'Exegetical violence'; Asghar Ali Engineer, *The Rights of Women in Islam* (London: Hurst, 1992); Haifaa Jawad, *The*

A new consciousness emerged, a gender discourse that came to be labelled 'Islamic feminism'.[51] This discourse, energised by new feminist scholarship in Islam, was further facilitated by the rapid spread of new technologies, notably the internet; and these new technologies have regularly shown their potential for the mobilization of campaigns for change.

By engaging with the tradition from within, these new feminist voices and scholarship in Islam have begun to insert women's concerns and voices into the processes of the production of religious knowledge and legal reform. In so doing, they can bridge two gaps in the Muslim family law debates and in the Muslim legal tradition. First, a majority of Muslim religious scholars are gender blind, being largely ignorant of feminist theories and unaware of the importance of gender as a category of thought. Secondly, in line with mainstream feminism, many women's rights activists and campaigners in Muslim contexts have long considered working within a religious framework to be counter-productive; choosing to work only within a human rights framework, they have avoided any religion-based arguments. They have tended to ignore that there is also an epistemological side to feminism, in the sense of examining how we know what we know about women in all branches of knowledge and in religious tradition. This knowledge not only sheds light on laws and practices that take their legitimacy from religion but enables a challenge, from within, to the patriarchy that is institutionalised in Muslim legal tradition.

Before considering, finally, the implication of feminist scholarship for twenty-first century debates over Muslim family laws, let me bring together the two elements that run through my narrative and argument in this chapter. First, the idea of gender equality, which became inherent to global conceptions of justice in the course of the twentieth century, has faced Muslim legal tradition with

---

Rights of Women in Islam: An Authentic Approach (London: MacMillan, 1998); Mir-Hosseini, 'The Construction of Gender in Islamic Legal Thought and Strategies for Reform'; Amira El-Azhary Sonbol, 'Rethinking women and Islam', in *Daughters of Abraham: Feminist Thought in Judaism, Christianity, and Islam*, ed. Yvonne Haddad and John Esposito (Gainesville: University of Florida Press, 2000); Zainah Anwar, ed., *Wanted: Equality and Justice in Muslim Family Law* (Kuala Lumpur: Sisters in Islam, 2009).

51 Although I was among the first to use the term 'Islamic feminism' to refer to the new gender consciousness emerging in Iran a decade after the 1979 revolution [Ziba Mir-Hosseini, "Stretching the Limits: A Feminist Reading of the Shari'a in Post-Revolutionary Iran," in *Islam and Feminism: Legal and Literary Perspectives*, ed. Mai Yamani (London: Ithaca, 1996)], more recently I have questioned its usefulness as an analytical or descriptive tool, given the heavy political and rhetorical baggage it has since acquired, Mir-Hosseini, 'Beyond "Islam" vs "Feminism"'.

an 'epistemological crisis'[52] that it has been trying to resolve with varying degrees of success. Secondly, the breakthrough came in the last two decades of the century with the emergence of feminist voices and scholarship in Islam, which, as I have argued elsewhere, is the 'unwanted child' of political Islam. The Islamists' attempt to turn patriarchal interpretations of the Shari'a into policy the made the intimate links between theology, law and politics more and more transparent. It led to new forms of activism among Muslims and the emergence of new discourses, which eventually opened the way for a constructive and meaningful dialogue between Muslim legal tradition and feminism.

By bringing the insights of feminist theory and gender studies into Islamic studies, feminist scholarship in Islam can enable us to ask new questions. For example, the *Maqasidi* approach[53] has captured the imagination of many Muslim reformist thinkers; what does it have to offer to those seeking gender equality? Does the concept of *qiwama* have positive elements that should be retained? Should the link affirmed by classical *fiqh* between maintenance (*nafaqa*) and obedience (*tamkin*) be redefined or severed? One of the basic necessities that the Shari'a aims to protect is *nasl:* progeny, family; so far, this has been done in a patriarchal form. What kind of family do Shari'a-based laws aim to protect? What do equality and justice mean for women and the family? Do they entail identical rights and duties in marriage? In other words, is legal equality good for women and the family?

These questions are at the centre of debates in feminist scholarship. There is a shift from 'formal' models of equality to 'substantive' models that take into account the differing needs of different women and the direct and indirect discrimination that they face.[54] A formal model of equality, which often simply requires

52 I borrow this concept from the philosopher Alasdair MacIntyre, who argues that every rational inquiry is embedded in a tradition of learning, and that tradition reaches an epistemological crisis when, by its own standards of rational justification, disagreements can no longer be resolved rationally. This gives rise to an internal critique that will eventually transform the tradition, if it is to survive. It is then that thinkers and producers in that tradition of inquiry gradually start to respond and assimilate the idea that is alien to the tradition. See Alasdair MacIntyre, *Whose Justice? Which Rationality* (Notre Dame, IN: University of Notre Dame Press, 1988), 350–52; Alasdair MacIntyre, 'The Rationality of Traditions', in *Moral Disagreements: Classic and Contemporary Readings*, ed. Christopher W. Gowans (London: Routledge, 2000). For a critique of MacIntyre's theory of justice and his neglect of gender, see Susan Moller Okin, *Justice, Gender and the Family* (Princeton: Princeton University Press, 1987), chapter 3, 'Whose traditions? Which Understanding?'

53 'Objectives of Shari'a'.

54 For instance, see Joan Scott, 'Deconstructing Equality-versus-Difference: OR, the Uses of Poststructuralist Theory for Feminism', *Feminist Studies* 14, no. 1 (1998); Sandra Fredman, 'Pro-

a reversibility and comparison between the sexes, does not necessarily enable women to enjoy their rights on the same basis as men. Feminist legal theorist Catherine MacKinnon tells us why such a model of equality rests on a false premise: neither the starting point nor the playing field are the same for both sexes.[55] Not only do women not have the same access as men to socio-economic resources and political opportunities, but women are not a homogeneous group; they do not experience legal inequality and discrimination in the same way; class, age, race, socio-economic situation, are all important factors. In short, what kind of laws and legal reforms are needed so that equality of opportunity and result can be ensured? For instance, CEDAW does not define equality, rather its provisions are directed at eliminating discrimination, and here it rightly adopts an abolitionist language. How useful is it to use such a language in Muslim contexts, given the primacy of law in Islamic discourses and the intimate links between *fiqh* and cultural models of the family? Is this the best way of approaching the tension between 'protection' and 'domination' that is inherent in the very concept of *qiwama*, however we define it? In Islamist and traditionalist discourses, *qiwama* is presented as a manifestation of 'protection', not of discrimination; such an approach could draw attention to the 'domination' side of *qiwama* and counter apologetic arguments that are based on ideologies and hypothetical cases rather than on lived realities and women's experience.

The search for answers to these questions takes us to realms outside Islamic legal tradition, to human rights law, feminist legal theory, and experiences of family law reform in other legal traditions. If, in the twentieth century, scholars like Tahir Haddad and Fazlur Rahman bridged the gap between classical *fiqh* and modern notions of justice by providing a framework for an egalitarian interpretation of Islamic sacred texts, in the twenty-first century the new feminist voices and scholarship in Islam have opened a dialogue with Muslim legal tradition. But a meaningful and constructive dialogue can only take place when the two parties can treat each other as equals and with respect, when they are ready to listen to each other's arguments, and to change position if necessary. This takes us once again to the realm of power relations; the theological is also necessarily – and intensely – political, in ways similar to the feminist understanding that the personal is political.

viding Equality: Substantive Equality and the Positive Duty to Provide', *South African Journal of Human Rights* 21 (2005).

55 Catherine MacKinnon, *Towards a Feminist Theory of the State* (Boston: Harvard University Press, 1989).

Bibliography

'Abd Al 'Ati, Hammudah. *The Family Structure in Islam.* Plainfield: American Trust Publications, 1997.

Abou El Fadl, Khaled. *Speaking in God's Name: Islamic Law, Authority and Women.* Oxford: Oneworld, 2001.

Abusulayman, Abulhamid A. *Marital Discord: Recapturing the Full Islamic Spirit of Human Dignity.* Occasional Paper Series 11. London, Washington: The International Institute of Islamic Thought, 2003.

Ahmed, Leila. *Women and Gender in Islam: Historical Roots of a Modern Debate.* New Haven: Yale University Press, 1992.

Al-Hibri, Aziza. 'A Study of Islamic Herstory: Or How Did We Ever Get Into This Mess?' *Islam and Women* 5, no. 2 (1982): 201–19.

—. 'An Islamic Perspective on Domestic Violence'. *Fordham Law Journal* 27 (2003): 195–224.

Ali, Kecia. 'Progressive Muslims and Islamic jurisprudence: The Necessity for Critical Engagement with Marriage and Divorce Law'. In *Progressive Muslims.* Edited by Omid Safi, 163–89. Oxford: Oneworld, 2003.

—. 'Understanding a Difficult Verse, Qur'an 4:34'. Accessed October 14, 2017. https://www.brandeis.edu/projects/fse/muslim/diff-verse.html.

—. *Sexual Ethics and Islam: Feminist Reflections on Qur'an, Hadith and Jurisprudence.* Oxford: Oneworld, 2006.

—. 'The Best of You Will Not Strike'. *Comparitive Islamic Studies* 2, no. 2 (2006): 143–55.

—. *Marriage and Slavery in Early Islam.* Cambridge, MA: Harvard University Press, 2010.

Anderson, James Norman. *Law Reforms in the Muslim World.* London: Athlone, 1976.

Anwar, Zainah, ed. *Wanted: Equality and Justice in Muslim Family Law.* Kuala Lumpur: Sisters in Islam, 2009.

Asad, Muhammad. *The Message of the Qur'an.* Bristol: Foundation Books, 2003.

Badran, Margot. 'From Islamic feminism to a Muslim Holistic Feminism'. *Institute of Development Studies Bulletin* 42, no. 1 (2011): 78–87.

Barlas, Asma. *Believing Women in Islam: Unreading Patriarchal Interpretations of the Qur'an.* Austin: University of Texas Press, 2002.

Bori, Caterina and Livnat Holtzman, eds. *A Scholar in the Shadow: Essays on the Legal and Theological Thought of Ibn Qayyim al-Ğawziyyah.* Rome: Istituto per l'Oriente; Herder, 2010.

Boulby, Marion. 'The Islamic Challenge: Tunisia since Independence'. *Third World Quarterly* 10, no. 2 (1988): 590–614.

Charrad, Mounira. *States and Women's Rights: The Making of Postcolonial Tunisia, Algeria and Morocco.* Berkeley: University of California Press, 2001.

Chiba, Masaji, ed. *Asian Indigenous Law in Interaction with Received Law.* London, New York: KPI, 1986.

Dunn, Shamon, and Rosemary B. Kellison. 'At the Intersection of Scripture and Law: Qur'an 4:34 and Violence against Women'. *Journal of Feminist Studies in Religion* 26, no. 2 (2010): 11–36.

Earle, Waugh H. and Frederic M. Denny, eds. *The Shaping of An American Islamic Discourse: A Memorial to Fazlur Rahman.* Atlanta: Scholars Press, 1998.

El-Azhary Sonbol, Amira, ed. *Women, Family and Divorce Laws in Islamic History.* Syracuse: Syracuse University Press, 1996.

—. 'Rethinking Women and ISLAM'. In *Daughters of Abraham: Feminist Thought in Judaism, Christianity, and Islam.* Edited by Yvonne Haddad and John Esposito, 108–46. Gainesville: University of Florida Press, 2000.

Elsaidi, and Murad H. 'Human Rights and Islamic law: A Legal Analysis Challenging the Husband's Authority to Punish "Rebellious Wives"'. *Muslim World Journal of Human Rights* 2 (2011): 1–25.

Engineer, Asghar Ali. *The Rights of Women in Islam.* London: Hurst, 1992.

Fredman, Sandra. 'Providing equality: Substantive Equality and the Positive Duty to Provide.' *South African Journal of Human Rights* 21 (2005): 163–90.

Guardi, Jolana. 'Women Reading the Qur'an: Religious Discourse in Islam'. *Hawwa: Journal of Women in the Middle East and the Islamic World* 2, no. 3 (2004): 301–15.

Günther, Ursula. 'Mohammad Arkoun: Towards a Radical Rethinking of Islamic Thought'. In Taji-Farouki, *Modern Muslim Intellectuals and the Qur'an*, 125–67.

Hassan, Riffat. 'Equal before Allah? Woman-Man Equality in the Islamic Tradition'. *Harvard Divinity Bulletin* 7, no. 2 (1987): 148–57.

Husni, Ronak, and Daniel Newman. *Muslim Women in Law and Society: Annotated Translation of al-Tahir al-Haddad's Imra'tuna fi 'l-shari'a wa l-mujtama' with an introduction.* London: Routledge, 2007.

Ibn Qayyim al-Jawziyya. *Iʿlām al-muwaqqiʿīn ʿan rabb al-ʿālamīn.* Beirut: Dār al-fikr al-ʿarabī, 1956.

Ibn Rushd. *The Distinguished Jurist's Primer: Bidayat al-Mujtahid wa Nihayat al-Muqtasid.* Translated by Imran Ahsan Khan Nyazee. 2 vols. Reading: Garnet Publishing, 1996.

Jawad, Haifaa. *The Rights of Women in Islam: An Authentic Approach.* London: MacMillan, 1998.

Keddie, Nikki. *Women in the Middle East: Past and Present.* Princeton: Princeton University Press, 2007.

Kelley, Patricia. 'Finding Common Ground: Islamic Values and Gender Equity in Tunisia's Reformed Personal Status Code'. In *Shifting Boundaries in Marriage and Divorce in Muslim Communities.* Edited by Homa Hodfar, 74–105. Grabels: Women Living Under Muslim Laws, 1996.

Kermani, Navid. 'From Revelation to Interpretation: Nasr Hamid Abu Zayd and the Literary Study of the Qur'an'. In Taji-Farouki, *Modern Muslim Intellectuals and the Qur'an*, 169–92.

MacIntyre, Alasdair. *Whose Justice? Which Rationality.* Notre Dame, IN: University of Notre Dame Press, 1988.

—. 'The Rationality of Traditions'. In *Moral Disagreements: Classic and Contemporary Readings.* Edited by Christopher W. Gowans, 204–16. London: Routledge, 2000.

MacKinnon, Catherine. *Towards a Feminist Theory of the State.* Boston: Harvard University Press, 1989.

Mahmood, Tahir. *Family Law Reforms in the Muslim World.* Bombay: N.M. Tripathi, 1976.

Mahmoud, Mohamed A. 'To Beat or Not To Beat: On the Exegetical Dilemmas over Qur'an, 4:34.' *Journal of American Oriental Society* 126, no. 4 (2006): 537–50.

Marin, Manuela. 'Disciplining Wives: A Historical Reading of Qur'an 4:34'. *Studia Islamica* 98 (2003): 5–10.

Masud, Muhammad Khalid. *Shatibi's Philosophy of Islamic Law.* New Delhi: Kitab Bhavan, 1997.
—. *Iqbal's Reconstruction of Ijtihad.* 2nd ed. Lahore: Sadat Art Press, 2003.
Mernissi, Fatima. *Women and Islam: An Historical and Theological Enquiry.* Translated by Mary Jo Lakeland. Oxford: Blackwell, 1991.
Mir-Hosseini, Ziba. 'Stretching the Limits: A Feminist Reading of the Shari'a in Post-Revolutionary Iran'. In *Islam and Feminism: Legal and Literary Perspectives.* Edited by Mai Yamani, 285–319. London: Ithaca, 1996.
—. *Islam and Gender: The Religious Debate in Contemporary Iran.* Princeton: Princeton University Press, 1999.
—. 'The Construction of Gender in Islamic Legal Thought and Strategies for Reform'. *Hawwa: Journal of Women in the Middle East and the Islamic World* 1, no. 1 (2003): 1–28.
—. 'Muslim Women's Quest for Equality: Between Islamic Law and Feminism'. *Critical Inquiry* 32, no. 1 (2006): 629–45.
—. 'Towards Gender Equality: Muslim Family Law and the Shari'a'. In *Wanted: Equality and Justice in Muslim Family Law.* Edited by Zainah Anwar, 23–63. Kuala Lumpur: Sisters in Islam, 2009.
—. 'Criminalizing Sexuality: Zina Laws as Violence Against Women in Muslim Contexts'. Accessed September 15, 2012. http://www.stop-stoning.org/node/882.
—. 'Beyond 'Islam' vs 'Feminism''. *Institute of Development Studies Bulletin* 42, no. 1 (2011): 67–77.
Moghissi, Haideh. *Feminism and Islamic Fundamentalism: The Limits of Post-Modern Analysis.* London: Zed Press, 1999.
Moosa, Ibrahim. 'The Poetics and Politics of Law after Empire: Reading Women's Rights in the Contestations of Law'. *UCLA Journal of Islamic and Near Eastern Law* 1, no. 1 (2001–2): 1–46.
Mubarak, Hadia. 'Breaking the Interpretive Monopoly: A Re-examination of Verse 4:34'. *Hawwa: Journal of Women in the Middle East and the Islamic World* 2, no. 3 (2004): 261–89.
Nashat, Guity, ed. *Women and Revolution in Iran.* Boulder, CO: Westview Press, 1983.
Okin, Susan Moller. *Justice, Gender and the Family.* Princeton: Princeton University Press, 1987.
Papanek, Hanna and Gail Minault, eds. *Separate Worlds: Studies of Purdah in South Asia.* Delhi: Chanakya Publications, 1982.
Rahman, Fazlur. 'A Survey of Modernization of Muslim Family Law'. *International Journal of. Middle East Studies* 11 (1980): 451–65.
—. 'Status of women in the Quran'. In *Women and Revolution in Iran.* Edited by Guity Nashat, 37–54. Boulder, CO: Westview Press, 1983.
—. *Islam & Modernity: Transformation of an Intellectual Tradition.* Chicago: The University of Chicago Press, 1982.
—. 'Islam and Political Action: Politics in the Service of Religion'. In *Cities of Gods: Faith, Politics and Pluralism in Judaism, Christianity and Islam.* Edited by Nigal Biggar, Jamie Scott and William Schweiker, 153–66. New York: Greenwood Press, 1986.
—. *Revival and Reform in Islam.* Oxford: Oneworld, 2000.
Rapoport, Yossef. *Marriage, Money and Divorce in Medieval Islamic Society.* Cambridge: Cambridge University Press, 2005.

Saeed, Abdullah. 'Fazlur Rahman: a Framework for Interpreting the Ethico-Legal Content of the Qur'an'. In Taji-Farouki, *Modern Muslim Intellectuals and the Qur'an*, 37–66.
Salem, Norma. 'Islam and the Status of Women in Tunisia'. In *Muslim Women*. Edited by Freda Hussain, 141–68. London: Croom Helm, 1984.
Scott, Joan. 'Deconstructing Equality-versus-Difference: OR, the Uses of Poststructuralist Theory for Feminism'. *Feminist Studies* 14, no. 1 (1998): 33–50.
Sheikh, Sa'diyya. 'Exegetical Violence: Nushuz in Quranic Gender Ideology'. *Journal for Islamic Studies* 17 (1997): 49–73.
Sonn, Tamara. 'Fazlur Rahman's Islamic Methodology'. *The Muslim World* 81 (1991): 212–30.
—. 'Fazlur Rahman and Islamic feminism'. In *The Shaping of An American Islamic Discourse: A Memorial to Fazlur Rahman*. Edited by Waugh H. Earle and Frederic M. Denny, 123–46. Atlanta: Scholars Press, 1998.
Soroush, Abdolkarim. *Reason, Freedom, & Democracy in Islam: Essential Writings of 'Abdolkarim Sorush*. Translated and edited with a critical introduction by Mahmoud Sadri and Ahmed Sadri. Oxford: Oxford University Press, 2000.
Taji-Farouki, Suha, ed. *Modern Muslim Intellectuals and the Qur'an*. Oxford: Oxford University Press, 2004.
Tucker, Judith. *In the House of Law: Gender and Islamic Law in Ottoman Syria and Palestine*. Berkeley: University of California Press, 2000.
Vahdat, Farzin. 'Post-Revolutionary Modernity in Iran: The Subjective Hermeneutics of Mohamad Mojtahed Shabestari'. In Taji-Farouki, *Modern Muslim Intellectuals and the Qur'an*, 193–224.
Wadud, Amina. *Qur'an and Woman: Rereading the Sacred Text from a Woman's Perspective*. New York: Oxford University Press, 1999.
—. *Inside the Gender Jihad: Women's Reform in Islam*, Oxford: Oneworld, 2006.
Zayzafoon, Lamia Ben Youssef. *The Production of the Muslim Woman: Negotiating Text, History, and Ideology*. New York: Lexington Books, 2005.

Mathias Rohe

Islamic Law and Justice

Introduction

Calls for injustice are not documented in world history. Striving for justice, however, seems to be an anthropological constant. This applies to individuals as well as to communities. Aristotle describes justice in the fifth book of his Nicomachean Ethics to be 'the greatest of virtues' and as 'the actual exercise of complete virtue'.[1] The expression 'iustitia fundamentum regnorum' is widely spread in the languages and cultures of past and present. The church father Augustinus[2] asks: Without justice, what distinguishes the state from a bunch of robbers? The writer of this article is in possession of an old copper plate from Aleppo, on which one can find the Arabic phrase *'al-ʿadl asās al-ḥukm'*. With this background, the following thoughts are based on premises which underlie modern comparative law analysis. It can be stated that all legal systems have to tackle certain needs of order in human coexistence. The solutions can be quite different, depending on social, economic and cultural circumstances and beliefs, while the subjects of regulation (e. g. protection of a person's life, body and goods against intrusion, fulfilment of demands by commitment to contract, regulation of rights and obligations within families etc.) appear to be quite similar.

This approach opposes a cultural exceptionalism according to the pattern 'Islamic law is immutable and insofar structurally different from other laws'. The orientation on concrete needs of order further thwarts superficial conclusions regarding differences or similarities. Instead of focusing on single laws of jurisprudence without taking their legal and extra-legal context into consideration, we have to analyse the answer to challenges of order within the interplay of material and procedural norms coming from possibly very different legal fields.[3]

What, however, is justice? In the fifth book of the Nicomachean Ethics of Aristotle, the still universally accepted assumption can be found which calls for a

1 Aristotle, *The Nicomachean Ethics: trans. David Ross* (Oxford: Oxford University Press, 2009), V.1 1129b 30 f.

2 De civitate dei IV, 4, 1. "Iustitia remota quid sunt regna nisi magna latrocinia."

3 Cf. e. g. Mathias Rohe, 'Gründe und Grenzen deliktischer Haftung: Die Ordnungsaufgaben des Deliktsrechts", *Archiv für die civilistische Praxis* 201, no. 2 (2001).

https://doi.org/10.1515/9783110574593-006

distributive justice that treats the equal equally and the unequal unequally.[4] The Corpus Iuris Civilis, which was compiled by Emperor Justinian in the sixth century, starts by combining justice and law: 'Justice is the steady and perpetual will to give dues to anybody,'[5] and gives a definition of justice that is, even today, conventional in vernacular ('to each his own'): 'iuris praecepta sunt haec: honeste vivere, alterem non laedere, suum cuique tribuere.'[6]

Lawyers of different cultures seem to be more focused on the law and its application than on the – rather abstract – term of justice, which also includes moral ways of living. Seemingly, there is a broad assumption that the law is an important, albeit not the most important tool for the implementation of justice.[7] This also applies to Islamic culture. There, legal scholars, especially judges, are held in high esteem – at least in legal literature. The judge's task is numbered among the most honourable religious activities, since the rightful legal decision brings out justice, and justice is the base for heaven and earth.[8]

But can law also be unjust? This dilemma can only be avoided on the basis of a pure legal positivism. There is an endless discussion about cases where a revolt against a regime is considered to be legally permissible or even necessary. In Germany, due to the experiences with the illegitimate state of the Nazi era, the so-called Radbruch Formula was established, named after the lawyer and Weimar minister of justice, Gustav Radbruch. His essay, published in 1946, titled 'Legal injustice and supra-legal justice', includes this formula for the first time, according to which a court, when confronted with a conflict of statute law and justice, can only (and has to) decide in favour of justice when the statute law is to be seen as 'unbearably unjust' or when it 'knowingly refuses'[9] the equality of people as a category which is inherent to law. Nevertheless, the debate on who/what is equal or unequal is an old one and will continue in all

4 Aristotle, *The Nicomachean Ethics*, 1131a 22–24.

5 "Iustitia est constans et perpetua voluntas ius suum cuique tribuens."

6 Institutiones 1, 3.

7 Aristotle equates them in his fifth work on Nicomachean ethics (1129b). The law philosopher Gustav Radbruch calls on the glosse 1.1. pr. D. 1, 1 "Est autem ius a iustitia, sicut a matre sua, ergo prius fuit iustitia quam ius" (Law however follows justice, just like she is its mother, hence justice comes before law) as well as the statement of the Archbishop of Freiburg, Konrad Groeber, in his speech on New Year's EVE 1940 against the unjust methods of the German National Socialists ("Law is what benefits the people"): "The idea of law cannot differ from the idea of Justice", cit. Gustav Radbruch, *Rechtsphilosophie: Studienausgabe*, 2nd ed. (Heidelberg: C.F. Müller, 2003), 34.

8 Shams al-Dīn al-Sarakhsī, *al-Mabsūṭ*, 31 vols. (Beirut: Dār al-maʿrifa, 1989), 16/59 f. with further references.

9 Quoted in Radbruch, *Rechtsphilosophie*, 211, 216.

legal orders: Are males and females, free people and slaves, citizens and non-citizens, followers of all religions or beliefs, adults and minors equal or unequal? The answers given differ tremendously in time and space.

In addition, legislators are normally fully aware of the fact that even the most diligent formulation of laws can lead to unreasonable and undesirable outcomes in exceptional cases. Consequently, normative or administrative corrections are made on the basis of justness or as an act of grace. This also applies to Islamic law, as will be shown below. Justice in law can therefore be only analysed by targeting certain groups of cases or situations of life. The dependence of this analysis on preconceptions with differing proveniences is quite apparent: Is it just or unjust to tax the poor and the rich equally? How can the search for materially right solutions be combined with the rather reverse necessity of establishing legal certainty?

How, and based on which benchmarks, can orientation and security be guaranteed by abstract laws, and in which cases is it necessary to consider justness or acts of grace? These are only some of the questions that describe the complexity of legal exercises of creating order. While an agreement on an abstract term of 'justice' is easy to achieve, the opinions on what in detail is equal or unequal and thereby has to be treated equally or unequally, also differs in Islamic law.

Justice as a Postulate in Islamic Norms Doctrine

Basic Texts

The Quran, being the first and most honourable normative source of Islam,[10] orders and teaches justice on its own accord[11] and allows assured decision[12]. Justice is an attribute of God. It is also required for decision-making between people, as can be seen the Quranic verse, which calls for a just judgement (*wa idhā ḥakamtum bayna al-nās, an taḥkumū bi l-ʿadl*)[13]. Hence, we also find here the personal ethic as well as the legal regulative components of justice.

10 Despite of the uncertain transmission story, Sunnis and Shi'ites mostly agree on this topic, cf.. Harald Löschner, *Die dogmatischen Grundlagen des šīʿitischen Rechts: Eine Untersuchung zur modernen imāmitischen Rechtsquellenlehre* (Cologne: Carl Heymanns Verlag, 1971), 72 and ff. with further references also on differing opinions on the Shia akhbārī school of thought.

11 E.g. Sura 4:135; 5:8; 6:152; 7:29; 16:90; 40:9; 57:25.

12 Cf. e.g. Sura 5:50.

13 Sura 4:58. See also Sura 5:42.

Nevertheless, no sole definition of justice has been developed. The great jurist al-Māwardī (d. 1058), the author of the most influential book on state legal theory, describes justice (*ʿadāla)* as a condition of moral and religious perfection. According to the scholar Ibn Rushd (d. 1198), who is also known in Europe by the name of Averroës, justice consists in avoiding severe sins and also staying clear of smaller ones. It is mostly taken for granted that such perfection is only rarely achieved. The first great codification of Islamic law in the 19th century, the Ottoman Mecelle in 1876, describes a suitable just witness as someone whose positive incentives outweigh the negative ones (article 1705 in the book on evidence and oath).[14]

The term justice has to be concretised with regard to single contents, depending on social preconceptions and legal landmark decisions. Hence, the fundamental question arises whether legislators or those applying the law are entitled to develop new interpretations of the laws and apply them. This might in theory collide with the traditional perception of God being the sole legislator, which is maintained not only by Islamists in our days.

On the other hand, there is the concept of sovereignty, delegated by God to the people. Its roots might already be found in the debate of the 8th century, in which the caliph was called 'God's representative'. In the constitutions of some Arab states, it is simply stated that state authority proceeds from the people (e. g. in article 24 of the Jordanian constitution). The Sudanese lawyer Abdullahi An-Naʿim pointedly expressed: 'Like all aspects of the legal system of each country, family law is really based on the political will of the state, and not on the will of God. After all, there is no way of discovering and attempting to live by the will of God except through the agency of human beings. Since that is the case, those responsible for the enactment and application of family law must be politically and legally accountable for their actions, instead of being allowed to hide behind claims of divine command.'[15]

---

14 Şāhidin ādil olması şarttır. Ādil, hasınātı sayyiātına ghalib olan kimsehdir, translated into English: "A witness must be an upright person. An upright person is one whose good qualities outweigh his bad qualities". Available at http://www.iium.edu.my/deed/lawbase/al_majalle/al_majalleb15.html (last accessed 26.09.2017).

15 Abdullahi A. An-Naʿim, *Islamic Family Law in A Changing World: A Global Resource Book* (London: Zed Books, 2002), 20.

Approaches to epistemological problems

Justice is not dealt with as an autonomous, theoretically-based concept[16] in the juristic or legal philosophical literature. Nevertheless, the scientifically most elaborate school of Islamic theology, the so-called Muʿtazila, is based on the presumption of God's justice as an important pillar of insight:[17] God *is* not only just – everybody agrees on that – but he is just *by necessity*, hence he cannot and must not be unjust. It is rationality which brings justice (by distinguishing between good and evil) to light.

In the latter aspect, the Muʿtazila differs fundamentally from other, later dominating readings like those by the Ashʿarites, who consider everything God does as being just. One consequence of the Muʿtazilite doctrine, even if not an exclusive one, is the rejection of a strict theory of predestination. If God is and has to be just, he cannot determine the belief or disbelief of a human in the future. On the contrary, the free will of the human being (*ikhtiyār*), decides on his/her ways, which are nevertheless judged by God.[18]

Sunni jurisprudence has unarguably widely settled for the assumption that the order created by God as the norm-giver (*shāriʿ*) completely fulfills the postulate of justice, so that only details have to be dealt with.[19] Respectively, the input on justice (*ʿadl*) is intellectually modest in the most comprehensive summary of the opinion on the four great Sunni schools of *fiqh*,[20] which is published by the Kuwaiti ministry for religious foundations and Islamic affairs in an encyclopedia containing 45 volumes. The article simply states that jurisprudence considers those to be just whose good features, motivations or actions outweigh the bad ones. After some philological explanations, only a few concrete cases are mentioned regarding the question whether the respective actors have to be just as a prerequisite for being entitled to fulfil certain tasks:

16 Cf. Emile Tyan, "ʿadl,", in Gibb; Kramers; Lévi-Provençal; Schacht; Lewis, *Encyclopaedia of Islam*.
17 Ibid.; Thomas Hildebrandt, *Neo-Muʿtazilismus? Intention und Kontext im modernen arabischen Umgang mit dem rationalistischen Erbe des Islam* (Leiden, Boston: Brill, 2007), 137 ff.
18 Cf. on all this Daniel Gimaret, "Muʿtazila", in *The Encyclopaedia of Islam: Second Edition, vol. VII*, ed. C.E. Bosworth et al. (Leiden: Brill, 1993); Hildebrandt, *Neo-Muʿtazilismus?*; Majid Khadduri, *The Islamic Conception of Justice* (Baltimore: The Johns Hopkins University Press, 1984), 41 ff.
19 This approach is similar to that of the ancient world and the Christian Middle Ages, which derive justice from divine destiny or cosmological order, differing from later rational approaches.
20 Wizārat al-awqāf wa al-shuʾūn al-islāmiyya, al-Kuwayt, ed., *al-Mawsūʿa al-fiqhiyya*, 4th ed., 45 vols. (Kuwait: Dhāt al-salāsil, 1993–2007). Entry can be found in issue 30 of 1414/1994 (p. 5–14).

There is consensus regarding the custodian of the alms taxes (*zakat*), who has to be just, as well as the one who recognises new moon in Ramadan, while there are different perceptions on the concrete requirements for justice here. Different perceptions are also discussed for the briefly touched issues such as the determination of the direction of prayer, the qualification of water for ritual washing, the exercise of marriage guardianship, the enforcement of wills, the observation of charities and the guardianship over minors. The literature on the judgeship, the administration of appeal instances (*maẓālim*), the institutions of giving expert opinions of normative issues (*iftā'*), and particularly on witnesses, is somewhat more explicit. The article closes with remarks on justice between spouses, where the postulate of equal treatment for all wives (Qur'an 4:3) is dealt with (*wa in khiftum allā taʿdilū, fa-wāḥida...*)[21].

Generally spoken, in Islam, as in other religions, simple-minded representatives have to deal with complex issues, and it happens that they try to enforce their interpretation with social pressure or brute force. Contemporary Islamists, last but not least the anti-intellectual neo-Salafists, claim exclusive knowledge of the truth – just like any religious or ideological fanatics. The badge that Islamist groups spread in the small Syrian town ʿAzāz 2013 after occupying it: 'Islam = justice, democracy = injustice'[22] may serve as an example of this simple-minded approach.[23]

More ambitious thinkers automatically have to deal with the question of how the norms set by God can be understood. Even though God should be the only lawgiver, the sense of his laws can only be interpreted via the human brain. The dilemma of a set of laws set by God, which accordingly gives the 'wrong' interpretation a transcendent dimension, is dealt with by the formula: '*kullu mujtahid*

21 For newer interpretations, which are followed by banning polygamy, cf. below III.4.

22 Article: *Nürnberger Nachrichten*, "Im Widerstand vereint", 3 April 2013, 4.

23 This is contrary e.g. to the statement of the influential General Secretary of the Organisation of Islamic Cooperation (OIC), Madani, from August 2014, where he together with the Indonesian president calls for the necessity of conveying the Islamic values like "Justice, Kindness, Fairness, Freedom of Religion and Coexistence" by education, to prevent and fight extremism as practiced by Boko Haram or the IS (*Bernama News*, "Promote Islamic Values to Combat Religious Extremism"). The speech recalls the statements of Mohammad Hashim Kamali, *Citizenship and Accountability of Government: An Islamic Perspective* (Cambridge: Islamic Texts Society, 2011), 178: "The Islamic ideals of human dignity, equality, justice and cooperation in good works tend to view the *homo sapiens* as a single entity without recognition of nationality and race or of divisive factors that would obstruct these values (...)."

muṣīb' – everybody, who sincerely tries to find the right solution, does so rightly and will be rewarded.[24]

Apart from this, two opinions were developed on the question of whether the norms of the Sharia consistently had a clear content. One of the schools (the *mukhaṭṭi'a*, or 'fallibilists'), agreed, but stated that only God knew the correct answer, which was to be made known on the day of the Last Judgement. The other school (the *muṣawwiba*, or 'infallibilists'), with prominent representatives like al-Juwaynī (d. 1085), al-Ghazālī (d. 1111) und al-Suyūṭī (d. 1505) already doubted the basic assumption of one righteous interpretation. For them, there was no exclusively right answer (*ḥukm mu'ayyan*), but God wanted the people to find it themselves. If there had been one correct answer, God would have made it clear and not send the people on their way to find it without having appropriate tools for the search. Hence, it would be enough to thoroughly care for one's own cognition (*ijtihād*).[25]

Justice and Rule

The small number of works on constitutional topics argue that the production of justice is an essential reason for the caliph's rule. Al-Māwardī[26] wrote in his standard work 'The ordinances of government', most probably addressing the caliph of the Abbasids[27] that the 'imāmate[28] was established as the succession of the Prophet in the protection of religion and the administration of worldly affairs.' According to the author, the Imam has to be entirely just, has to fulfil all the preconditions for independent legal reasoning (*ijtihād*) and have intact senses, be physically healthy, insightful, courageous and fearless and has to belong to the clan of the Prophet, the Quraysh. His tasks include the preservation and enforcement of religion and of the law, the protection the realm, the execution of Qur'anic criminal law, the defence of the external borders, the *jihād* against

---

24 In detail: Josef van Ess, "Kull mujtahid muṣīb", in *Dirāsāt islāmiyya*, ed. Fahmī Jad'ān (Irbid: Manshūrāt Jāmi'at al-Yarmūk, 1983), 123 ff.; Birgit Krawietz, *Hierarchie der Rechtsquellen im tradierten sunnitischen Islam* (Berlin: Duncker & Humblot, 2002), 327 ff. with further references.
25 Cf. Khaled Abou El Fadl, "The Centrality of Shari'ah to Government and Constitutionalism in Islam", in *Constitutionalism in Islamic Countries: Between Upheaval and Continuity*, ed. Rainer Grote and Tilmann Röder (Oxford: Oxford University Press, 2011), 58 f. with further references.
26 Abū al-Ḥasan al-Māwardī, *al-Aḥkām al-sulṭāniyya* (Beirut: n.p., n.d., before 1988), 5.
27 Cf. Hamilton A.R. Gibb, "Al-Māwardī's Theory of the Caliphate", in *Studies on the Civilization of Islam*, ed. Hamilton A.R. Gibb (Boston: Beacon Press, 1962), 152.
28 The term "imām" in this kind of literature in Sunni Islam addresses the caliph.

those who fight Islam, ensure the collection of war booty shares and of the alms taxes, setting the level of state benefits and payments, the organisation of the administration and its oversight.[29]

The eminent scholar al-Juwaynī identifies the correction of discrepancies and injustices, the support of those having been treated unfairly and the proper allocation of rights the central tasks of the ruler.[30] The scholar Ibn Qayyim al-Jawziyya (d. 1350) states that God has sent his message to guide the people in justice. Hence, just rule was the way to God, and Muslims had to follow every way that lead to the right and just.[31]

This corresponds with the perception of Ibn Abī al-Rabīʿ (d. 1258), namely that humans might be unjust by nature, but also have the natural desire for justice and the urge to consolidate to bring justice back. This is why rulers came to power through a contract with their people, which promised to create a just society or at least the maximum of potential for justice.[32] However, according to Ibn Abī al-Rabīʿ, the Sharia itself substantially determinates justice.[33] In consequence, he refrains from any elaboration of concrete parameters for justice.

A certain specification of ideas of justice can also be found in mediaeval literature. The important universal historian and 'sociologist' Ibn Khaldūn (d. 1406), describes three kinds of political system: The first level is a primitive-natural system, in which only the power of the fittest, who tyrannises the others, counts. The second, 'dynastic' system can also be considered tyrannical. It is based on laws of the king/ruler. However, these rules are arbitrary and are only followed on the basis of coercion. The highest level is achieved with the caliphate, which is based on the norms of Sharia. The Sharia fulfills all criteria of justice and legitimacy and binds the ruling as well as the ruled, hence is not exposed to the arbitrariness of the ruler.[34]

Khaled Abou El Fadl[35] states that on this basis a ruling system, which acts in accordance with the law, is created. However, it does not necessarily include the (modern) premise of the rule of law, which will only be established through spe-

29 Al-Māwardī, *al-Aḥkām al-sulṭāniyya*, 18 f.

30 Cited in Abou El Fadl, "The Centrality of Shariʿah to Government and Constitutionalism in Islam", 35, 42 with n. 25.

31 Cited in ibid., 42 with n. 26. On the Shiʿite view see Abdulaziz Sachedina, *The Just Ruler in Shiite Islam* (Oxford: Oxford University Press, 1988).

32 Cited in Abou El Fadl, "The Centrality of Shariʿah to Government and Constitutionalism in Islam", 43 in nn. 27–29.

33 Ibid., 44.

34 Summary in ibid., 35, 38.

35 Ibid., 39.

cific contentious decisions and procedural guaranties like checks and balances. Also, it has to be examined under which conditions even an unjust ruler can claim loyalty or should not be toppled. Ultimately, this deals with weighing up different evils, which is also a central aspect of Islamic law.

After the complete loss of power of the Abbasids in the 10th century (with a short break in the late 12th and the early 13th centuries) the legitimacy of state rule was evaluated rather generously. Ibn Taymiyya (d. 1328) who is widely quoted until today, held the view that Muslims only had to act obediently before God and his messenger; the faithful had to discuss and counsel themselves with the expertise of their respective branches.[36] In this reading, Muslim society can exist as a variety of political entities under different rulers. With this interpretation, Ibn Taymiyya was able to preserve his crucial concern, the enforcement of the norms of Sharia, irrespective of particular structures of worldly rule.[37] The scholar and judge Badr al-Dīn ibn Jamāʿa (d. 1333)[38] added little to the theoretical construction of al-Māwardī.[39] His theory of the Imamate is largely embedded in the current political situation, even though he differentiated between an Imamate by choice and an enforced Imamate.[40] The Imamate which was only established by military means was also valid, so that 'the unity of Muslims and their unanimity remains'; insecurity and the sinfulness of the ruler do not change it.[41] Even if the Imam or the sultan acted in a sinful manner, it was better not to degrade them to avoid disturbances.

His interpretation of Qur'an 4:59 is remarkable: not only were caliphs to be commanders, but also their 'representatives', namely the usurpers. Finally, constitutional law developed the pragmatic rationale that injustice was preferable to

---

36 Aḥmad Ibn Taymiyya, *al-Siyāsat al-sharʾiyya fī iṣlāḥ al-rāʿī wa l-raʿiyya*, ed. Muḥammad Mubārak (Beirut: Dār al-kitāb al-ʿarabī, 1966), 135 f.; Henri Laoust, *Essai sur les Doctrines Sociales et Politiques de Taḳī-d-Dīn Aḥmad B. Taymiyya* (Cairo: Imprimerie l'Institut français d'archéologie orientale, 1939), 301 f.

37 Cf. on this Dietrich Pohl, *Islam und Friedensvölkerrechtsordnung: Die dogmatischen Grundlagen der Teilnahme eines islamischen Staates am modernen Völkerrechtssystem am Beispiel Ägyptens* (Wien, New York: Springer, 1988), 41 ff.; Peter Heine, "Staat/Staatslehre", in *Islam-Lexikon: Geschichte – Ideen – Gestalten*, 3 vols. (Freiburg: Herder, 1991), 3/688.

38 On his biography and its meaning, see Hans Kofler, "Handbuch des islamistischen Staats- und Verwaltungsrechtes von Badr-ad-dīn ibn Ǧamā'ah", *Islamica* 6 (1934), 349, 350 f.

39 Cf. Ann K. Lambton, *State and Government in Medieval Islam: An Introduction to the Study of Islamic Political Theory* (Oxford: Pyschology Press, 1981), 138 ff. on his and Ibn Taymiyyas teachings.

40 Kofler, "Handbuch des islamistischen Staats- und Verwaltungsrechtes von Badr-ad-dīn ibn Ǧamā'ah", 349, 356.

41 Ibid., 357.

anarchy.[42] The statement that sixty years under an unjust Imam were better than one night without a sultan is widely quoted.[43] The Shi''ites, who were rarely in charge of power, had to develop strategies to deal with a rule they perceived as unjust.[44].

It might not be too daring to draw parallels to the Radbruch formula. Unjust and inappropriate law generally also has to be followed. Otherwise the peace-keeping impact of the state monopoly on the use of force might break down, legal security might go astray, necessary common codes of behaviour might be endangered and the generally rather thin layer of civilization might be blown away by the right of the stronger. Consequently, according to a Syrian legal handbook from the 8th/14th century,[45] the appointment of judges by an unjust ruler is valid, as long as the judge is capable of performing jurisdiction. But then what remains of justice?

Specific Cases

Introduction

Despite the actual power relations and the rather pragmatic arrangements with them, Islamic law provides a wide range of different methods, institutions and principles of consideration, which can be applied to the making of justice. The function of the law as the basis for lasting peace based on just norms and decisions is of core importance.

Such functional, general considerations can already be found in the writings of the prominent Hanafi lawyer al-Sarakhsī[46] (d. 1090) on homicide. Al-Sarakhsī firstly emphasises the harmfulness of these actions with reference to the Qur'an and Muhammad. He also underlines the importance of punishment of the perpetrators in this world: If the pressure (on possible perpetrators) was restricted to

42 Cf. on this Ulrich Haarmann, "Lieber hundert Jahre Zwangsherrschaft als ein Tag Leiden im Bürgerkrieg: Ein gemeinsamer Topos im islamischen und frühneuzeitlichen europäischen Staatsdenken", in *Gottes ist der Orient – Gottes ist der Okzident: Festschrift für Abdoldjavad Falaturi zum 65. Geburtstag*, ed. Udo Tworuschka (Cologne, Vienna: Böhlau, 1991).

43 Ibn Taymiyya, *al-Siyāsat al-shar'iyya fī iṣlāḥ al-rā'ī wa l-ra'iyya*, 139.

44 Cf. Heinz Halm, *Der schiitische Islam* (Munich: Beck, 1994), 101ff.; Mathias Rohe, *Islamic Law in Past and Present.* Translated from the 3rd ed. in German by Gwendolyn Goldbloom (Leiden, Boston: Brill, 2015), 28ff., 186f. with further references.

45 Gabriela L. Guellil, *Damaszener Akten des 8. – 14. Jahrhunderts nach aṭ-Ṭarsūsīs Kitāb al-I'lām: Eine Studie zum arabischen Justizwesen* (Bamberg: Aku, 1985), 330.

46 Al-Sarakhsī, *al-Mabsūṭ*, 26/59.

punishment in the hereafter, only a very small percentage of people might be stopped by it. For an effective deterrence, the regime of the worldly punishment (*ʿuqūba*) and respective mechanisms of revenge (*qiṣāṣ*) had been implemented. The legal exercise of order – securing human life by effective deterrence of perpetrators – is defined there.

Differing statement can even be found regarding topics related to both the application of the law in this world as well as religion and the hereafter, and the consequential question about equal or unequal legal treatment of the followers of different religions. Al-Sarakhsī[47] for instance, deals with different opinions on the question whether the same amount of money (blood money, Arabic. *diya*)[48] is to be paid for Muslim and protected non-Muslim (e.g. Jews and Christians, so-called *dhimmīs*[49]) victims of murder or bodily harm. Some scholars call for unequal treatment to the detriment of the non-Muslims (e.g. reduction of the amount to one half or a third of it). They mainly argue on the basis of Qur'anic statements, saying that there is no equality (*musāwāt*) between Muslims and Disbelievers (e.g. in Qur'an 59:20) and further traditions (of the Prophet).

Al-Sarakhsī counters these statements by quoting other verses of the Qur'an and other traditions, but also delivers a justification based on keeping worldly order: The parts of the Qur'an calling for unequal treatment, he states, only dealt with incidents related to the hereafter. The content of the protection contract with the *dhimmīs* called for their equal treatment in this world. Furthermore, *dhimmīs* were legally capable, just like Muslims, to acquire property; hence the same should apply for their physical integrity (this is the meaning of *'nafs'* in this context). Also, the purpose of *diya* was the protection of security (*iḥrāz*); and this was a matter related to life on earth (this is the meaning of *'dār'* in the present context), not to religion (*dīn*), and relevant for Muslims and non-Muslims alike. This example shows, how misguided the prejudice of the inseparableness of religion and law in Islam really is.

The implementation of the postulate of justice in actual cases is of course highly dependent on changing social and economic parameters and on cultural, religious or philosophically coined preconditions. This becomes clear when looking at the gender relations, as we will do below. However, in other important questions the conditio humana is often stronger than sole economic, social or religious and/or cultural factors (e.g. communal life in the family, aspects of protection of minors, allocation of rights and property to persons and their protec-

---

47 Ibid., 26/84–86.

48 Cf. Rohe, *Islamic Law in Past and Present*, 178 ff. with further references.

49 Cf. ibid., 196 ff. with further references.

tion against intrusion, necessities of binding relationships in economies based on the distribution of labour). This demonstrates a broad range of problems and tasks to be tackled in all civilizations, which are solved through specific juristic approaches.[50]

There is, for example, a universal approach with respect to the legal capacity of minors regarding private contractual transactions. The basic idea is that minors should gradually obtain legal capacity in that respect depending on their age and maturity level. Respective legal rules can be found in European laws, but also in Islamic law, partly with astonishingly similar debates throughout the ages. Only an adult person who is mentally healthy (*bāligh ʿāqil*[51]) and free is legally capable without restrictions (*mukallaf*) and hence able to create civil law obligations. The mentally ill (*majnūn*) and the minor who is unable to make decisions (*ghayr mumayyiz*) are legally incapable. The minor who can make decisions[52] (*mumayyiz*) is legally capable in part: He generally needs the approval of a legal representative, but is independent with regard to favourable transactions.[53] A certain age is not required here.[54] The stance of imbeciles (*maʿtūh*[55]) is contested: Some consider them being mentally ill, some see them as partly legally capable youngsters.

On the other hand, some problems and many writings are incomprehensible to readers lacking legal education, even if they are fluent in the respective language. Some Islamicists who lack legal knowledge tend to overlook this fact, and hence practice an historicizing and essentialist view of Islamic law[56].

---

50 A current example, which is by no means meant to criticise the author, is the intellectually very appealing essay by Brinkley Messick, "Indexing the Self: Intent and Expression in Islamic Legal Acts", *Islamic Law and Society* 8, no. 2 (2001), 151 ff. For an anthropologist, it may be surprising that outside formal elements are comparatively strict considered, when it comes to legally relevant actions in cooperation with others, while the inner will is weighted more heavily when it comes to unilaterally appearing legal actions. For lawyers, this is an insight from the very beginning of their career: The topic is the intensively discussed balance of the relationship between private autonomy and protection of traffic.

51 Cf. Wizārat al-awqāf wa al-shuʾūn al-islāmiyya, al-Kuwayt, *al-Mawsūʿa al-fiqhiyya*, 7/154 f. (Tz. 11)

52 What is meant is the ability to differentiate between advantages and disadvantages, cf. ibid., 14/32.

53 Ibid., 14/34 f.

54 Ibid., 27/21 (Tz. 8) with further references

55 Cf. on different approaches ibid., 29/275 f.

56 A prominent example is the legally uneducated Islamic scholar Tilman Nagel, see Rohe, *Islamic Law in Past and Present*, 3; Mathias Rohe, "Der Islam im demokratischen Rechtsstaat", *Erlanger Universitätsreden* 80, no. 3 (2012), 31 f. with further references, available at https://

All in all, Islamic law is by no means singularly and structurally different from other legal orders. This awareness is especially important when dealing with Islamic law in the West. Specific legal thinking can be found across different cultures and is in fact comparable, as long as similar issues have to be tackled in both systems.

Procedural Rules

The enforcement of just solutions depends to a great measure on suitable procedures. In some regard, justice can only be produced via procedure: If there is no superior person or institution providing a just solution, participational procedures are necessary for everybody involved, e. g. for price building when transferring goods or services. In Islamic law, we also find a general freedom of market operators: 'Just' is, what everybody agrees on. The law is restricted to providing the parameters for this freedom of decision. Of course, the market pricing fails when deceit leads to erroneous perceptions or someone's emergency situation is abused.

Islamic contract and business law deals with those questions. It emerged in an economically quite developed environment. Muhammad was a merchant, just like many people from the area. Qur'an 4:29 shows this strong foundation: 'You believers! Do not fraudulently cheat[57] yourselves out of one another's wealth! But this does not apply to businesses that all of you agree on (*tijārat ʿan tarāḍin minkum*).' Economic operations are not only perceived as acceptable, but are desirable.

However, they shall not, as the Qur'an states, happen in an unjust way – and this renders the control of economic transactions necessary. The striving for serious exchange relationships and prevention of overreaching is a remarkable characteristic of Islamic contract law. Any promise of performance without a consideration is not binding.[58] Usury, conjectures and exploiting of monopolies

www.fau.de/files/2013/10/Der-Islam-im-demokratischen-Rechtsstaat.pdf (last accessed 26.09.2017).

57 The term *bi 'l-bāṭil* is translated too narrowly by Paret [*Der Koran: transl. Rudi Paret*, 10th ed. (Stuttgart: Kohlhammer, 2006)]. The author agrees with Wichard's [*Zwischen Markt und Moschee: Wirtschaftliche Bedürfnisse und religiöse Anforderungen im frühen islamischen Vertragsrecht* (Paderborn, Munich, Vienna, Zurich: Schöningh, 1995), 89 n. 1] critical remarks; *bāṭil* means the negligible, opposing the law, and has found its respective place in law terminology.

58 This corresponds with English teaching of consideration.

are prevented as far as possible.[59] A certain regulative for disparities (which are seen as a reaction to 'natural inequality' due to patriarchal understandings) can also be found in family and inheritance law, where individually preferred solutions, which normally improve the situation of women or non-Muslims, can be achieved through wills and contractual regulations.[60]

Another important element of contract is the attempt of neutrality and fairness when enforcing the law. The literature on Islamic law here especially deals with the actions of lawyers and with the preconditions for suitability of witnesses.

The demands for judicial actions are normally dealt with in tractates and chapters on '*Adab al-qāḍī*'. They include functional, characteristic and procedural preconditions, which serve to enable just decision-making. Even though the ideal picture of a judge could never really be established in reality,[61], it does not reduce its significance as a benchmark for achieving justice.

Hence, there is consensus on a certain amount of specific education. The great lawyer al-Shāfiʿī[62] (d. 820), called for the following knowledge as a prerequisite for a *qāḍī*'s work regarding his crucial task of independent reasoning by *qiyās* (analogies and argumentum e contrario[63]): knowledge of Qur'anic norms, of its deontology and ethics, of the abrogating and abrogated parts of it, of its specific and general rules and its guidance, as well as the ability to interpret in conformity with the Sunna of the Prophet and in lack of it, in conformity with Muslim consensus, and when consensus is missing, via *qiyās*, knowledge of the already established Sunna, of the statements of the forefathers, of general consensus and existing disputes as well as sufficient knowledge of Arabic, plus mental health, *the ability to distinguish what seems similar* (emphasis added), and no hasty statements without justification. Finally, one needed the willingness to listen to opposing opinions to avoid any possible neglect and achieve a sounder reasoning for the decision made. The jurist would have to let efforts and neutrality prevail, to recognise the advantages of his decision compared

---

59 For more details see ibid; Rohe, *Islamic Law in Past and Present*, 135 ff., 298 ff. with further references.

60 See ibid., 120 ff., 127 ff.

61 Cf. Muhammad Khalid Masud, 'The Award of *Matāʿ* in the Early Muslim Courts', in *Dispensing Justice in Islam: Qadis and their Judgements*, ed. Muhammad Khalid Masud, Rudolph Peters and David Powers (Leiden, Boston: Brill, 2012), 349.

62 Muḥammad ibn Idrīs al-Shāfiʿī, *al-Risāla*, ed. Aḥmad Muḥammad Shākir (Cairo: Muṣṭafā al-bābī al-ḥalabī, 1940), 509 ff.; translation in Majid Khadduri, *Al-Shāfiʿī's Risāla: Treatise on the Foundations of Islamic Jurisprudence, translated with an introduction, notes, and appendices* (Cambridge: Islamic Texts Society, 1997), 306 f.

63 For more details, see Rohe, *Islamic Law in Past and Present*, 79 ff., with further references.

to the discarded outcomes. Apart from this general features, the jurist needs specific knowledge when it comes to concrete factual issues.

When looking at the respective literature, further important elements are found: the parties of a lawsuit have to be treated equally, no matter what social rank or religion (the latter is contested) they have, they have to be invited to the court at the same time and should be greeted the same way.[64] In addition, one can find regulations on predilections or the explicit ban of taking presents from any party to the proceedings[65] or doing business which might endanger legal neutrality.[66] If any partisanship is to be feared, the jurist cannot act. The normative base for this ban is the institute of '*sadd al-dharā'i'*': What might lead to something forbidden is equally forbidden.[67] Furthermore, it is prohibited to act while in anger.[68]

Comparably, rules are established that enable the integrity and reliability of witnesses statements as central evidence in Islamic law. Part of this is the consultation of professional witnesses (*'udūl*).[69] Predilection causes the ignoring of the witnessing statements of one husband in favour of another due to possible – inheritance law – advantages.[70]

Some statements on the claimed personal integrity are a rich repository off social history at the same time. The witness proof on the massively punished Qur'anic crime of theft (*sariqa*) can only be brought up by two Muslim, male,[71] free, full-aged and respectable witnesses. According al-Qudūrī no one is respectable who enters the public bath without a loincloth, who takes interest, who plays chess or nard, who eats on the streets or who urinates there.[72]

---

64 Irene Schneider, *Das Bild des Richters in der adab al-qāḍī-Literatur* (Frankfurt am Main: Peter Lang, 1990), 131 ff. with further references.

65 E.g. in al-Māwardī, *al-Aḥkām al-sulṭāniyya*, 96 f.

66 Schneider, *Das Bild des Richters in der adab al-qāḍī-Literatur*, 69 ff. with further references; Franz Rosenthal, 'Gifts and Bribes: The Muslim View', *Proceedings of the American Philosophical Society* 108, no. 2 (1964), 135, 138 ff.

67 On this: Rohe, *Islamic Law in Past and Present*, 91 f., with further references.

68 Schneider, *Das Bild des Richters in der adab al-qāḍī-Literatur*, 60 ff. with further references

69 Cf. Emile Tyan, *Histoire de l'organisation judiciaire en pays d'Islam*, 2nd ed. (Leiden: Brill, 1960), 236 ff.; Mathias Rohe, *Das islamische Recht: Geschichte und Gegenwart* (München: Beck, 2011), 38 ff.

70 Cf. Ibrāhīm Salqīnī, *al-Muyassar fī uṣūl al-fiqh al-islāmiyya* (Damascus: Dār al-fikr, 2000), 185 f.

71 Al-Sarakhsī, *al-Mabsūṭ*, 9/169; derives this from sura 2, 282.

72 Aḥmad al-Qudūrī, *Mukhtaṣar al-Qudūrī* (Istanbul: al-Maṭba'a al-'uthmāniyya, 1892), 125. Plural of *maẓlama*, here: unjust act. For more see Tyan, *Histoire de l'organisation judiciaire en pays d'Islam*, 433 ff.

Additionally, there are correcting mechanisms for decisions of administrations or court houses, which the affected parties regard as unjust. Complaints against injustice (*maẓālim*)[73] could be brought forward to the caliph or his ministers (*wazīr*, plural *wuzarā'*) as well as to the governors of the province.[74] Administrative decisions[75] in taxation matters or state salary payments were submitted as well as complaints about incapable or corrupt judges or activities of the administration charities. Furthermore, one could step in when court positions were vacant or judges were unable to implement their decisions.[76]

There are several historical examples for this: In the last parts of its work on judges' salary the Baghdad chief justice and prominent Hanafite jurist Abū Yūsuf (d. 798) deplores the many judges who did not fulfil their duty and did not prevent their subordinates from wasting the fortune of orphans and the beneficiaries of legacies.[77]

Last but not least, the social level apart from formal, state structures has to be taken into account, which is especially important for administratively weak states or regions. Here, individual solutions on the basis of socially accepted habits that have been established are widespread. Surely, in this scientifically only sparsely investigated area,[78] one can find fundamentally differing perceptions on the relevant perspective for evaluating the fairness of solutions. Where the social stability of families or clans is seen as a necessary condition to survive, the perspective of collective interests will prevail over individual ones.

---

73 Qudūrī, *Mukhtaṣar al-Qudūrī*, 125. Plural of *maẓlama*, here: unjust act. For more details see Tyan, *Histoire*, 433 ff.

74 Both are adressed by e.g. al-Māwardī, *al-Aḥkām al-sulṭāniyya*, 97, in connection with the *maẓālim*, cf. Wahba al-Zuhaylī, *al-Fiqh al-islāmī wa adillatuhu*, 8 vols. (Damascus: Dār al-fikr, 1984), 6/759.

75 Ibid., 6/757, interprets them as a kind of administrative jurisprudence.

76 Cf. al-Māwardī, *al-Aḥkām al-sulṭāniyya*, 101 ff.; Wael Hallaq, *The Origins and Evolution of Islamic Law* (Cambridge: Cambridge University Press, 2005), 100 f.

77 Abū Yūsuf, Ya'qūb ibn Ibrāhīm, *Kitāb al-Kharāj* (Beirut: Dār al-ma'rifa, 1979), 187; many more items of evidence at Tyan, *Histoire de l'organisation judiciaire en pays d'Islam*, 295 f., 299 ff.

78 'Normative Pluralism in Indonesia: Regions, Religions, and Ethnicities', in *Multiculturalism in Asia*, ed. Will Kymlicka and Baogang He (Oxford: Oxford University Press, 2005), available at: https://anthropology.artsci.wustl.edu/files/anthropology/imce/Bowen-Normative_Pluralism_in_Indonesia.pdf (last accessed 26.09.2017).

Substantive Rules

Generally speaking, all regulations of material law can be interpreted in light of the intention to find just solutions. However, we have to remind ourselves of the already mentioned complexity of legal exercises of order and the changing preconceptions. Only a few fundamental aspects that document the perception of justice in Islamic law shall be presented here.

One key element of justice is the question of which goods and interests need the protection of legislation and also deserve it. This question has only been dealt with by a few important scholars, but plays an important role in the daily practice of applying the law. When it comes to legal theory and the interpretation of norms, this question becomes essential: It demands the reflection of the interpretation of legal norms. Those who interpret the norms have to clarify whether the norm is applicable to everyone at any place and at all times, or whether it is restricted to certain persons, to particular places or in time. This key question usually cannot be answered when looking at the respective norm alone. Instead, it is more promising to apply the well-established and revived theory of the higher goals *(maqāṣid)* of Sharia.

Other than the regulations of religious ritual practice, which are mostly considered to be immutable, the law has to serve the common interest (*maṣlaḥa*) first and foremost, which is accessible to human perception.[79]

Classical references like Ibn Qayyim al-Jawziyya (1292–1350), al-Shāṭibī[80] (d. 1388), as well as some other prominent scholars[81] are frequently referred to in this context. In nuce, the core of this theory can already be found in the works of the eminent scholar al-Ghazālī (d. 1111).[82]

---

79 See e.g. Muhammad Khalid Masud, *Shatibi's Philosophy of Islamic Law* (New Delhi: Kitab Bhavan, 1997), 127 ff. On this background, explicit, quranic rules in their exact wording can be exclused from application; cf. Sachedina, *The Just Ruler in Shiite Islam*, 4; also see Khadduri, *The Islamic Conception of Justice*, 136 ff.

80 Abū Isḥāq al-Shāṭibī, *al-Muwāfaqāt fī uṣūl al-sharīʿa*, 4 vols., ed. Muḥammad ʿAbd al-Qādir al-Fāḍilī (Sayda, Beirut: al-Maktaba al-ʿaṣriyya, 2000), 2/7 ff. Cf. on this Masud, *Shatibi's Philosophy of Islamic Law*; Ahmad al-Raysuni, *Imam al-Shatibi's Theory of the Higher Objectives and Intents of Islamic Law* (London: International Institute of Islamic Thought, 2005).

81 Mohammad Hashim Kamali, *Principles of Islamic Jurisprudence*, 2nd ed. (Petaling Jaya: Pelanduk Publications, 1999), 395 ff, esp. 400 ff.; cf. also David Johnston, 'Maqāṣid al Sharī'a: Epistemology and Hermeneutics of Muslim Theologies of Human Rights', *Die Welt des Islams* 47, no. 2 (2007).

82 See Abū Ḥ. M. al-Ghazālī, *al-Mustaṣfā min ʿilm al-uṣūl*, 2 vols. (Cairo: Būlāq, 1904); Reprint Beirut, n.d., 1/345 ff.; 2/393

Abū Isḥāq al-Shāṭibī, who is the most prominent and most cited representative of this school of thought, concretises the higher purposes of Sharia in a benchmark setting way.[83] He defines these by five general and universally recognised goods ('necessities', Arabic. *ḍarūriyāt*): religion (*dīn*), life (*nafs*), progeny (*nasl*), property (*māl*) and reason (*'aql*); social recognition (*'irḍ*) might also considered a necessity. These purposes were absolute and could not be abrogated, but only be changed in singular aspects and in accordance with their lasting purpose.[84]

The Sharia-based actions were not aims in themselves: If the objective conditions for any action under Sharia were given, but did not realise the purpose protected under Sharia, their application would be wrong and contradict the norm in fact, since it has only been established for a certain purpose.[85] Whoever states that these purposes could not be discerned and understood – which he accuses the religious philosophical school of the *bāṭiniyya*[86] of pretending – would in fact destroy the Sharia.[87] The norms (*adilla,* 'signs', in Arabic) of the Sharia cannot contradict reason, since the prerequisite for the norm's validity and applicability in concreto (Arabic *taklīf*) is its potential to be understood it on a rational basis.[88]

Only ritual obligations (*'ibādāt*) stood above human-rational understanding, while all other norms were accessible to human ratio.[89] The fact that the revelation of the Qur'n and the life of Muhammad took place in the 7th century CE

---

83 Al-Shāṭibī, *al-Muwāfaqāt fī uṣūl al-sharī'a*, 2/8, 39 and more often; see on this Raysuni, *Imam al-Shatibi's Theory of the Higher Objectives and Intents of Islamic Law*, especially 137 ff.; Kamali, *Principles of Islamic Jurisprudence*, esp. 400 ff. For it's contemporary reception, see Masud, *Shatibi's Philosophy of Islamic Law*, 108 ff.; Mohamed Ibrahim, *Maqāsid al šarī'a: Islamische šarī'a versus Menschenrechte?* (Darmstadt: Averroes Institut für wissenschaftliche Islamforschung, AWIS, 2007), 6 ff.; 'Abd al-'Azīz Ibn 'Abd al-Raḥmān, *'Ilm maqāṣid al-shāri'a* (Riyadh: n.p., 2002); Johnston, 'Maqāṣid al Sharī'a', 149 ff.,157 ff.

84 Al-Shāṭibī, *al-Muwāfaqāt fī uṣūl al-sharī'a*, 3/77.

85 Ibid., 2/285.

86 This is what specifically the Shi'i Ismailis were called, but also more generally those who opposed an literal understanding of the text in favour of the inner meaning (Arabic *bāṭin)*; cf. M.G.S. Hodgson, 'Bāṭiniyya', in Gibb; Kramers; Lévi-Provençal; Schacht; Lewis, *Encyclopaedia of Islam.*

87 Al-Shāṭibī, *al-Muwāfaqāt fī uṣūl al-sharī'a*, 2/291.

88 Ibid., 3/16.

89 Ibid., 2/294 and others. A good summary of the main standpoints is provided by Raysuni, *Imam al-Shatibi's Theory of the Higher Objectives and Intents of Islamic Law*, 317 ff.

opens broad space for a far-reaching new interpretation of Islamic law by taking the respective historical circumstances into account.[90]

In a considerable number of particular legal questions, the principle of proportionality is recognised as an important element of justice: The draconic punishment for *sariqa* (Qur'anic theft), which is amputation of a hand or a foot according to traditional penal law, is inter alia linked to a sizeable minimum value of the stolen goods (*niṣāb*).[91] Taxation has to be based on the financial capability of the taxable person (even though this did and does not hold true in reality).[92] Furthermore, Islamic law contains the universal rule of 'necessity knows no law'. Necessity (*ḍarūra*) in this sense e. g. allows minor theft of food in case of need, or self-defence.[93].

Islamic contract and economic law is furthermore coined by the fundamental concern to bring together chances of profit and risks of loss, as well as to prevent the exploitation of ignorance or the plights of others. This is achieved by procedural rules as well as through material regulations, which for instance forbid contractual stipulations that enable any one-sided allocation of chances of profit or shifting of risks as well as by prohibiting usury.[94]

The Concepts of Justice through the Ages: The Example of Gender Relations

Traditional marital, family and succession law is characterised by patriarchal structures. Rights and obligations are attributed to both sexes; both are respected and protected in their respective roles in family and society, but these roles are fixed and not interchangeable.[95] Unequal treatment of the sexes under the law is based on several verses in the Qur'an, which refer to the woman's position under family or inheritance law, or her suitability for giving evidence in court. A

---

90 On the question of dress code see Zekeriya Beyaz, *İslam ve Giyim-Kuşam: Başörtüsü sorununa dini çözüm* (Istanbul: Sancak Yaynlar, 2000), 259 ff.

91 Cf. Rohe, *Islamic Law in Past and Present*, 162 ff. with further references

92 See ibid., 209 ff. with further references

93 See ibid., 84 f., 244 f. with further references.

94 Cf. ibid., 136 ff., 142 ff. with further references.

95 It also tackles the heir of the hermaphrodite (*khuntā*): Some scholars attribute half of the male plus half of the female shares, others would confine it to the female share, since only that had a factual basis; cf. Wizārat al-awqāf wa al-shu'ūn al-islāmiyya, al-Kuwayt, *al-Mawsū'a al-fiqhiyya*, vol. 20, article '*khuntā*', n. 29.

central statement in this context (in the tradition of other religious texts)[96] is found in Qur'an 4:34: "Men are the managers of the affairs of women because God has preferred in bounty one of them over the other, and because they have expended of their property."[97]

This is one of the Medinan suras and can be interpreted from a historical point of view. The reason given for men's superior role on the one hand is the maintenance they have to provide, in the broadest sense. This is linked to functional, not intrinsic 'superiority'.[98] If, however, as in the present-day Islamic world, the circumstances are or may be inverted, the basis of this superior role becomes non-existent.[99] 'Preference in bounty', the second reason, is a very vague expression. It is interpreted as referring to the man's role as a protector, due to his superior physical strength.[100] The basis for this role is also becoming non-existent. In Balić's words, this Qur'anic passage resembles 'a sociological statement characterising the status quo of a patriarchal society. It does not contain a rule of conduct.'[101]

Corresponding regulations are considered time-dependent by other authors and thus alterable. Abdullahi An-Naʿim[102] rejects a timeless validity of Sharia-norms on male supremacy (*qawwāma*), the hegemony of Muslims over Non-Mus-

---

96 Cf. also Genesis 3:16: 'Unto the woman he said (...) thy desire shall be to thy husband, and he shall rule over thee', and Ephesians 5:22 f.: 'Wives, submit yourselves unto your own husbands, as unto the Lord. For the husband is the head of the wife, even as Christ is the head of the church (...)'.

97 Following Arberry's translation of the Quran, http://web.archive.org/web/20071219022352/, http://arthursclassicnovels.com/arthurs/koran/koran-arberry10.html, last accessed 26.09.2017.

98 Fazlur Rahman, *Major Themes of the Qur'an* (Chicago: University of Chicago Press, 2009), 49; Smail Balić, *Islam für Europa: Neue Perspektiven einer alten Religion* (Cologne: Böhlau, 2001), 85 f. calls it an indicative statement reflecting the social reality of the time, but without normative character.

99 Khaled Abou El Fadl, *Speaking in God's Name: Islamic Law, Authority and Women* (Oxford: Oneworld, 2001), 210 ff.

100 Cf. the translation "Men are the protectors and maintainers of women, because God has given the one more (strength) than the other, and because they support them from their means" (trans. Yusuf Ali).

101 Smail Balić, *Ruf vom Minarett: Weltislam heute – Renaissance oder Rückfall?* (Hamburg: EB-Verl. Rissen, 1984), 88, 90; concerning new interpretations arriving at comparable results cf. Murad Wilfried Hofmann, *Der Islam im 3. Jahrtausend* (Kreuzlingen, Munich: Hugendubel, 2000), 140 f.; cf. also Ghada Karmi, "Women, Islam and Patriarchalism", in *Feminism and Islam: Legal and literary perspectives*, ed. Mai Yamani and Andrew Allen (New York: New York University Press, 1996), 69 ff., esp. 80.

102 Abdullahi A. An-Naʿim, *Islam and the Secular State: Negotiating the Future of Shariʿa* (Cambridge, MA: Harvard University Press, 2010), 283 f. and *passim*.

lims (*dhimma*) and the offensive and violent interpretation of *jihād*. According to him, all this contradicts the opposite Meccan revelations and was only declared for historical reasons, as a concession to the difficult circumstances of the Islamic community in an extremely hostile environment.

A dynamic interpretation of rules according to their higher (and ever-lasting) objectives is equally possible. In this sense, the uncontested provisions about women's rights in the Qur'an include a significant improvement of their legal status as compared to the previous situation. According to Islamic tradition, in the times before Islam women did not possess any rights and for example were part of the deceased husband's assets rather than being included in the distribution of the deceased's estate.[103] On this basis, the true message of a 'progressive' Qur'an is contrasted with traditionalist jurisprudence of the classical era. This approach is largely based on the recourse to the higher objectives of rules (*maqāṣid*). These rules are aimed at serving human beings, at enabling them a decent and peaceful life. While the purposes are fixed, their realization is dependent on the circumstances of time and space and may thus vary accordingly. In consequence, the 'actual' content of the Qur'anic messages has to be separated from the 'outdated' traditional texts and the unfounded elements of popular practice.[104]

Regarding divorce law Hüseyin Atay refers to suras 4:35 and 65:2 and comes to the conclusion that after an unsuccessful attempt at mediation, a judicial divorce could take place in front of two witnesses. He does not recognise any further requirements, either for husbands or for wives seeking a divorce, assigning them to the outdated patriarchal understanding of legal scholars of the past which misinterprets the gender equality inherent in the Qur'an.[105]

In a comparable approach, some rules which were considered by classical jurists not to be legally binding, but 'only' of moral quality in the sense of mere recommendations, have been reinterpreted in recent times. This applies for instance to the statements of gender equality.[106] If such statements are now understood as legally binding, previous decisions based on a different in-

103 Cf. Hamid Khan, *Islamic Law of Inheritance: A Comparative Study of Recent Reforms in Muslim Countries*, 2nd ed. (Karachi: Oxford University Press, 1999), 21f., 26; Rohe, *Islamic Law in Past and Present*, 129f.

104 To this: Osman Taştan, 'Hüseyin Atay's approach to understanding the Qur'an', in *Modern Muslim Intellectuals and the Qur'an*, ed. Suha Taji-Farouki (Oxford: Oxford University Press, 2004), 241, in particular 252ff.

105 Conversation with Atay quoted in ibid., 252f.

106 Cf. Mohammad H. Kamali, 'Divorce and Women's Rights: Some Muslim Interpretations of S. 2:228', *The Muslim World* 74, no. 2 (1984).

terpretation are overtaken.[107] In particular, Muslim female authors, distinguishing between Islam as such and the impact of the dominant patriarchate in many regions, foster such an approach. [108] The Pakistani jurist Shaheen Sardar Ali is thinking along the same lines when she adds the apt subtitle 'Equal before Allah, Unequal before Man?' to her book on women's rights in Islam.[109]

Muslim feminists and others frequently argue on this basis.[110] For instance, a prominent Iranian jurist interprets the rule on guardianship over minor children (*wilāya*), which is in principle restricted to men, as a merely personal relationship between the guardian and the child; other 'protective measures' for children were not covered by this term.[111] In consequence, the *wilāya* is separated from legal relations – in contrast to the predominating understanding – with the effect that the protective role can also be attributed to females.

One characteristic example of the freedom of interpretation which courts in the Islamic world allow themselves in particular is a judgement on appeal by the Bangladesh High Court in the matter of Hefzur Rahman v. Shamsun Nahar Begum et al. of 9 January 1995.[112] The point at issue was whether divorced wives may claim alimony from their husbands beyond the three-month period of waiting (*ʿidda*). One of the major works of classical legal literature, the Hana-

---

107 Cf. Ziba Mir-Hosseini, 'Stretching the limits: A feminist reading of the Shariʿa in post-revolutionary Iran', in *Islam and Feminism: Legal and Literary Perspectives*, ed. Mai Yamani (London: Ithaca, 1996), 285 ff., in particular 315.

108 Cf. Karmi, 'Women, Islam and Patriarchalism'; Asghar Ali Engineer, *The Rights of Women in Islam* (New York: St. Martin's Press, 1996), Reprint, 11 and more often; Amina Wadud, *Inside the Gender Jihad: Women's Reform in Islam* (Oxford: Oneworld, 2006), in particular 187 ff.; Asma Barlas, *Believing Women in Islam: Unreading Patriarchal Interpretations of the Qur'an* (Austin: University of Texas Press, 2002); Haya al-Mughni, *Women in Kuwait: The Politics of Gender* (London: Saqi Books, 2001), 184; Mohamed Fathi Osman, *The Children of Adam: An Islamic Perspective on Pluralism* (Washington D.C.: Georgetown University, 1996), 20.

109 Shaheen Sardar Ali, *Gender and human rights in Islam and international law: Equal before Allah, unequal before man?* (The Hague: Kluwer Law Internat., 2000).

110 Cf. Mohammad Muslehuddin, *Islamic Jurisprudence and the Rule of Necessity and Need* (New Delhi: Kitab Bhavan, 1982), 21 f. about the contrast with pre-Islamic law; Nasr Hamid Abu Zayd, 'Die Frauenfrage zwischen Fundamentalismus und Aufklärung', in *Islam, Demokratie, Moderne: Aktuelle Antworten arabischer Denker*, ed. Erdmute Heller and Hassouna Mosbahi (Munich: Beck, 1998), 193, 204 and more often; Engineer, *The Rights of Women in Islam*, 20 ff., 62 ff. and more often.

111 Seyyed Mostafa Mohaghegh-Damad at a German-Iranian legal conference at the Max-Planck-Institute for foreign and international private Law in Hamburg on 4 July 2003.

112 Civil Revisional Case No. 2067 of 1992, 47 DLR (1995), 54.

fite scholar al-Marghinānī's (1135–1197) *Hidāya*, which has had a particular impact on the Indian subcontinent and to which the verdict refers,[113] is against this.

The conclusion is determined by the interpretation of sura 2:241 which says (in Arberry's translation): "There shall be for divorced women provision honourable – an obligation on the godfearing." The nub of the problem is the interpretation of the phrase 'appropriate goods' (*matāʿ bi-l-maʿrūf*): does this refer to household utensils and suchlike, or does it refer to continuing alimony for needy wives after the end of the marriage? In the end the court went with the opinion which translates the passage as 'maintenance on a reasonable scale' and consequently agrees to the continuing claim to alimony (up to a possible remarriage).

The court started by saying that in God's own words the Qur'an is easy to understand. Of course, it admitted, there are Muslims who insist that everyone must follow one of the interpretations by recognised scholars of the early period, and that the door to new interpretations is closed. This, however, would go against the constitution of Bangladesh, which states that God's commandments must be followed to the letter and without any deviation. The Qur'an requires continuous study in order for it to do justice to the dynamic, progressive and universal nature of Islam. There follows a quote from a judgement by the Lahore High Court in 1960: "It is quite clear that reading and understanding the Quran is not the privilege or the right of one individual or two. It is revealed in easy and understandable language so that all Muslims, if they try, may be able to understand and act upon it. It is thus a privilege granted to every Muslim which cannot be taken away from him by anybody, however highly placed or learned he may be to read and interpret the Quran. In understanding the Quran one can derive valuable assistance from the commentaries written by different learned people of yore, but then that is all. Those commentaries cannot be said to be the last word on the subject. Reading and understanding the Quran implies the interpretation of it and the interpretation in its turn includes the application of it which must be in the light of the existing circumstance and the changing needs of the world (...). If the interpretation of the Holy Quran by the commentators who lived thirteen or twelve hundred years ago is considered as the last word on the subject, then the whole Islamic society will be shut up in an iron cage and not allowed to develop along with the time. It will then cease to

113 Cf. Abū al-Ḥasan al-Marghīnānī, *al-Hidāya fī sharḥ bidāyat al-mubtadī*, 2 vols., ed. Ṭalḥa Yūsuf (Beirut: Dār al-kutub al-ʿilmiyya, 1995), 2/290.

be a universal religion and will remain a religion confined to the time and place when and where it was revealed (...)."[114]

A civil court, they argued, is consequently authorised to follow Qur'anic law and disregard everything else, even if the latter was argued by early, much-respected jurists and observed for a long time. Consequently, a conflicting judgement by the Privy Council formerly responsible for British India from 1897, which followed the traditional interpretation, should not be observed any more for the reasons named, and also because the non-Muslim judges were very careful not to decide against the views of established Muslim jurists in similar cases. Apart from everything else this illustrates that colonialism not infrequently led to the conservation of traditional views and the interruption of an older vitality in the application of the law.

The time-oriented reinterpretation can be found in a wide range of individual issues below the threshold of general reinterpretation. The short weighting of female testimony in Qur'an 2: 282 (the declaration of two women is equal to one male testimony) is one example. This regulation is set in the context of a proving documentation of certain financial transactions. The modern opinion can now argue that the rule requires a lack of female versatility facing such points. But if women were also well informed, their testimony would be equal to the male.[115]

On the other hand extreme patriarchal cultural traditions may be perpetuated, or even re-instituted, with the support of traditionalist sharia scholars. In her impressive study on women and Islam in Bangladesh the Bangladeshi scientist Taj Hashmi examined among other things the activities of rural arbitration courts ('Salish courts'). She says that the myth of the connection between the judgments of rural mullahs, 'self-styled guardians of Islam', and sharia law must be destroyed. She describes even non-practising and non-believing men insisting on so-called Sharia law being applied in order to deprive their relations, usually sisters, of an inheritance to which the latter have an equal claim. The mullah (supporting this) should be seen as nothing more than the assistant and collaborator of powerful village elders, but due to his position as interpreter of the Sharia he has great influence with the populace.[116] 'The bulk of the peasant and non-peasant population favour patriarchy and both "islamists" and

---

114 Mst. Rashida Begum vs. Shahan Din et al., PLD 1960, Lah 1142.

115 Cf. Rahman, *Major Themes of the Qur'an*, 48 f.; Balić, *Ruf vom Minarett*, 90 f. with further references; J. Badawi, Gender Equity in Islam, Neudruck Plainfield 1999, 35 ff.; Engineer, *Status of Women*, 63 f.; al-Alwani, Taha Jabir, *Issues in Contemporary Islamic Thought*, London, inter alia 1426/2005, 161 ff.

116 Taj Hashmi, *Women and Islam in Bangladesh: Beyond Subjection and Tyranny* (Basingstoke: Palgrave Macmillan, 2000), 96 ff. (quote from p. 98); cf. also op. cit., 61 ff.

"secular" Bangladeshi Muslims ardently legitimise the subjection and deprivation of women in the name of Islam (...) In sum, (...) patriarchy has been the main stumbling-block in the way of the empowerment of Bangladeshi women. The marriage of convenience between patriarchy and popular Islam has further aggravated the situation.'[117]

Approaches improving women's rights culminating in equality are currently developed especially in the geographical periphery of the Islamic world, such as in Turkey and in Southeast Asia, but also in Tunisia or Morocco as well as in Iran, and meet massive resistance in particular within the Arab world and from the current Iranian regime. Some pioneers have fled from threats and coercive measures to the West. Their opponents are not only Islamists, but also within a broad spectrum of the traditionalist mainstream among the scholars. While they only accept de facto the implemented reforms without resistance, they put up massive resistance to completely new interpretations. The former Pakistani minister of justice, Brohi, is worth quoting here: 'In the Islamic world, research on the field of the law must assert itself against the intolerance of the so-called ulama (...) as well, who see themselves as the guardians of the faith. They will also, and this is worse, note the smallest possible deviation in writings by academically trained authors on the subject of law and institutions of the law, and then brand the writers responsible as heretics. As a result there are hardly any contributions worth mentioning from the pen of thinkers in Muslim countries on the literature of Islam; only in non-Muslim countries do we find a few attempts at supporting a re-establishment of Islamic thought, law and institutions of the law.'[118]

Conclusion

Islamic law, like other legal systems, seeks to offer justice. Theoretical explanations and specifications of this term are rare. Instead, the search for justice is documented in the treatment of concrete legal issues. The concretization of justice – like in other legal systems – depends greatly on the social, economic and cultural framework of the time. Islamic law is by no means limited to (allegedly) clear and immutable rules. This can even be demonstrated on the epistemological level of the Qur'an, e.g. regarding the legal status of women. It can be shown how strongly the pre- understanding of the legal interpreters influences the out-

117 Op. cit., 209.
118 Cf. Rohe, *Islamic Law in Past and Present*, 252.

come of legal interpretation. However, there are also anthropological constants, for instance the ubiquitous conviction that protection has to be granted for minors or against usury inter alia.

New issues still await broader debates: Can non-Islamic secular states and their legal systems offer justice to Muslims and non-Muslims alike? Is justice in a Muslim perspective universal in the sense that non-Muslim institutions can fulfil its prerequisites, once the contents of justice are offered by the respective legal order? A European-Muslim answer has been given: The prominent Bosnian scholar Enes Karić emphasised,[119] based on the ground-breaking work 'Islam and the Foundations of Governance' (*al-Islām wa uṣūl al-ḥukm*) by the Egyptian scholar ʿAlī ʿAbd al-Rāziq in 1925,[120], that the caliphate, i.e. the secular governance by a Muslim ruler, was not a part of the religion of Islam. The Sharia (the Islamic norm system) was a compendium of rules achieving moral objectives which could be implemented by secular states alike. A state with an appropriate system of social care, e.g. financial support for students and senior citizens, that planned to establish economic and social justice and respected and implemented human rights, was an Islamic state in such sense. He quoted in this context the proverb '*ʿadl al-dawla īmānuhā, ẓulm al-dawla kufruhā*' – the faith of a state is justice, his its unbelief is injustice. On the basis of this maxim, Islam and a secular constitutional state can be convincingly reconciled in an overlapping search for justice.

Bibliography

Abou El Fadl, Khaled. *Speaking in God's Name: Islamic Law, Authority and Women.* Oxford: Oneworld, 2001.

—. 'The Centrality of Shariʿah to Government and Constitutionalism in Islam'. In *Constitutionalism in Islamic Countries: Between Upheaval and Continuity.* Edited by Rainer Grote and Tilmann Röder, 35–62. Oxford: Oxford University Press, 2011.

Abū Yūsuf, Yaʿqūb ibn Ibrāhīm. *Kitāb al-Kharāj.* Beirut: Dār al-maʿrifa, 1979.

Abu Zayd, Nasr Hamid. 'Die Frauenfrage zwischen Fundamentalismus und Aufklärung'. In *Islam, Demokratie, Moderne: Aktuelle Antworten arabischer Denker.* Edited by Erdmute Heller and Hassouna Mosbahi, 193–210. Munich: Beck, 1998.

Ali, Shaheen Sardar. *Gender and Human Rights in Islam and International Law: Equal Before Allah, Unequal before Man?* The Haque: Kluwer Law International, 2000.

An-Naʿim, Abdullahi A. *Islamic Family Law in A Changing World: A Global Resource Book.* London: Zed Books, 2002.

119 At a conference at the theological faculty in Sarajevo in 2007.

120 Cf. Rohe, *Islamic Law in Past and Present*, 250 f., 313 f. with further references.

——. *Islam and the Secular State: Negotiating the Future of Shari'a.* Cambridge, MA: Harvard University Press, 2010.

Aristotle. *The Nicomachean Ethics: trans. David Ross.* Oxford: Oxford University Press, 2009.

Balić, Smail. *Ruf vom Minarett: Weltislam heute – Renaissance oder Rückfall?* Hamburg: EB-Verl. Rissen, 1984.

——. *Islam für Europa: Neue Perspektiven einer alten Religion.* Cologne: Böhlau, 2001.

Barlas, Asma. *"Believing Women" in Islam: Unreading Patriarchal Interpretations of the Qur'an.* Austin: University of Texas Press, 2002.

Beyaz, Zekeriya. *İslam ve Giyim-Kuşam: Başörtüsü sorununa dini çözüm.* Istanbul: Sancak Yaynlar, 2000.

Bowen, John. 'Normative Pluralism in Indonesia: Regions, Religions, and Ethnicities'. In *Multiculturalism in Asia.* Edited by Will Kymlicka and Baogang He, 152–169. Oxford: Oxford University Press, 2005.

Dupret, Baudoin, Barbara Drieskens, and Annelies Moors, eds. *Narratives of Truth in Islam.* London, New York: I.B. Tauris, 2007.

Engineer, Asghar Ali. *The Rights of Women in Islam.* New York: St. Martin's Press, 1996. Reprint.

Ess, Josef van. 'Kull mujtahid muṣīb'. In *Dirāsāt islāmiyya.* Edited by Fahmī Jadʿān, 123–141. Irbid: Manshūrāt Jāmiʿat al-Yarmūk, 1983.

Ghazālī, Abū Ḥāmid Muḥammad al-. *Al-Mustaṣfā min ʿilm al-uṣūl.* 2 vols. Cairo: Būlāq, 1904; Reprint Beirut, n.d.

Gibb, H.A.R., J.H. Kramers, É. Lévi-Provençal, J. Schacht, and B. Lewis, eds. *Encyclopaedia of Islam: Second Edition, vol. I.* Leiden: Brill, 1960.

Gibb, Hamilton A.R. 'Al-Mawardī's Theory of the Caliphate'. In *Studies on the Civilization of Islam.* Edited by Hamilton A.R. Gibb, 151–165. Boston: Beacon Press, 1962.

Gimaret, Daniel. 'Muʿtazila'. In *The Encyclopaedia of Islam: Second Edition, vol. VII.* Edited by C.E. Bosworth et al., 783–93. Leiden: Brill, 1993.

Guellil, Gabriela L. *Damaszener Akten des 8. — 14. Jahrhunderts nach aṭ-Ṭarsūsīs Kitāb al-Iʿlām: Eine Studie zum arabischen Justizwesen.* Bamberg: Aku, 1985.

Haarmann, Ulrich. 'Lieber hundert Jahre Zwangsherrschaft als ein Tag Leiden im Bürgerkrieg: Ein gemeinsamer Topos im islamischen und frühneuzeitlichen europäischen Staatsdenken'. In *Gottes ist der Orient – Gottes ist der Okzident: Festschrift für Abdoldjavad Falaturi zum 65. Geburtstag.* Edited by Udo Tworuschka, 262–69. Cologne, Vienna: Böhlau, 1991.

Hallaq, Wael. *The Origins and Evolution of Islamic Law.* Cambridge: Cambridge University Press, 2005.

Halm, Heinz. *Der schiitische Islam.* Munich: Beck, 1994.

Hashmi, Taj. *Women and Islam in Bangladesh: Beyond Subjection and Tyranny.* Basingstoke: Palgrave Macmillan, 2000.

Heine, Peter. 'Staat/Staatslehre'. In *Islam-Lexikon: Geschichte – Ideen – Gestalten.* 3 vols., 3/685–689. Freiburg: Herder, 1991.

Hildebrandt, Thomas. *Neo-Muʿtazilismus? Intention und Kontext im modernen arabischen Umgang mit dem rationalistischen Erbe des Islam.* Leiden, Boston: Brill, 2007.

Hodgson, M.G.S. 'Bāṭiniyya'. In Gibb; Kramers; Lévi-Provençal; Schacht; Lewis, *Encyclopaedia of Islam*, 1098–1100.

Hofmann, Murad Wilfried. *Der Islam im 3. Jahrtausend*. Kreuzlingen, Munich: Hugendubel, 2000.
Ibn ʿAbdarraḥmān, ʿAbd al-ʿAzīz. *ʿIlm maqāṣid al-shāriʿa*. Riyadh: n.p., 2002.
Ibn Taymiyya, Aḥmad. *al-Siyāsa al-sharʾiyya fī iṣlāḥ al-rāʿī wa l-raʿiyya*. Edited by Muḥammad Mubārak. Beirut: Dār al-kitāb al-ʿarabī, 1966.
Ibrahim, Mohamed. *Maqāsid al šarīʻa: Islamische šarīʻa versus Menschenrechte?* Darmstadt: Averroes Institut für wissenschaftliche Islamforschung, AWIS, 2007.
Nürnberger Nachrichten. 'Im Widerstand vereint'. 3 April 2013.
Johnston, David. 'Maqāṣid al Sharīʻa: Epistemology and Hermeneutics of Muslim Theologies of Human Rights'. *Die Welt des Islams* 47, no. 2 (2007): 149–187.
Kamali, Mohammad Hashim. 'Divorce and Women's Rights: Some Muslim Interpretations of S. 2:228'. *The Muslim World* 74, no. 2 (1984): 85–99.
—. *Principles of Islamic Jurisprudence*. 2nd ed. Petaling Jaya: Pelanduk Publications, 1999.
—. *Citizenship and Accountability of Government: An Islamic Perspective*. Cambridge: Islamic Texts Society, 2011.
Karmi, Ghada. 'Women, Islam and Patriarchalism'. In *Feminism and Islam: Legal and literary perspectives*. Edited by Mai Yamani and Andrew Allen, 69–85. New York: New York University Press, 1996.
Khadduri, Majid. *The Islamic Conception of Justice*. Baltimore: The Johns Hopkins University Press, 1984.
—. *Al-Shāfiʿī's Risāla: Treatise on the Foundations of Islamic Jurisprudence, translated with an introduction, notes, and appendices*. Cambridge: Islamic Texts Society, 1997.
Khan, Hamid. *Islamic Law of Inheritance: A Comparative Study of Recent Reforms in Muslim Countries*. 2nd ed. Karachi: Oxford University Press, 1999.
Kofler, Hans. 'Handbuch des islamistischen Staats- und Verwaltungsrechtes von Badr-ad-dīn ibn Ǧamāʻah'. *Islamica* 6 (1934): 349–414.
Krawietz, Birgit. *Hierarchie der Rechtsquellen im tradierten sunnitischen Islam*. Berlin: Duncker & Humblot, 2002.
Lambton, Ann K. *State and Government in Medieval Islam: An Introduction to the Study of Islamic Political Theory*. Oxford: Pyschology Press, 1981.
Laoust, Henri. *Essai sur les Doctrines Sociales et Politiques de Takī-d-Dīn Aḥmad B. Taymiyya*. Cairo: Imprimerie l'Institut français d'archéologie orientale, 1939.
Löschner, Harald. *Die dogmatischen Grundlagen des šīʿitischen Rechts: Eine Untersuchung zur modernen imāmitischen Rechtsquellenlehre*. Cologne: Carl Heymanns Verlag, 1971.
Marghīnānī, Abū al-Ḥasan al-. *Al-Hidāya fī sharḥ bidāyat al-mubtadī*. Edited by Ṭalḥa Yūsuf. 2 vols. Beirut: Dār al-kutub al-ʿilmiyya, 1995.
Masud, Muhammad Khalid. *Shatibi's Philosophy of Islamic Law*. New Delhi: Kitab Bhavan, 1997.
—. 'The Award of *Matāʿ* in the Early Muslim Courts'. In *Dispensing Justice in Islam: Qadis and their Judgements*. Edited by Muhammad Khalid Masud, Rudolph Peters and David Powers, 349–381. Leiden, Boston: Brill, 2012.
Māwardī, Abū al-Ḥasan al-. *Al-Aḥkām al-sulṭāniyya*. Beirut: n.p., n.d., before 1988.
Messick, Brinkley. 'Indexing the Self: Intent and Expression in Islamic Legal Acts'. *Islamic Law and Society* 8, no. 2 (2001): 151–178.

Mir-Hosseini, Ziba. 'Stretching the limits: A feminist reading of the Shari'a in post-revolutionary Iran'. In *Islam and Feminism: Legal and Literary Perspectives.* Edited by Mai Yamani, 285–319. London: Ithaca, 1996.
Mughni, Haya al-. *Women in Kuwait: The Politics of Gender.* London: Saqi Books, 2001.
Muslehuddin, Mohammad. *Islamic Jurisprudence and the Rule of Necessity and Need.* New Delhi: Kitab Bhavan, 1982.
Osman, Mohamed Fathi. *The Children of Adam: An Islamic Perspective on Pluralism.* Washington D.C.: Georgetown University, 1996.
Pohl, Dietrich. *Islam und Friedensvölkerrechtsordnung: Die dogmatischen Grundlagen der Teilnahme eines islamischen Staates am modernen Völkerrechtssystem am Beispiel Ägyptens.* Wien, New York: Springer, 1988.
Bernama News. 'Promote Islamic Values to Combat Religious Extremism'.
Qudūrī, Aḥmad al-. *Mukhtaṣar al-Qudūrī.* Istanbul: al-Maṭbaʿa al-ʿuthmāniyya, 1892.
Radbruch, Gustav. *Rechtsphilosophie: Studienausgabe.* 2nd ed. Heidelberg: C.F. Müller, 2003.
Rahman, Fazlur. *Major Themes of the Qur'an.* Chicago: University of Chicago Press, 2009.
Raysuni, Ahmad al-. *Imam al-Shatibi's Theory of the Higher Objectives and Intents of Islamic Law.* London: International Institute of Islamic Thought, 2005.
Rohe, Mathias. 'Gründe und Grenzen deliktischer Haftung: Die Ordnungsaufgaben des Deliktsrechts'. *Archiv für die civilistische Praxis* 201, no. 2 (2001): 117–164.
—. *Das islamische Recht: Geschichte und Gegenwart.* München: Beck, 2011.
—. 'Der Islam im demokratischen Rechtsstaat'. *Erlanger Universitätsreden* 80, no. 3 (2012): 5–38.
—. *Islamic Law in Past and Present.* Translated from the 3rd ed. in German by Gwendolyn Goldbloom. Leiden, Boston: Brill, 2015.
Rosen, Lawrence. *The Justice of Islam: Comparative Perspectives on Islamic Law and Society.* Oxford: Oxford University Press, 2000.
Rosenthal, Franz. 'Gifts and Bribes: The Muslim View'. *Proceedings of the American Philosophical Society* 108, no. 2 (1964): 135–44.
Sachedina, Abdulaziz. *The Just Ruler in Shiite Islam.* Oxford: Oxford University Press, 1988.
Salqīnī, Ibrāhīm. *al-Muyassar fī uṣūl al-fiqh al-islāmiyya.* Damascus: Dār al-fikr, 2000.
Sarakhsī, Shams al-Dīn al-. *Al-Mabsūṭ.* 31 vols. Beirut: Dār al-maʿrifa, 1989.
Schneider, Irene. *Das Bild des Richters in der adab al-qāḍī-Literatur.* Frankfurt am Main: Peter Lang, 1990.
Shāfiʿī, Muḥammad ibn Idrīs al-. *Al-Risāla.* Edited by Aḥmad Muḥammad Shākir. Cairo: Muṣṭafā al-bābī al-ḥalabī, 1940.
Shāṭibī, Abū Isḥāq al-. *Al-Muwāfaqāt fī uṣūl al-sharīʿa.* Edited by Muḥammad ʿAbd al-Qādir al-Fāḍilī. 4 vols. Sidon, Beirut: Maktaba al-ʿaṣriyya, 2000.
Taştan, Osman. 'Hüseyin Atay's approach to understanding the Qur'an'. In *Modern Muslim Intellectuals and the Qur'an.* Edited by Suha Taji-Farouki, 241–62. Oxford: Oxford University Press, 2004.
Tyan, Emile. "ʿadl'. In Gibb; Kramers; Lévi-Provençal; Schacht; Lewis, *Encyclopaedia of Islam*, 209–10.
—. *Histoire de l'organisation judiciaire en pays d'Islam.* 2nd ed. Leiden: Brill, 1960.
Wadud, Amina. *Inside the Gender Jihad: Women's Reform in Islam.* Oxford: Oneworld, 2006.

Wichard, Johannes. *Zwischen Markt und Moschee: Wirtschaftliche Bedürfnisse und religiöse Anforderungen im frühen islamischen Vertragsrecht.* Paderborn, Munich, Vienna, Zurich: Schöningh, 1995.

Wizārat al-awqāf wa al-shuʾūn al-islāmiyya, al-Kuwayt, ed. *al-Mawsūʿa al-fiqhiyya.* 4th ed. 45 vols. Kuwait: Dhāt al-salāsil, 1993–2007.

Zuhaylī, Wahba al-. *Al-Fiqh al-islāmī wa adillatuhu.* 8 vols. Damascus: Dār al-fikr, 1984.

Abbas Poya

Jihād and Just War Theory: A Conceptual Analysis*

Abstract

The idea of a 'just war' has long occupied a central position in legal, ethical, and philosophical discussions. The body of thought on the topic goes beyond the contradiction of the act of war itself and how to conduct war in a just manner. This work asks to what extent the Arabic-Islamic term *jihād* (jihad) can be usefully understood within the context of just war theory, if at all. The text begins with a linguistic and conceptual analysis of *jihād*, including its occurrence in classical and modern Islamic literature. The work concludes with the following points: within the framework of legal-sharia interpretations, the term *jihād* has strongly combative connotations. Modern interpretations of the term have tended to be defensive, although many scholars continue to define it as an offensive act of war. With regard to internationally recognised human rights legislation however, an offensive interpretation of *jihād* is increasingly untenable. Islam's rich theoretical discourse surrounding the term however, can make meaningful contributions to today's controversial just war debates, if *jihād* is understood as an act of defence against aggression.

Introduction

If justice is a concept that applies to all humans and human communities equally, regardless of national, religious, ethnic, or other affiliations, with the corresponding advantages and disadvantages of communal living being equally distributed among all,[1] then war can only ever be unjust. The global or cosmopolitan normative understanding of justice today is based on a moral uni-

* This article will also be published in German in: Dagmar Kiesel/Cleophea Ferrari (eds.), Gerechter Krieg, (Frankfurt am Main: Klostermann, 2018), 151–168.

1 This 'ideal' understanding of justice is rooted in the globalized world of today, defined by its strong pluralistic tendencies, as evinced in diverse and increasingly closely-knit cultural and religious ideas and practices. The theoretical origin of this global conception of justice however, lies in the Kantian idea of a universal peace and rights order. See Otfried Höffe, *Gerechtigkeit: Eine philosophische Einführung*, 4th ed. (Munich: Beck, 2010), 94.

https://doi.org/10.1515/9783110574593-007

versalism, in which all humans, everywhere, are of precisely equal moral importance.[2] It is further based on a concept of responsibility that applies to all humans, regardless of nationality, religion, and culture.[3] If justice is understood in this holistic sense, the problem of war must still be confronted, with efforts being made to find 'just' solutions to any given conflict. However, within this framework, war itself can hardly be described as just. For, in war, there is always an opponent, to whom the arguments legitimating war for the first party are perceived as unjust; not to mention the so-called collateral damage that accompanies all wars, revealing how they are no more than ugly and unjust affairs. If justice is defined, on the other hand, as being particular,[4] it becomes easy to speak of war as a just or an unjust affair. Particular, in this sense means, particular to a specified group of people. This means, that in order to determine the just course of action in a given conflict, the starting point for deliberation is one's own particular position within a given framework (e. g., national, religious, or cultural). The theoretical grounding of particular justice is based on the empirical finding that there is no form of global authority or over-arching sovereignty, that can meet the demands of justice in a form analogous to that of the state. It thus supports the normative assumption that in the case of conflicting national and global principles of justice, members of one's own group will be prioritised.[5] Justice is still called for in a general sense, even in this particularistic form, for one's own position is taken to be absolute. Others however, are not party to this definition of justice. It is irrelevant whether the position is perceived as legitimated via conceptualizations of natural law, religion, or nationality.

It is precisely this 'particular' understanding of justice that formed the bases for initial theories of 'just war' in Antiquity, not only that of Aristotle, but also of later ecclesiastical theories, such as that of Thomas Aquinas. These scholars theorised about just war (*bellum iustum*) in a world that differentiated between two groups of human beings: the free, the chosen, followers of the Lord, the civilised,

2 Christoph Broszies and Henning Hahn, 'Die Kosmopolitismus-Partikularismus-Debatte im Kontext'. In *Globale Gerechtigkeit: Schlüsseltexte zur Debatte zwischen Partikularismus und Kosmopolitismus*, ed. Christoph Broszies and Henning Hahn, 3rd ed. (Berlin: Suhrkamp, 2016), 10.
3 See Elke Mack, *Eine christliche Theorie der Gerechtigkeit* (Baden-Baden: Nomos, 2015), 93.
4 Particular here is not meant in its Aristotelian sense. Aristotle differentiated between universal and particular justice. He wrote of universal justice as corresponding to 'virtue as a whole', noting that when justice was identified with 'complete virtue', it was always 'in relation to another person.' He wrote of particular justice as narrower in scope, with reference to concrete areas, such as justice in the distribution of material or non-material goods such as honour. See Günther Bien, 'Gerechtigkeit bei Aristoteles', in *Aristoteles: Die Nikomachische Ethik*, ed. Otfried Höffe (Berlin: Akademie-Verlag, 1995), 135–164.
5 Broszies and Hahn, 'Die Kosmopolitismus-Partikularismus-Debatte im Kontext', 11.

and believers, on the one hand, and slaves, barbarians, the Lord's enemies, heretics, and non-believers, on the other.[6]

Similarly, the term *jihād*, as a meritorious (and at times bellicose) act, must also be contextualised against the background of a particular conception of the world, or of humans within it. Traditional Islam groups people based on their religious affiliations, whereby the community of Muslims is the just, or the more just, of the religious groupings, and deserving of struggle: "You are the best community produced for humans [as an example]. You enjoin what is right and forbid what is wrong and believe in God!"[7] During the Middle Ages, it was in reference to this verse, that the Ḥanafi legal scholar al-Sarakhsī (d. 1090) claimed that if the message of Islam was delivered to non-believers and they rejected it, then they must be fought.[8]

War or Just War

This work is concerned with whether the Arabic (and by now also English and German) term *jihād* (Jihad) can be equated with 'war' or 'just war'. Before elaborating my thoughts on the matter however, this section briefly discusses the terms 'war' and 'just war'.

As mentioned above, war is often associated with violence, the shedding of blood, destruction, suffering, and pain. Consequently, it may sound grotesque and cynical to describe wars as being just. Nonetheless, the formulation of the 'just war' forms not only part of the rhetorical repertoire of warlike conflicts, but also has a long tradition in legal, theological-ethical, and philosophical dis-

---

6 Aristotle, for example, considered some people to be masters by nature, and others to be slaves by nature. For him, "the science of acquiring slaves is different both from their ownership and their direction – that is, the just acquiring of slaves, which is akin to the art of war or that of the chase." Further, it is fully in accordance with the laws of nature and is a just battle. See Ulrike Kleemeier, *Grundfragen einer philosophischen Theorie des Krieges* (Berlin: Akademie-Verlag, 2002), 27. Justice, in the end, for him is an ideal that is only ever realized for the free male citizens amongst one another and within the polis. Relations between men, their wives, and their children, and relations between masters and slaves are characterized by dominance and submission. See Ernst-Wolfgang Böckenförde, *Geschichte der Rechts- und Staatsphilosophie* (Tübingen: UTB, 2002), 116.

7 Q. 3:110.

8 See Shams al-Dīn al-Sarakhsī, *al-Mabsūṭ*, 31 vols. (Beirut: Dār al-maʿrifa, 1989), 10/2.

course, extending back to Greek Antiquity, across the Middle Ages, and down to the present.[9]

Over the last several decades, the negative associations accompanying the term 'war' have resulted in official statements largely abandoning use of the word altogether, heedless of the reality that warring activities continue to affect the everyday lives of many people around the world. Avoidance of the term is also an attempt to evade specific problems concerning its legality and definition. It is hardly possible to arrive at a consensus on the definition of war, since it can take diverse forms (wars between states, world wars, civil wars, colonial wars, wars of independence, etc.) and can have numerous causes (of a political, economic, religious, territorial, national, racist, freedom-related, or anti-colonial nature). Thus, more recent international treaties avoid the term 'war' altogether, in favour of expressions such as 'armed conflict', and 'armed violence'.[10] Furthermore, euphemisms such as 'humanitarian intervention' are common features of diplomatic discourse.[11]

Regardless of how we signify the facts on the ground: a violent conflict is designated as 'war' today, if it is armed and collective, carried out between states. In order to be designated a just war, it must be carried out a) for the purpose of self-defence, that is thus, b) based on a just cause (*ius ad bellum*), and c) its conduct must be in accordance with the laws governing the conduct of war (*ius in bello*).[12]

What then does the term *jihād* mean, and can it be equated with Just War or only with 'war'?

---

9 The genesis of the just war has been analyzed in numerous works. See e.g., the contributions in Georg Kreis, ed., *Der "gerechte Krieg": Zur Geschichte einer aktuellen Denkfigur* (Basel: Schwabe, 2006).

10 At the Geneva Conference in December 1932, the Big Five Powers for example, replaced the expression 'war' with the formulation 'application of armed violence' (article III). In the United Nations charter, it is written, 'all members shall refrain in their international relations from the threat of use of force against the territorial integrity or political independence of any state' (article II, 4). The use of force, or threat thereof, was henceforth permitted only when decided upon in the Security Council as a form of sanction (article 42), or as an act of defense (article 51).

11 The problem of international law that complicates humanitarian intervention was clearly illustrated during the Kosovo war. See Nasimi Aghayev, *Humanitäre Intervention und Völkerrecht: Der NATO-Einsatz im Kosovo* (Berlin: Köster, 2007). For critical reflection on the topic see Jean Bricmont, *Humanitärer Imperialismus: Die Ideologie von der humanitären Intervention als Rechtfertigung für imperialistische Kriege* (Berlin: Homilius, 2009).

12 See Peter Rudolf, 'Krieg', in *Lexikon der Politikwissenschaft, Bd. 1 A – M*, ed. Dieter Nohlen and Rainer-Olaf Schultze (Munich: Beck, 2010), 526.

On the term *jihād*

The root of the term *jihād* is j-h-d and means to make an effort, to strive, and to struggle. *Ijtihād*, a term that is central to Islamic legal discourse, is an eighth form verbal noun from the same root. It refers to the effort, striving, and studiousness of a scholar to arrive at independent formulations of opinion concerning religious questions.[13] If we examine the use of the term *jihād* in religious contexts (concerning Islamic duties for example), and in religious scripture (Qur'an and hadith),[14] these efforts are always connected to God and the spiritual cause, as illustrated in the following example of a Qur'anic verse: "And strive for Allah with the striving due to him."[15] At the same time, in most cases there is also a warlike or conflictual aspect that accompanies personal efforts. The use of the term in the Qur'an is almost exclusively connected with this aspect, as is shown in the following verse: "The ones who have believed, emigrated and striven in the cause of Allah, with their wealth and their lives are greater in rank in the sight of Allah."[16] The one leading a *jihād*, a *mujāhid*, is someone who is committed to the cause of God, someone who seeks to undertake deeds that are deserving in religious terms, and such a person is valued more than one who stays at home: "Allah has preferred the *mujtahidūn* those who strive for the cause of God/ on the path of God with their wealth and their lives over those who remain behind/ remain in the home, by degrees."[17]

This combative aspect of *jihād* also dominates the legal texts and in the hadith compendia. Usually, classical legal and hadith-studies contain a separate chapter under the heading of *jihād* or *siyar* (singular, *sīra*; in the sense of *sunna*, tradition, custom, way of conduct),[18] or *jihād wa siyar* (jihad and con-

---

13 See Hans Wehr, *Arabisches Wörterbuch für die Schriftsprache der Gegenwart* (Wiesbaden: Harrassowitz, 1998). On the term *ijtihād* specifically, see Abbas Poya, *Anerkennung des Iğtihād: Legitimation der Toleranz. Möglichkeiten innerer und äußerer Toleranz im Islam am Beispiel der iğtihād-Diskussion* (Berlin: Klaus Schwarz, 2003).

14 Hadiths (Arabic: *aḥādīth*, singular: *ḥādīth*) are the sayings of the Prophet Muhammad, collected as a set of traditions, containing also accounts of his daily practices and the practices of others that he tacitly endorsed. Hadiths enjoy a normative status and constitute the second source of Islamic learning and guidance after the Qur'an.

15 Q. 22:78.

16 Q. 9:20. In this verse and similar ones the term *jihād* is translated by Rudi Paret as war or the conduct of war.

17 Q. 4:95.

18 The Ḥanafi legal scholar al-Sarakhsī chose the title *Kitāb al-siyar* (Book of Conduct) for the topic. On the choice of title, he wrote, '... for in this book the conduct of Muslims is described in

duct),[19] discussing the normative details of war. These sections include questions raised in the just war discourse: What conditions must pertain in order to justify going to war, and to what factors must one pay attention during the conduct of war? On the whole, *jihād* is taken to compromise a legal category within sharia that cuts across schools of thought and belief and is understood to mean fighting against non-believers.[20]

There have been numerous recent attempts, especially within the European diaspora, to strip *jihād* of its militant associations and motivations, promoting a translation of the term as committing oneself to the faith, that is, to Islam. If texts or history reveal cases in which the term comprises indisputably concrete warlike actions, these are presented as particular modes of this more general effort of self-improvement. The more important and more valuable *jihād* is proclaimed to be that against one's own ego and against 'the evil forces of the soul'.[21] Scholars base this analysis on a disputed hadith wherein the prophet is supposed to have said, following a battle, "Good, this battle has been won. It is only the lesser Jihad, however, the greater Jihad lies ahead of us."[22] By greater *jihād* he allegedly meant the inner *jihād*, the mental battle and battling against one's ego (*jihād al-nafs*).[23]

Surely, the meaning of terms and their use in varying contexts can change over time, for historical and other reasons. History bears out countless examples of terms with differing interpretations at varying points in time. The term tolerance (Latin: tolerantia), for example, today signifies a recognition of the Other, or at least putting up with them. In Antiquity however, the term denoted the endurance of pain, torture, misfortune, or military defeat. The same word was then claimed in scholasticism to express the toleration of sinful behaviour in order

their treatment of polytheists as the parties of war (*ahl al-ḥarb*) and as parties to a contract (*ahl al-ʿahd*).' [al-Sarakhsī, *al-Mabsūṭ*, 10/2].

19 The well-known hadith-collector Muslim, for example, chose for the chapter the title, *kitāb al-jihād wa al-sīra* (The Book of Jihad and Conduct), See Muslim b. al-Ḥajjāj, *al-Ṣaḥīḥ*, 5 vols. (Damascus: Dār iḥyāʾ al-kitāb al-ʿarabī, 1955), 3/1356.

20 See ʿAbdallāh bin Aḥmad al-Qādirī, *al-Jihād fī sabīl Allāh: Ḥaqīqatuhu wa ghāyatuhu*, 2 vols. (Jeddah: Dār al-manāra, 1992), 49.

21 Albrecht Noth, 'Der Dschihad: Sich mühen für Gott', in *Die Welten des Islam: Neunundzwanzig Vorschläge, das Unvertraute zu verstehen*, ed. Gernot Rotter (Frankfurt am Main: Fischer, 1993), 23.

22 Patrick Franke, 'Rückkehr des Heiligen Krieges? Moderne Dschihad-Theorien im modernen Islam', in *Religion und Gewalt: Der Islam nach dem 11. September*, ed. A. Stanisavljević and R. Zwengel (Potsdam: Mostar Friedensprojekt e.V., 2002), 48.

23 On this interpretation of *jihād*, see Muhammad Moghaddam, *"Jihad" – nicht "Heiliger Krieg"* (Hamburg: Islamisches Zentrum Hamburg, 1984).

to avoid greater evil. It was only during the sixteenth century in the context of religious conflicts within Christianity that the term gradually gained entry into European political and philosophical debates and took on the meaning of a peaceful acknowledgment and recognition of the worldviews and practices of others.[24] With the term *jihād*, however, the violent aspect is not only dominant in the context of the Qur'an and the classical legal and hadith literature. Contemporary use of the term is also generally understood to be associated with acts of war or violence that are, however, held to be favourable to the cause of Islam, and thus, meritorious and just.[25] Expressions such as *jihād al-nafs* (in the sense of fighting against one's inner ego) or *jihād al-shayṭān* (in the sense of fighting the evil forces within one's soul) do come up in classical legal literature.[26] At times they are also ascribed to the prophet.[27] These cases do not represent the dominant use of the term, however. Rather, the inner *jihād*, as Noth observes, is in all likelihood a later image derived from the concrete war-related *jihād:* to suppress the sinful desires of the soul requires strong effort and motivation in the same way as armed battle against a dangerous and tenacious enemy.[28]

There are two other Arabic terms that are used in the sense of 'war', namely *ḥarb* and *qitāl*. Both also appear in the Qur'an.[29] The roots of the nouns *ḥarb* and *qitāl*, as also in the case of *jihād*, are used as active verbs in the third form with the meaning of battling or fighting. In terms of the roots of both words: in *ḥarb* the root implies an aspect of fighting and war; in *qitāl* the aspect of killing and slaughter is inherent. This distinction is most clear in the expression *qatīl al-ḥarb* (someone killed in war, a war victim, war dead). In the Qur'an also, the varying nuances in the meaning of the terms can be observed.[30] The apparent differentiation between *jihād* on the one hand, and *ḥarb* or *qitāl* on the other indicates that *jihād* happens exclusively as a force for good, in the name of God (*fī sabīl*

---

24 See Gisela Schlüter and Rudolf Grötker, 'Toleranz', in *Historisches Wörterbuch der Philosophie*, ed. Joachim Ritter et al., 13 vols. (Basel: Schwabe, 1971–2007), 1251.

25 See Rudolph Peters, 'The Doctrine of Jihad in Modern Islam', in *Jihad in Classical and Modern Islam*, ed. Rudolph Peters (Princeton: Markus Wiener Publishers, 1995), 103–148; some contemporary works are also mentioned that still illustrate the use of the term only in the sense of a violent activity.

26 See e.g. al-Sarakhsī, *al-Mabsūṭ*, 10/270.

27 See ibid., 10/270.

28 Noth, 'Der Dschihad' 24.

29 See e.g. Q. 5:33 and 2:190.

30 "The penalty for those who *fight against* (*yuḥāribūna*) Allah and his messenger and who strive upon earth to spread evil, is that they be *killed* (*yuqtalū*) or crucified [...]" (Q. 5:33). Emphasis added.

allāh), while *ḥarb* and *qitāl* can be carried out for God and for good (God)[31] as well as against God and for evil (idols).[32]

When the intended meaning is war in a general sense, then the terms *ḥarb* or *qitāl* are used rather than *jihād*. If, however, within the warring context a war is being discussed that is legitimated by the cause of religion, and is by extension a justified war, then the term *jihād* is used. In the following section, the term is employed in this sense and examined via a selection of classical and modern legal works.

Offensive or Defensive *jihād*

A central question of war, and in our case of *jihād*, is whether it should be understood as an offensive or as a defensive act. The answer to this question will determine whether or not *jihād*, as an act of war, can be categorised as just. Within Islam, there is both an offensive and a defensive interpretation of the term *jihād*.[33] The offensive interpretation of the term is based on the assumption that the prophet Muhammad conducted offensive wars, wars of aggression, against non-believers (*kuffār*; singular: *kāfir*). There are numerous Qur'anic verses that confirm this assumption, including the so-called 'sword-verses' (Q. 9:5 and 9:29). Proponents of a defensive interpretation of the term by contrast, see no proof in the Qur'an, or in the life of the prophet, that would favour an offensive doctrine of *jihād* – and if there were any, it would be a gross anachronism to assume applicability in the present. They consider all significations to be either exclusively defensive, or to be limited in their applicability to their historical context. The fact is, however, that the offensive interpretation of the *jihād* term was widespread, particularly during the time of the Umayyads (661–750) and the Abbasids (750–1258), as well as in the course of military expansions.[34]

31 See Q. 2:279 and 4:76.

32 See Q. 5:33 and 4:76.

33 The following analysis is based on the majority Sunni position, and within the ramifications of the sources taken into account here. Twelver-Shiism also traditionally divides *jihād* into offensive (*ibtidāʾī*) and defensive (*difāʿī*) forms. But they are generally of the opinion that an offensive *jihād* can only be considered in the presence of the prophet or the infallible imam. Thus, today there can only be defensive *jihād*. For more on the *jihād* term within Twelver-Shiism, see Murtaḍā Muṭahharī, *Jihād* (Qom: Intishārāt-i ṣadrā, 1994); and Niʿmatullāh Ṣāliḥī Najafābādī, *Jihād dar islām* (Tehran: Nay, 2015).

34 See Emile Tyan, 'Djihād', in *Encyclopaedia of Islam: Second Edition*, ed. P. Bearman et al. (2002); and Mathias Rohe, *Das islamische Recht: Geschichte und Gegenwart* (Munich: Beck, 2011), 149.

The offensive interpretation of *jihād* is also represented in the classical *fiqh*,[35] or hadith literature. When *jihād* is mentioned in these works, it is in reference to war-like activity, including wars of aggression. In the hadith collection of Muslim, one finds in *The Book of Jihad and Expedition* (*kitāb al-jihād wa al-siyar*), for example, the following subtitle: 'The chapter on the permissibility of attacking unbelievers, who have been informed of the message of Islam, without notifying them of the attack' (*bāb jawāz al-ighāra ʿalā al-kuffār alladhīna balaghathum daʿwat al-islām min ghayr taqaddum al-iʿlām bi-l-ighāra*).[36] In *fiqh* literature also, it is common for *jihād* to be divided into offensive (*hujūmī*) and defensive (*difāʿī*) battles.[37]

It is important to take into account that the classical theories pertaining to *jihād*, some of which continue to be handed down to this day, discuss the term as a tool of domination, an instrument of power. That is, they assume the existence of a central authority, defined solely by its religious identity, knowing no national or other bases for identification, and that considers itself duty-bound to deliver the message of Islam – which it considers to be just – to all humans.[38] It is not imperative that all accept the message of Islam and convert, but its message has to reach them.[39] The manner in which *jihād* and its conditions are discussed reveals how the term's understanding presumes an existing Islamic governing entity.[40] This point is further reinforced if one looks at the

35 *Fiqh* is the scientific discipline within Islam that is concerned with religious norms. The term is often translated as Islamic legal theory or jurisprudence. Since *fiqh* however, is not only concerned with legal matters, but also comprises ritual practice and ethical norms, the phrase 'religious norms' is more suitable.

36 See Muslim b. al-Ḥajjāj, *al-Ṣaḥīḥ*, 3/1356. As is known, Muslim did not insert chapters or titles in his *Ṣaḥīḥ*. Generally, editions that are published nowadays include chapter descriptions and titles that go back to the Shafiʿī scholar of legal studies and hadith, Muhyī al-Dīn Abū Zakariyā al-Nawawī (1233–1277). Al-Nawawī compiled the insertions so as to match the usual titles in Shafiʿī *fiqh* literature. Nonetheless, the title cited here is an accurate description of the content of the following hadith as transmitted by Muslim. See, ibid.

37 See e.g. Muṣṭafā Saʿīd al-Khunn, Muṣṭafā al-Bughā and ʿAlī al-Sharbajī, *al-Fiqh al-manhajī ʿalā madhhab al-imām al-Shāfiʿī*, 8 vols. (Damascus: Dār al-qalam, 1992), 8/115.

38 For this reason, *jihād* is also interpreted as an extension of the enforcement of 'the promotion of virtue and the prevention of vice' (*al-amr bi-l-maʿrūf wa-l-nahy ʿan al-munkar*), and is only permissible when the enemy has already been offered Islam. See al-Sarakhsī, *al-Mabsūṭ*, 10/2.

39 That is why there exists, for example, the category of the *ahl al-kitāb* (People of the Book), that includes Jews and Christians. In exchange for the payment of a special 'tax' (*jizya*), members within this category enjoy protection under Muslim rule. See al-Khunn, Bughā and Sharbajī, *al-Fiqh al-manhajī ʿalā madhhab al-imām al-Shāfiʿī*, 8/127.

40 For example, that *jihād* and its execution be dependent on Muslim rulers and their competence. See Ibn Qudāma al-Maqdisī, *al-Mughnī*, 10 vols. (Cairo: Maktabat al-qāhira, 1968), 9/202.

story of the term's formation: while the prophet and his few followers remained in Mecca (610 – 621), no physical confrontations took place between them and their opponents. Quite the opposite: people were called upon to maintain peaceful relations with one another. It is only with the founding of the first political community in Medina under the prophet's leadership, that *jihād* begins to emerge in both the Qur'an and the hadith. Muslims were now in a position in which they had to critically confront and determine guidelines for social and political concerns, including the question of war.[41] Thus, the traditional conception of *jihād*, which provides also for an offensive variation, is based on the assumption that a) rulership is defined via religious affiliation, and that b) a legitimate, Islamic, central authority exists.

In the present, however, there is no Islamic central authority, not even one that is nominally recognised. People live within nation-states in which they are recognised as citizens in accordance with the constitution of each state, and are not defined by their religious identities. In this context, the traditional interpretation of *jihād* is no longer tenable. Tellingly, in the present, the only people or organizations calling for an offensive *jihād* are concerned with the recreation of the conditions of early Islam and yearn for an Islamic global empire. Today, most Muslim scholars and religious institutions, such as al-Azhar University and Representatives of the Muslim Brotherhood, assume a defensive understanding of *jihād*. It is interpreted as an act of defense against aggressors and not as an act in the context of spreading Islam.[42]

Jihād as Just War?

If *jihād* is understood as an act of defence, then it can be categorised within the realm of just war theory, in accordance with the criteria for a just war within contemporary human rights discourse.[43] Those who continue to discuss *jihād* as an offensive matter, however, see it as a just act nonetheless. The core of their argument is that Islam promotes just goals and that war in the name of Islam, then, can only ever be just.

41 Contemporary scholars also distinguish between the position of the prophet whilst in Mecca and whilst in Medina, or the differing positions within Islam pertaining to the correct conduct in dealing with opponents. See for example, al-Khunn, Bughā and Sharbajī, *al-Fiqh al-manhajī ʿalā madhhab al-imām al-Shāfiʿī*, 8/119.

42 See Rohe, *Das islamische Recht*, 261 f.

43 See footnote 9.

This interpretation is promoted, for example, by the contemporary scholar ʿAbdallāh bin Aḥmad al-Qādirī, of Yemeni origin, who received his education in Medina. In his two-volume work, *Jihād in the name of God. Its Essence and its Goal* (*al-jihād fī sabīl Allāh. ḥaqīqatuhu wa ghāyatuhu*), he enumerates some of the goals of Islam, and how their realization legitimates *jihād*;

1. Islam is a religion of *iḥsān* (beneficence). In accordance with Islam one should obey God's commands to the best of one's abilities and in accordance with one's conscience. These include *saʿādat* (felicity), *adāʾ al-ḥuqūq* (the performance of justice), and *ṣiyānat al-nufūs wa ʿuqūl wa amwāl* (the protection of life, mind, and property).[44]
2. Further, via the command to act in a manner pleasing to God, Islam gives meaning to human life: one must pursue one's duties as requested by God, and in doing so, will find fulfilment.[45]
3. In addition, Islam illustrates to humans their most suitable positioning within the universe, whereby they find their cosmological and ontological placement among God, the angels, and spirits.[46]
4. Islam guarantees the equality of humans. In other cultures, people are judged based on their skin colour, lineage, or nationality, whilst in Islam all that counts, is piety, regardless of skin colour or ancestry.[47]
5. Islam guarantees safety and forbids all 'aggression' (*iʿtidāʾ*), regardless of whether it affects an individual or a group, a simple citizen or a ruler. Citizens are legally protected before the ruler, for the ruler is subject to the same rights as citizens. The author brings the example of *qiṣāṣ* (retribution). The lax talionis principle of 'an eye for an eye, a tooth for a tooth', according to al-Qādirī, is equally valid for all, acknowledging neither rank nor name. Further, in Islam, one is sure of one's honour (*ʿirḍ*). Here, the author specifically addresses legal punishments for the crimes of 'slander' (*qadhf*) or 'adultery' (*zināʾ*). Individual property is also ensured in Islam. Hence there are also punishments for 'stealing' (*sirqa*) and 'corruption' (*fasād fi-l-arḍ*). One's private life is untouchable, as spying (*tajassus*) is prohibited within Islam.[48]

---

44 See al-Qādirī, *al-Jihād fī sabīl Allāh*, 35 ff.
45 Ibid., 37–40.
46 Ibid., 40 ff.
47 Ibid., 43 ff. The author refers to the well-known verse Q. 49:13, which reads, "O mankind, indeed We have created you from male and female and made you people and tribes that you may know one another. Indeed, the most noble of you in the sight of Allah is the most righteous of you. Indeed, Allah is Knowing and Acquainted."
48 Ibid., 45.

6. Finally, the cohesion of the community is a central concern within Islam and is directly addressed in the Qur'an: "And hold firmly to the rope of Allah all together and do not become divided" (3:103).[49]

In summary, according to the enumeration of al-Qādirī, Islam offers a comprehensive and just concept for how to lead one's life. It takes into account that which is visible and that which is concealed, providing regulations and guidelines for the individual, as well as for society and the state.[50]

Al-Qādirī attempts to elaborate upon the traditional interpretation of *jihād* as an instrument of war for spreading the message and rule of Islam. He seeks to continue to write *jihād* into the present, to update it, using modern modes of argumentation. He thus ascribes to Islam desirable goals in the name of which to carry out *jihād*. He is not the only contemporary scholar to do so. Many traditional scholars employ a similar mode of argumentation. These include scholars in secular Syria, such as Muṣṭafā Saʿīd al-Khunn, Muṣṭafā al-Bughā and ʿAlī al-Sharbajī, as demonstrated in their joint work, *al-Fiqh al-manhajī ʿalā maḏhab al-imām al-shāfiʿī*.[51]

Regardless of whether *jihād* is interpreted in a defensive or offensive manner, scholars have meticulously discussed the conditions to be considered before, during, and after an act of war. Some of the main discussion points are summarised below.

Jihād is principally seen as a duty that must be carried out by every Muslim. For many scholars, the object of discussion often pertains to whether and under what conditions it is an individual obligation (*farḍ ʿayn*; everyone is obligated) or a collective one (*farḍ kifāya*; one is only obligated if needed). Most represent the opinion however that *jihād* is essentially a collective obligation.[52] It can become an individual duty if a) it is a case of defence, b) if the current Muslim ruler has called upon all Muslims to carry out *jihād*, or c) when standing directly before battle as a soldier. In these cases, there can be no turning back, and it is impermissible to flee before an impending battle.[53]

---

49 Ibid., 45 f.

50 Ibid., 46 ff.

51 See al-Khunn, al-Bughā and al-Sharbajī, *al-Fiqh al-manhajī ʿalā madhhab al-imām al-Shāfiʿī*, 8/120 – 123.

52 Ibn Qudāma al-Maqdis, *al-Mughnī*, 9/196, and al-Qādirī, *al-Jihād fī sabīl Allāh*, 53 ff. There is also an opinion that *jihād* is not a duty but simply a legal recommendation (*mandūb*) within the sharia. ibid., 64 ff.

53 See Ibn Qudāma al-Maqdisī, *al-Mughnī*, 9/197, and al-Qādirī (1992), 72 f. There is a scholarly difference in opinion concerning the third case. Three questions in particular are disputed: is

Although the legal literature treats *jihād* as an individual duty of each Muslim, comparable to ritual prayer or pilgrimage, its execution is dependent on the competence of the leader (*imām*) of the Muslim community.[54] It is not possible for any individual to issue a call to *jihād*. The duties of tactical organization and strategic execution are those of the imam; others are obligated to follow his lead.[55] This is in reference to, among other factors, the following hadith: "The imam is truly like a shield. With him one fights and through him one is protected. If he commands fear of God and justice, he shall be rewarded; if he espouses something else, accusation shall be levelled against him."[56]

Another topic in relation to *jihād*, is that the person participating in it (*mujāhid*) must be a Muslim, male, and of age. Hence, it is forbidden for a non-Muslim, woman, or child to take part in *jihād*.[57] There have been recurring cases in the history of Islam in which a war effort was supported by non-Muslims,[58] but the act is referred to as *jihād* only if it is carried out by a Muslim. Despite the prohibition of *jihād* for women, there have also been numerous historical exceptions that have witnessed the participation of women.[59] Another condition for *jihād* is that the participants meet the necessary financial and physical requirements. Thus, if someone suffers from a disability or their family is not adequately provided for, they are not obligated to execute *jihād*.[60] In the case of a collective obligation (insofar as there is a sufficient number of *jihād*-abled Muslims), it is also imperative that the parents of participants give their consent.[61] In the case of individual obligation to *jihād*, each male, whether father or son, is obligated to pursue his personal duty.[62]

Muslims must also take into consideration certain issues as they pertain to their opponents. On principle, people who are not involved in warring against

---

fleeing a battle categorically forbidden? Or is this permissible if the number of Muslim soldiers is ominously low when compared to that of the opponents? And how low should one's fighting force be in order to permit retreat? See al-Qādirī, *al-Jihād fī sabīl Allāh*, 73 ff.

54 See Ibn Qudāma al-Maqdisī, *al-Mughnī*, 202.

55 See ibid.

56 For example, Muslim b. al-Ḥajjāj, *al-Ṣaḥīḥ*, 3/1471, hadith number 1841.

57 Al-Khunn, al-Bughā and al-Sharbajī, *al-Fiqh al-manhajī ʿalā madhhab al-imām al-Shāfiʿī*, 8/121 f.

58 See al-Qādirī, *al-Jihād fī sabīl Allāh*, 84 f.

59 Ibid., 88.

60 Al-Khunn, al-Bughā and al-Sharbajī, *al-Fiqh al-manhajī ʿalā madhhab al-imām al-Shāfiʿī*, 8/122.

61 Ibid., 123.

62 See Q al-ādirī, *al-Jihād fī sabīl Allāh*, 91.

Muslims are not allowed to be fought.[63] In concrete terms, this means that Muslims may not wage war against the following: those to whom they have already granted asylum; those with whom they have already entered into a contractual agreement; and those whom they have taken on with an obligation to protect, the People of the Book (*ahl al-dhimma*).[64] It is thus forbidden for Muslims to commit a breach of contract.[65]

In this sense also, no child or woman may be killed, insofar as they do not participate in the war effort.[66] Likewise, monks, the elderly, and servants may not be killed either.[67]

On principle, Muslims are forbidden to pursue a scorched earth policy in war, for they are tasked with ensuring the prosperity and thriving of the earth.[68] Consequently, it is not admissible to destroy the abodes or trees of the opponent; unless they are being used to protect the enemy.[69] Further, there is very unambiguous warning against the defilement or burning of the bodies of the deceased.[70]

In addition, Muslims are obligated to treat prisoners in a considerate manner and to set them free under specific conditions.[71] They must meet the defeated with dignity and demonstrate to them that the victory of Islam is not a degradation, but a blessing and benefaction.[72]

Conclusion

In summary, the following should be noted: within Islamic discourse, and in particular within the context of sharia/legal discourse, the term *jihād* is generally strongly associated with war. The act of war, as connoted by the term *jihād*, has positive associations. Contrary to the expressions of *ḥarb* or *qitāl*, which can, depending on the context, signify neutral, positive, or negative motivations, *jihād* only has good, godly, and just intentions. That is why the legal literature is

63 See ibid., 210.

64 Al-Khunn, al-Bughā and al-Sharbajī, *al-Fiqh al-manhajī ʿalā madhhab al-imām al-Shāfiʿī*, 8/123f.

65 Al-Sarakhsī, *al-Mabsūṭ*, 10/5.

66 See ibid., and al-Qādirī, *al-Jihād fī sabīl Allāh*, 212f.

67 Ibid., 213ff.

68 Ibid., 235f.

69 Ibid., 237.

70 Al-Sarakhsī, *al-Mabsūṭ*, 10/5, and al-Qādirī, *al-Jihād fī sabīl Allāh*, 239f.

71 Ibid., 250.

72 Ibid., 269.

filled with meticulous discussions of what must be taken into consideration, in order for *jihād* to be permissible, and by extension, just. Many of these conditions make up the definition of a just war, such as the treatment of prisoners of war, or the prohibition of *jihād* for children, the impermissibility of defiling the deceased, and of pursuing a scorched earth policy. The decisive point remains however, whether *jihād* is interpreted as defensive or offensive. An offensive interpretation assumes the particularistic position that there is only one legitimate authority. Nonetheless, *jihād* can meet many of the preconditions of a just war as they pertained in the Middle Ages.[73]

An offensive understanding of *jihād*, however, is hardly tenable in the present. With regard to Muslim-majority nation-states today, such an interpretation appears anachronistic, in its legitimizing the attacks on other communities of belief, and in its encouragement of violent clashes within the Muslim community. If *jihād* is understood as an act of defence against aggression, then Muslims are able to fall back on a rich theoretical discussion of the term within Islamic legal literature, and can make significant contributions to the general discourse surrounding the just war topic today.

Bibliography

Aghayev, Nasimi. *Humanitäre Intervention und Völkerrecht: Der NATO-Einsatz im Kosovo.* Berlin: Köster, 2007.

Bien, Günther. 'Gerechtigkeit bei Aristoteles'. In *Aristoteles: Die Nikomachische Ethik.* Edited by Otfried Höffe, 135–64. Berlin: Akademie-Verlag, 1995.

Böckenförde, Ernst-Wolfgang. *Geschichte der Rechts- und Staatsphilosophie.* Tübingen: UTB, 2002.

Bricmont, Jean. *Humanitärer Imperialismus: Die Ideologie von der humanitären Intervention als Rechtfertigung für imperialistische Kriege.* Berlin: Homilius, 2009.

Broszies, Christoph, and Henning Hahn. 'Die Kosmopolitismus-Partikularismus-Debatte im Kontext'. In *Globale Gerechtigkeit: Schlüsseltexte zur Debatte zwischen Partikularismus und Kosmopolitismus.* Edited by Christoph Broszies and Henning Hahn. 3rd ed., 9–52. Berlin: Suhrkamp, 2016.

Franke, Patrick. 'Rückkehr des Heiligen Krieges? Moderne Dschihad-Theorien im modernen Islam'. In *Religion und Gewalt: Der Islam nach dem 11. September.* Edited by A. Stanisavljević and R. Zwengel, 47–68. Potsdam: Mostar Friedensprojekt e.V., 2002.

Gräf, Erwin. 'Religiöse und rechtliche Vorstellungen über Kriegsgefangene in Islam und Christentum'. In *Die Welt des Islams* 3 (1963): 89–139.

Höffe, Otfried. *Gerechtigkeit: Eine philosophische Einführung.* 4th ed. Munich: Beck, 2010.

---

73 See Erwin Gräf, 'Religiöse und rechtliche Vorstellungen über Kriegsgefangene in Islam und Christentum', *Die Welt des Islams* 3 (1963), 89–139.

Ibn Qudāma al-Maqdisī. *Al-Mughnī.* 10 vols. Cairo: Maktabat al-qāhira, 1968.
Khunn, Muṣṭafā Sa'īd al-, Muṣṭafā al-Bughā, and 'Alī al-Sharbajī. *Al-Fiqh al-manhajī 'alā madhhab al-imām al-Shāfi'ī.* 8 vols. Damascus: Dār al-qalam, 1992.
Kleemeier, Ulrike. *Grundfragen einer philosophischen Theorie des Krieges.* Berlin: Akademie-Verlag, 2002.
Kreis, Georg, ed. *Der "gerechte Krieg": Zur Geschichte einer aktuellen Denkfigur.* Basel: Schwabe, 2006.
Mack, Elke. *Eine christliche Theorie der Gerechtigkeit.* Baden-Baden: Nomos, 2015.
Moghaddam, Muhammad. *"Jihad" — nicht "Heiliger Krieg".* Hamburg: Islamisches Zentrum Hamburg, 1984.
Muslim b. al-Ḥajjāj. *Al-Ṣaḥīḥ.* 5 vols. Damascus: Dār iḥyā' al-kitāb al-'arabī, 1955.
Muṭahharī, Murtaḍā. *Jihād.* Qom: Intishārāt-i ṣadrā, 1994.
Noth, Albrecht. 'Der Dschihad: Sich mühen für Gott'. In *Die Welten des Islam: Neunundzwanzig Vorschläge, das Unvertraute zu verstehen.* Edited by Gernot Rotter, 22–32. Frankfurt am Main: Fischer, 1993.
Peters, Rudolph. 'The Doctrine of Jihad in Modern Islam'. In *Jihad in Classical and Modern Islam.* Edited by Rudolph Peters, 103–48. Princeton: Markus Wiener Publishers, 1995.
Poya, Abbas. *Anerkennung des Iǧtihād: Legitimation der Toleranz. Möglichkeiten innerer und äußerer Toleranz im Islam am Beispiel der iǧtihād-Diskussion.* Berlin: Klaus Schwarz, 2003.
Qādirī, 'Abd Allāh bin Aḥmad al-. *Al-Jihād fī sabīl Allāh: Ḥaqīqatuhu wa ghāyatuhu.* 2 vols. Jeddah: Dār al-manāra, 1992.
Rohe, Mathias. *Das islamische Recht: Geschichte und Gegenwart.* Munich: Beck, 2011.
Rudolf, Peter. 'Krieg'. In *Lexikon der Politikwissenschaft, Bd. 1 A — M.* Edited by Dieter Nohlen and Rainer-Olaf Schultze, 526. Munich: Beck, 2010.
Ṣāliḥī Najafābādī, Ni'matullāh. *Jihād dar islām.* Tehran: Nay, 2015.
Sarakhsī, Shams al-Dīn al-. *Al-Mabsūṭ.* 31 vols. Beirut: Dār al-ma'rifa, 1989.
Schlüter, Gisela, and Rudolf Grötker. 'Toleranz'. In *Historisches Wörterbuch der Philosophie.* Edited by Joachim Ritter et al. 13 vols., 1251–62. Basel: Schwabe, 1971–2007.
Tyan, Emile. 'Djihād'. In *Encyclopaedia of Islam: Second Edition.* Edited by P. Bearman et al., 538–40., 2002.
Wehr, Hans. *Arabisches Wörterbuch für die Schriftsprache der Gegenwart.* Wiesbaden: Harrassowitz, 1998.

Bernd Ladwig

The Islamic Veil and Justice

Abstract

Based on a judgment of the German High Court of Justice, some federal states passed laws holding that a female teacher is not allowed to wear an Islamic headscarf in a public school, whereas Christian symbols can be allowed due to their general cultural significance. The article argues that such a differentiation is incompatible with the equal concern and respect a secular state owes to each of its citizens. The arguments are based on an ethical understanding of liberalism that takes the difference between weak and strong evaluations seriously. Apart from pragmatic considerations, ethical liberalism supports a moderate multiculturalism in dealing with conflicts around religious signs and symbols.

Contested Clothing

Imagine a teacher at a public primary school in Dortmund appeared in class wearing the jersey of the Bayern München soccer club. The teacher would likely cause a great deal of commotion among the student body. Their natural partiality for the home team Borussia Dortmund would surely squash any hopes at a calm, constructive learning experience. Would it be right for the educational authority to prohibit the teacher to wear this contested item of clothing?

Surely, it would be. Whoever teaches at a public school does so voluntarily and in full knowledge of the consequences of his employment: being responsible for minors who cannot escape his gaze. Pupils may refuse to actively participate or pay attention in class, or they might make use of other forms of 'Great Refusal' (Herbert Marcuse). And the teacher will certainly not succeed in converting his wards to the Munich team – this is Dortmund, after all. This notwithstanding, it is surely within the rights of the pupils that the teacher's appearance be conducive to their education. And outside the context of an ethics class about the burdens of tolerance, the jersey does not meet this criterion.

Undoubtedly then, there do exist circumstances where public school teachers have no choice but to accept that they must obey certain rules concerning their appearance. Further still, if the teacher is a civil servant, then he/she stands before the class as representatives of the government. He/she is an embodiment

https://doi.org/10.1515/9783110574593-008

of the state he/she has chosen to serve. This choice bears consequences for the freedoms the teacher enjoys while serving. And in any case, according to classical liberalism, claims to freedom are primarily aimed at protecting citizens from the state. Citizens' claims to freedom are related to those of civil servants in an asymmetrical manner, in favour of the former.

But the latter are not completely without rights either. Civil servants, as citizens, have a right to the free development of their personalities. Any job-related infringements on their freedoms must therefore be accompanied by a justification: infringements must be both objectively necessary and proportional. The more central the freedom being infringed upon, or the more severe the infringement, the more securely grounded its justification must be. In addition, civil servants have the right not to be discriminated against. In our example: if the educational authority decided to move against teachers in jerseys, it would have to do so regardless of which particular team might be considered offensive. So, a new rule would have to apply equally to a Borussia Dortmund jersey.

Just as a jersey, a veil too can be perceived as offensive. It can be understood as the symbol of a religious community and as the marker of a political positioning: veils covering the hair on the head of a female are nowadays primarily associated with Islam or even with its fundamentalist formations. Many people think it conveys missionary intent or, in any case, the refusal to fully assimilate. It is taken to signify aggression, or at least a separation from the majority of society. The potential for these and similar interpretations has determined legal rulings in some 'veil cases'. The most important of these cases, and the one that carried the most juridical weight, was that of Ludin.

The Case of Ludin and its Consequences: Some Fundamental Questions

Fereshta Ludin, a German national of Muslim belief, wanted to become a teacher in the federal state of Baden-Württemberg. She was not prepared, however, to remove her veil in the classroom; the item of clothing, she claimed, formed part of her Islamic identity. The educational authority of the federal state revoked her qualification to serve as a teacher at primary and secondary schools. It ruled that the veil had an objective effect of cultural disintegration that was incompatible with state's requirement of neutrality. A teacher wearing an Islamic veil would offend both the positive and negative freedom of belief of pupils and their parents.[1]

Taking her case to specialised courts – from the Higher Administrative Court in Stuttgart, all the way up to the Federal Administrative Court – the federal state maintained that it was in the right against the plaintiff Ludin. The tone of the rulings was to the effect that the veil was a conspicuous symbol, that it was likely to confuse pupils religiously and to make them feel insecure, even if worn with no missionary intent. None of the courts even presumed Miss Ludin to harbor such intentions. They did, however, all refer to the 'objective effect' of the veil: they ruled that the item of clothing in question was open to religious and political interpretations. The fact of its being worn by a person holding a position of authority whom students have no choice but to be in contact with, bears the potential of bringing conflict into the classroom as well as into the relationship between teacher and parents.

Miss Ludin finally took her case to the Federal Constitutional Court. The second senate voted five to three in her favour. It ruled that the federal state of Baden-Württemberg may not bar Miss Ludin from the teaching profession without a relevant legal basis[2] and that no such basis was in place at the time of ruling. Thus, in order to justify the exclusion, there would have to be a concrete danger to the maintenance of peace in the school. In contrast, the 'objective effect' of the veil only represents an abstract danger. It does not justify the teacher's expulsion in the absence of an explicit legal provision. After all, the decision infringed on the teacher's right to freedom of belief, a basic and unconditional right. The court thus also acknowledged the plaintiff's argument that its own former 'crucifix-ruling' was not applicable in this case. Whereas in that former case a state institution had maintained the right to mount religious symbols, now an individual bearer of the most fundamental rights was expressing her own personal religious conviction.

The Federal Constitutional Court based its ruling on the principle of 'open neutrality'. The Federal Republic, the court reasoned, is a secular – and not a laic – state. It not only respects, but also promotes freedom of belief. The state is not permitted to equate itself with any particular community of belief or religious conviction. It must, however, provide space for religious and spiritu-

---

1 The negative freedom of belief is freedom from state intervention and compulsion in questions of belief; the positive freedom of belief is the freedom to lead one's life in accordance with religious convictions. In the case of the veil, this generally applies to the freedom of parents raise their children in a religious manner.

2 See, concerning this and what follows: Ruling of the Federal Constitutional Court: bVerlG, 2 BvR 1436/02, dated March 6th, 2003, paragraph (1–140).

al convictions to be lived, even when these seek to appear publicly. And thus, the Federal Constitutional Court ruled that any legal prescriptions concerning clothing regulations in public service that might infringe upon expressions of religious belief must have a justification that does justice to the normative importance of the basic right to freedom of belief.

The judges added that a change in the general societal framework could speak for a re-formulation of the principle of neutrality. They reasoned it would in principle be permissible for the state to re-interpret its obligation to neutrality in stricter terms, since increased social diversity also means increased risk of religious conflict. Thus, it could be permissible for the state to forbid religious symbols that were previously permitted. In order to do so, however, it would require a sufficiently explicit legal basis. State legislators would be permitted to rule differently, so long as they maintained the principle of strict equality in the treatment of all religious persuasions, in legislation as well as in practice [with potential constraints]. Such was the statement of the majority judges at the federal constitutional court.[3]

Following the ruling many federal states passed new laws concerning the veil. States with conservative governments, such as Baden-Württemberg, emphasised the state's obligation to neutrality, while maintaining, however, a distinction between strictly religious symbols and Christian-Occidental symbols that express educational and cultural value. According to this reasoning, Christianity occupies two roles, a religious and a cultural one; consequently, due to its cultural importance, it should be accrued certain privileges. In practice this means a veil can be forbidden on the grounds that it is a religiously imprinted item of clothing; a crucifix, or even a nun's habit, on the other hand, not necessarily. Or at least that is what the federal legislators must have envisioned. At the other end of the spectrum is the law based on article 29 of the Constitution of Berlin. It prohibits any visible religious symbols or religiously imprinted items of clothing at public schools except during religion class. Berlin's response to the fact of religious plurality is almost laic.

The ruling of the federal constitutional court and the laws passed in its aftermath throw up a number of fundamental questions. Why does the state need to be religiously neutral in the first place? Is it permissible for state legislators to

---

3 The minority sided with the federal state of Baden-Württemberg and the specialized courts. Their primary argument was that public servants cannot simply refer to the freedoms guaranteed to them as basic rights, in the same way that normal citizens can. There is no space within the scope of their contractual commitment to public service for personal avowals. Accordingly, it should be permitted for a federal state to prohibit veiled women from serving at public schools even without a legal basis.

prevent veiled women from teaching, while permitting nuns to teach in their habit, without violating the legal requirement of strict equality, as upheld and reaffirmed by the Federal Constitutional Court? And if not, then should the state keep all religiously toned items of clothing away from schools? Or should it generally permit them all? To answer this last question, it is also necessary to clearly define what makes an item of clothing religiously significant. How is it different from a styling accessory – or a soccer jersey which can also elicit a heated reaction?

As I will demonstrate, the Federal Constitutional Court should have at least clarified that state legislators who are permitted to favour Christianity under the pretext of cultural preservation, are acting in violation of the constitution of a secular state. The Court should have set clearly defined guidelines for state legislators. Setting aside for a moment any concrete danger, prohibiting the veil while permitting the Jewish skull-cap, the cross, or even a nun's habit is clearly discriminatory. It is not in line with the requirement of strict equality of all religious persuasions.

Two possible solutions remain. One is the more laic of a general prohibition of any religious attire. The second is moderately multi-cultural: generally to permit these items of clothing. Of the two, the latter appears to be preferable to me. A general authorization of veiling, even in public office, is the best answer a secular state may offer in response to religious pluralism, because it is the fairest possible solution. In addition there are also a number of pragmatic considerations that favour such a response. Further, the state would still be permitted to prohibit teachers from wearing the jersey of Bayern München, or that of any team for that matter. The intuition I appealed to in my introductory example remains intact.

This opinion is not only in opposition to the conservative position that privileges for Christianity could be justified by appealing to its general cultural significance. I am also opposing those liberals who do not distinguish between expressions of religious conviction and mere fashion accessories or fan paraphernalia. The liberalism I hold to be plausible is an ethical liberalism that acknowledges the importance of particular values to personal identity formation. Acknowledging the importance of these values means favouring approaches that are moderately multicultural with regard to peoples' need for expressions of religious belief.

Normative Foundations

Equal Concern and Respect

For a state to be impartial in matters of religious belief, it must treat all religious convictions equally in the sense of not taking sides with any one religious community or belief system. But this does not mean that there are never situations in which the state may be permitted or even required to take sides. The principle of neutrality is based, not least, in morality. It is a consequence of the requirement that the state treat all its citizens as equals, with equal concern and respect.[4] It must give equal weight to the life, well-being, and self-determination of each and every individual member of the political community. For the state's laws apply to all citizens equally, and every citizen must be able to abide by them, not merely out of fear or prudence, but also out of respect for law's content. As a consequence, legislators, governments, administrations, and courts, as well as we ourselves, as citizens, we all bear the responsibility of preventing segregation and discrimination among the citizenry. A reasonably fair state will not accept that there are any second-class citizens or even citizens without rights. In the words of the American legal philosopher Ronald Dworkin:

> A political community that exercises dominion over all its own citizens, and demands from them allegiance and obedience to its laws, must take up an impartial objective attitude towards them all, and each of its citizens must vote, and its officials must enact laws and form governmental policies, with that responsibility in mind. Equal concern, as I said, is the special and indispensable virtue of sovereigns.[5]

The equality of respect and regard is a basic norm in need of clarification. It can call for strictly equal treatment, but need not necessarily entail it. The emphasis here is not so much on equal treatment, but rather on everyone counting equally.[6] Undoubtedly, this entails having the same basic rights. Where this is not the case, there, by definition, exists discrimination. When it comes to the interpretation and exercise of rights, however, some consideration of morally relevant dif-

---

4 An important basic reading on neutrality: Stefan Huster, *Die ethische Neutralität des Staates: Eine liberale Interpretation der Verfassung* (Tübingen: Mohr Siebeck, 2002).

5 Ronald Dworkin, *Sovereign Virtue: The Theory and Practice of Equality* (Cambridge, MA, London: Harvard University Press, 2002), 6.

6 On the difference between equal treatment and being treated as an equal, see Ronald Dworkin, *Bürgerrechte ernstgenommen* (Frankfurt am Main: Suhrkamp, 1990), 370. Dworkin also emphasizes that the right to be treated as an equal is basic, whilst the right to equal treatment is derivative.

ferences is required. Some individuals or communities are likely to be more vulnerable and/or needy than others. Abstract principles of human rights, such as respect for physical and psychological integrity, or the promotion of autonomy, can only be exercised as rights in a meaningful way and in an equal manner, where morally relevant differences between groups and individuals are taken into account. Thus, for example, one would not be treating someone suffering from a chronic illness as equals by overlooking their specific needs for expensive medication or by expecting the same level of performance from them as one would from healthy individuals. Neither are children regarded as equal without taking into account their special need for attention, care, and protection.

If we are to judge truly impartially, that is, if we are to search for justifying reasons that all can share,[7] we will understand that some deviation from equal treatment does not create undue privilege for some. On the contrary, it is but an attempt – however insufficient – to strike a balance against specific disadvantages or against undeserved inferior starting conditions. Impartial grounds for a deviation from the principle of equal treatment may include: unequal needs, unequal contribution to some common good, a past discrimination that may still be momentous, or previous entitlements that were legitimately acquired, such as in contractual form. In any case, the list is not especially long where all count as equals. If no moral grounds speak for unequal treatment, then the logical conclusion is equal treatment, following from the principle that all are to be treated as equals. This is nothing more and nothing less than a necessary moral fallback position for those cases in which no shared grounds for unequal treatment can be found.[8]

Equal treatment is *prima facie* also called for when it comes to religious and other comprehensive doctrines that are disputed amongst citizens who judge them critically, conscientiously, and in a morally responsible manner. Laws cannot stand on theoretical foundations that are baseless to non-believers, or people of differing persuasions. Whosoever is systematically disadvantaged through legislation influenced by religious convictions would be fully justified in considering themselves to be second-class citizens.

---

7 More extensively on this, see Bernd Ladwig, 'Begründung von Normen', in *Einführung in die Politische Theorie und Methodenlehre*, ed. Sven-Uwe Schmitz and Klaus Schubert (Opladen: Barbara Budrich, 2006), 255 ff. On impartiality, see also Georg Lohmann, 'Unparteilichkeit in der Moral', in *Die Öffentlichkeit der Vernunft und die Vernunft der Öffentlichkeit: Festschrift für Jürgen Habermas*, ed. Lutz Wingert and Klaus Günther (Frankfurt am Main: Suhrkamp, 2001), 434 ff.

8 I am here presupposing equality. For more on this see Stefan Gosepath, *Gleiche Gerechtigkeit: Grundlagen eines liberalen Egalitarismus* (Frankfurt am Main: Suhrkamp, 2004), esp. 200–211.

However, the limitations of the principle of equal treatment become visible at the point where its own moral foundations are at stake. Belief systems that do not grant equal rights to all, or that infringe upon (other) basic legal interests have to face justifiable limitations and even sanctions. No community of belief may, for example, prohibit its members from leaving that community. Equally, no community may attempt to occupy the role of the sovereign. The equality of the entire citizenry remains the basis for positive and negative freedoms of belief and religious expression.

Ethical Liberalism

A more difficult question is whether a liberal state is permitted to promote certain ways of life over others. Some liberals hold that the secular state must remain strictly neutral in all questions pertaining to how to lead a good and meaningful life; and if the state does intervene it can only do so rightfully in order to promote basic rights such as the right to life and to physical integrity. I hold this view to be unworldly and also untenable from a normative perspective. Wherever a state, even a liberal one, actively sets guidelines for rational self-determination, it is promoting a certain way of life over another. This is the case in public schools, for example, where education is intended to promote maturity [*Mündigkeit*] by training male as well as female children's' ability to make informed decisions and pass judgement by thinking through matters in a critical manner. Even traditionalist parents have to live with the fact that their children attending public schools will become familiar with ways of thinking that they might then turn against the values that their parents revere.

It is clear to me that there is no such thing as total impartiality in this respect (possible and desirable). Although the state should not be partial to any particular set of goals, it will show some partiality by promoting a certain way of life: well informed, guided by independent thought and action, and with the potential to scrutinise and even revise the conception of the good.[9] This position is not

9 In the partiality to individual autonomy, there is a joining together of the political liberalism of the later John Rawls and of the ethical liberalism of the later Dworkin. See John Rawls, *Gerechtigkeit als Fairness: Ein Neuentwurf* (Frankfurt am Main: Suhrkamp, 2006), 44; Ronald Dworkin, 'Foundations of Liberal Equality', in *The Tanner Lectures on Human Values, vol. 11*, ed. Grethe B. Peterson (Salt Lake City: University of Utah Press, 1990). W. Kymlicka puts forward a similar line of argument to that of Dworkin in Will Kymlicka, 'Two Models of Pluralism and Tolerance', in *Toleration: An Elusive Virtue*, ed. David Heyd (Princeton: Princeton University Press, 1996), 81 ff. A perfectionist justification for the principle of autonomy, adjusted for the special circum-

based in the misguided assumption that we can choose such a conception at random. On the contrary: anyone seriously committed to a certain way of life should be interested in how to justify it and in what makes – or fails to make – it viable and meaningful. Openness to critique does not indicate a loss of the strong, stable bonds that hold together one's self-conceptualization. On the contrary, it is the only rational and responsible way to foster them.

This general conviction is the hallmark of ethical liberalism. It assumes that a good life is also always one of self-determination. And it does not shy away from obligating the state to promote personal autonomy. This ethical liberalism, it seems to me, is superior to the kind of liberalism that seeks to remain neutral even when confronted with communities that hold minors in heteronomy in order to protect them from a 'sinful' outside world or from world views that unsettle their beliefs such as the theory of evolution.

This might create the impression that followers of ethical liberalism would have to favour the promotion of non-religious lifestyles. After all, believers pass their lives into the hands of God. They believe that not they themselves, but God should have the last say in all of life's big questions. Instead of freely choosing the good, they see themselves bound to God's resolution. But it would be invalid to infer that, as a consequence, religious people must oppose individual autonomy. When someone leads a self-determined life, they are guided by reasons they consider good and valid, under conditions of judgment that promote rational thought.[10] Leading an autonomous life at the least requires self-respect and self-confidence, the mental and physical capacities for independent thought and action, a certain level of material security, basic education, and the knowledge of relevant alternatives, in a social context sufficiently rich with valuable options. Whoever leads a religious life within such a framework, will count as self-determined until the opposite is proven.

And in any case, strictly speaking nobody is in a position to choose freely among different conceptions of the good. We do not just have a set of convictions which we may trade in at will. Whatever convictions we have, we find ourselves

---

stances of modern societies, is provided by Joseph Raz, *The Morality of Freedom* (Oxford: Clarendon Press, 1986). I myself have defended the centrality of autonomy for liberalism in Bernd Ladwig, *Gerechtigkeit und Verantwortung: Liberale Gleichheit für autonome Personen* (Berlin: Akademie-Verlag, 2000).

10 See on this Bernd Ladwig, 'Der Wert der Wahlfreiheit: Eine Kritik von Isaiah Berlins Verständnis von negativer Freiheit', *Deutsche Zeitschrift für Philosophie* 55, no. 6 (2007), 877 ff.

committed to them, be it through argumentation or evidence-based thought.[11] This is equally the case for religious and non-religious beliefs. The freedom of an autonomous being consists in a disposition to critically evaluate their beliefs when necessary. Even religious people can recognise that they bear responsibility for their beliefs and should thus remain open to new perspectives, experiences, and arguments.

An ethical liberal will thus differentiate between rational and irrational forms of belief. But this will be just a special case of distinguishing between rational and irrational forms of commitment more generally. Ethical liberals prefer open-minded and oppose narrow-minded attitudes regarding our most important convictions. And if the educational system within a secular state were to favour open-mindedness and contribute to dogmatism losing ground, such a person would welcome this development.

At the end of the day, some belief systems will find such an arrangement more problematic than others. But equality in the end-result cannot be expected from a liberal state anyway. A community without open-ended debate and free competition between worldviews cannot be a liberal one. It is the state's responsibility to ensure that such confrontations take place within a context of respect that all citizens owe to each other. And it must ensure that the formally granted equal rights also have real value for all. In other words, the state must guarantee that communal conflicts within the citizen body take place within a framework characterised by fairness. However, this is not to be equated with an obligation to protect and preserve any and all religious orientations.[12] They can only survive so long as enough people practice the respective beliefs voluntarily.

If the state is to function in accordance with ethical liberalism, then it will, among other things, be in favour of an educational system that encourages independent thinking and critical judgment by pupils of any gender. This puts any community and belief system under pressure: they must prove that they can attract and maintain the loyalty of people who call for justifying reasons. They must be able to survive in a society of self-critical and reflective individuals, who perform self-respect as confident subjects of equal rights.[13] If they cannot

---

11 More extensively on this, see: Robert B. Brandom, *Making it Explicit: Reasoning, Representing, and Discursive Commitment* (Cambridge, MA: Harvard University Press, 1998), esp. Part One, chapter 3.

12 J. Habermas has already made this observation, see Jürgen Habermas, 'Anerkennungskämpfe im demokratischen Rechtsstaat', in *Multikulturalismus und die Politik der Anerkennung*, ed. Charles Taylor and Jürgen Habermas (Frankfurt am Main: Fischer, 1997), 173.

13 For more on this, see Henning Hahn, *Moralische Selbstachtung: Zur Grundfigur einer sozialliberalen Gerechtigkeitstheorie* (Berlin: De Gruyter, 2008).

manage this task, then there is no reason to be saddened by their declining influence.[14]

Justifiable Inequality? Five Attempts to Defend the Prohibition of the Veil

What follows from the Ludin case and related cases concerning the veil? I would like to examine some of the arguments brought forward in order to justify a ban on the Islamic veil without being equally restrictive towards *other* religiously worn items of clothing. In that regard, I am dismissing, from the outset, reasoning based on majority structures in a current population. The mere fact that a structural majority is in favour or against a certain practice cannot in and by itself justify unequal treatment with regard to goods relevant to religious freedoms. In order to legitimise such treatment, we need generally shareable reasons that apply to all citizens. A just community must thereby also remain open to change in the composition of the demos. All recent arrivals, too, have a right to equal regard and respect. Traditions that might have shaped the legal system legitimately under conditions of relative homogeneity may no longer be tenable when the composition of society changes. Minorities need not tolerate the majority stance against regulations that justice demands for the sake of ethnic and cultural plurality.

Are there other arguments for privileging Christian symbols and clothing? I am going to examine five attempts to justify this favouritism. These arguments are allegedly non-discriminatory; an important factor on which the legitimacy of any basic liberal order depends. The formulation of the question, however, already hints at the difficulty of finding such a justification. Beliefs with a partic-

---

14 A possible, and tragic, exceptional case indigenous communities whose constitutive norms and values are simply not compatible with the ways of life of a modern, functionally differentiated and socially mobile community, no matter how hard one strives for reconciliation. They may make basic claims to special protection and claim a need for increased promotion, but this is in no way a right to ignore the human rights of people belonging to the respective community. Truly tragic are situations in which the freedoms of human rights and of autonomous position-taking will almost inevitably result in the extinction of these ways of life. We have reason to find this regrettable not only because many of these communities have suffered major injustices in the past. Even more importantly, their decline in the present regularly creates anomic situations among its members: apathy, malnutrition, alcoholism, violence and other trademarks of moral self-surrender disproportionately affect all indigenous populations, from the Australian Aborigines to the New Zealand Maoris, all the way to the Indians of North, Middle and South America.

ular content that is rightfully contested among conscientious and morally responsible citizens can play no part in these arguments. What remains then, are first, pragmatically justified measures, second, impartially justifiable norms such as human rights, and third, generalisable evaluations, such as those made by ethical liberalism in favour of the basic value of personal autonomy.

Offensiveness

A first set of arguments claims that some items of clothing that carry spiritual significance are particularly offensive. This could be because they are especially conspicuous, presenting an uncommon sight for the majority of the population, are rejected by the majority and/or are perceived to be worn for missionary purposes. As the list illustrates, an item of clothing can be perceived as offensive for a variety of reasons, and each one must, in turn, be analysed.

It is true that some items of clothing are more readily visible than others, possibly due to their size or their location on the body. When it comes to conflicts in schools we need only discuss items of clothing that are visible to pupils. A small cross hung around a teacher's neck will probably only rarely be seen by pupils, e.g. if the teacher bends down before them. A veil or Jewish skull-cap on the other hand, is permanently visible. But here we must mention the possibility that for precisely this reason one might not notice these items of clothing after some time of familiarization; likewise, punks in large cities have had to realise that the power of habit works to subvert the offensiveness of even those symbols that *are intended* to promote insecurity or offense. Further, the type of symbol or spiritual item of clothing depends on the content of the doctrine in question; this also applies, in part, to where on the body it is to be worn and how large it should be. No one who seriously follows a belief system has a real choice in this respect. A skull-cap or a veil is an item of clothing which believers place on or over their hair as a sign of humility before God. If that alone were sufficient justification for unequal treatment in favour of Christians, who are allowed to wear their crosses around their necks, then we would be penalizing a community based on circumstances beyond its control, and that would be unfair.

What one can surely ask of teachers is that their choice of clothing be as discreet and unobtrusive *as possible*. But what this actually entails depends on what substantively matters to the teacher. A remaining argument in favour of exclusion might then be that certain items of clothing are objectively unsuitable to carrying out some of the tasks of a teacher. An item of clothing might be so peculiar and outlandish for example, that some pupils are not able, by any standard, no matter how hard they try, to concentrate in class. This might apply to clothing that conceals the entire body, such as the Afghan-style burka. But as we shall see, in such a case a very different objection becomes relevant. In any case, it appears quite implausible not to expect of ordinary pupils to concentrate in class because their teacher is wearing a veil. Even in the great arsenal of pupils' excuses this one is but a dull sword.

Does the veil have such a strong effect of unfamiliarity? This will probably be the case, at least as long as few women are allowed or want to teach whilst wearing it. However, the objection to using this as an argument for exclusion is straightforward: the state may not generate the self-fulfilling prophecy of sustaining the unfamiliarity of an item of clothing that is then used to legitimate its prohibition. A justifiable reason for prohibition cannot be that the prohibition will result in exactly the effect that justified said prohibition. Besides, the familiarity of an item of clothing is a function of majoritarian social structures within a community. It is quite reasonable to expect majorities to endure moderate cultural shocks brought about by changes in the composition of the population. This is an undeniable component of the modernity we inhabit. The better communities are in the practice of dealing with unfamiliarity, the less disoriented they will be, and the faster change will be readily adapted into the realm of one's own. (Modern humans are familiar with, amongst others things, the constant possibility of encountering unfamiliarity.)

What to do, however, when the majority, or at least a noteworthy minority, seriously rejects the veil? What if they perceive women wearing the veil as not only annoying but as seriously aggravating? Well, annoyance, anger, and aggravation might be justified or not. Nobody can demand of a teacher to respond to idiosyncratic reactions of some of her pupils by renouncing all forms of personal expression that are especially meaningful to her. The mere fact of rejection is not reason enough to interfere with her basic religious freedoms.

However, even a justified rejection would not suffice to warrant such an intrusion. The justification may be based on ideological principles that the wearer of the veil can reasonably reject. This is a classic application for the virtue of tolerance: a serious and not unreasonable rejection, whose justification however does not sufficient to warrant state interference. Tolerance can be owed to co-citizens for they must acknowledge each other, in a general and reciprocal manner, as subjects of equal rights. Respect for the person then entails accepting their convictions and practices, even if grudgingly so.[15] And just as dealing

15 See, more comprehensively on tolerance: Rainer Forst, *Toleranz im Konflikt: Geschichte, Ge-*

with experiences of unfamiliarity in a civil manner is a skill that pupils should acquire sooner rather than later, so is tolerance. This line of argument thus favours wearing the veil at public schools rather than prohibiting it. For the school is, in effect, intended to prepare pupils for life within a religious and ideologically pluralistic community.

But what if the veil indicates missionary purposes? Well, if this intention is present, then it will not be solely expressed through this one item of clothing. Rather, it will come to bear on teacher's everyday practices that may then warrant sanctioning. The veil may, in such a case, have been an indicator for a concrete and present danger. But it would not have been the only, let alone the most important indicator of that kind. To justify legal sanctions, there must be a direct relation to real or acutely feared behavior. The wearing of a veil as such is not the relevant kind of behavior.

Thus, from whichever angle the argument is examined, the potential offensiveness of the veil is not a strong enough basis for its prohibition in public schools. Believers can only partly control whether or not items of clothing that are meaningful to them are offensive to others. People may take offense for no reason, or for morally invalid reasons, but then the problem lies with them and not in the object in which they take offense. They may be obliged to tolerance, or they might make pessimistic predictions about the wearer's behavior, but these will then concern activities other than veiling. And if such actions are worthy of sanction, then it is not due to the mere fact that veiling is a part of them.

The Flag of Islamism

A further argument goes that donning the veil can be interpreted as an expression of a misogynistic belief system that harbors contempt for women and is thereby morally reprehensible. It is, as inimitably stated by Alice Schwarzer, the 'flag of Islamism'.[16]

Now, it is of course true that many female Islamists wear the veil. It is also true that some Islamists force women to wear the veil and threaten those who do

---

halt und Gegenwart eines umstrittenen Begriffs (Frankfurt am Main: Suhrkamp, 2003); as well as the collections of David Heyd, ed., *Toleration: An Elusive Virtue* (Princeton: Princeton University Press, 1996), and Rainer Forst, *Toleranz: Philosophische Grundlagen und gesellschaftliche Praxis einer umstrittenen Tugend* (Frankfurt am Main: Campus-Verlag, 2000).

16 Alice Schwarzer, 'Die Islamisten meinen es so ernst wie Hitler', *Frankfurter Allgemeine Zeitung*, 4 July 2006, Interview with Alice Schwarzer.

not. It also appears to me to be true that there is some connection between the advancement of conservative, or even reactionary, interpretations of religion among Muslims on the one hand, and the increase in the number of veiled women on the other.

In countries ruled by radical Islamists women no longer have the choice to leave their homes veiled or unveiled – that is, if they are even allowed to leave their homes, and if it is only a matter of covering their hair and not of total disappearance beneath a full body veil, leaving only small slits for the eyes. Radical Islamism has elevated archaic practices to the rank of law. It prescribes that women's primary purpose is to bear male children. As potential or present mothers they are not much more than the mediums of family or tribal 'honour'. An independent female claim to freedom and happiness is not provided for in the radical Islamist worldview. This is clearly morally reprehensible: a veritable apartheid that affects millions of women all over the world, deserving of no less radical condemnation than racial segregation in Apartheid South Africa did. It is scandalous that many cultural relativists apparently take less issue with oppression when it is embellished with religion and affects mostly women.[17] And it is such relativism to the detriment of women that authors such as Schwarzer, Necla Kelek, Taslima Nasreen, or Ayaan Hirsi Ali justifiably criticise.

However, not all veiled Muslims profess Islamism by covering their hair. Not all veiled Muslims thereby aim at the same restrictive regulations for Germany as exist today in Saudi Arabia, Iran, or parts of Pakistan. A study by the Konrad-Adenauer-Stiftung, though it cannot claim to be representative, found clear indications that Muslim women in Germany cover their hair for a variety of reasons.[18] Despite all the inherent difficulties of assessing true motives, there is clear evidence that Islamist ambitions is only one of them – and probably not even the main one. Also, a significant number of women and girls credibly claim that their decision to don the veil was freely taken and that no coercion was involved. Against this finding, one might argue that families are likely to have more subtle methods of convincing women to conform to reactionary role models than the use of brute force. The very minimum however, that opponents of the veil and practitioners of ideological critiques more generally should take upon them-

---

17 As stated also by Susan Moller-Okin, 'Konflikte zwischen Grundrechten: Frauenrechte und die Probleme religiöser und kultureller Unterschiede', in *Philosophie der Menschenrechte*, ed. Stefan Gosepath and Georg Lohmann (Frankfurt am Main: Suhrkamp, 1998), 310 ff.

18 Frank Jessen and Ulrich von Wilamowitz-Moellendorff, 'Das Kopftuch: Entschleierung eines Symbols', Konrad-Adenauer-Stiftung, accessed 31 July 2008, http://www.kas.de/wf/de/33.9095/.

selves is the burden of proof: a false consciousness is surely not the norm among Muslim women.

Thus, the *general* suspicion of Islamist motivations behind veiling is not justified. It may well be justified in individual cases, but these would have to be investigated and proven case by case. Such a context-specific individual case examination was not considered necessary, however, in the Ludin case in Stuttgart. The new Federal State School Law (§ 38 II) declares that an outward behavioral appearance is not permissible if it could generate the impression, amongst pupils or parents, that a teacher is acting against human dignity, against the equality of all as stated in article 3 of the *Grundgesetz*, or against the free and democratic order. It is noteworthy here that the law does not specify any reasons that might count in favour of such an impression. Could it not, in individual cases, be wholly unfounded? And could such a – wrong – impression that the teacher was acting against the principles of human dignity even be used against her?

The state should not add authority to unfounded impressions by basing legal action on them. In the face of error, critical assessment is to be promoted. It would do pupils and some parents much good to realise that not every head covered by a veil contains dubious thoughts and evil intentions. The phrasing, however, of the new school law of Baden-Württemberg permits the interpretation that mere prejudice on the part of parents and pupils is sufficient to infringe upon the basic freedoms of teachers or even to prevent them from practicing their profession.

A Political Symbol?

The same basic response can be given for the argument that the Islamic veil is not a solely religious symbol, but that it expresses a certain political ethos as well. Who would deny that teachers in public schools have to accept infringements to their basic rights to freedom, in order to avoid politically influencing pupils? Now, some opponents of the veil argue that in the case of Islam it is not possible to separate religious and political expressions. After all, they claim, since its inception Islam has not allowed room for mundane forces outside religion.

Here, I would like to remain open as to what the disciplines of History and Islamic Studies have to say concerning these debates.[19] Does the argument involve the claim that veiling is an expression of the desire for theocracy or of a legal system that is constructed along the lines of the Sharia? In either case, the same response as stated above, about the suspicion of fundamentalism, is applicable: this would have to be proven in individual cases. As a general suspicion, it is surely untenable. In individual cases, the political associations of a woman with her veil are likely to be highly variable. There exist veiled women of a social democratic orientation as well as politically conservative ones. A unified political message does not automatically emit from the veil. So, how and to what could it be seducing pupils politically?

Pre-Political Bases

A fourth argument is based on the alleged ideological foundations of liberal democracy. It states that both Christianity and Judaism have made significant contributions to this field, but Islam has not.[20] On the contrary, according to this argument, Islam contains many problematic clauses that are, at best, not suited to the foundation of a secular state. This applies, for example, to the already stated difficulty of separating worldly and religious powers. And it is a principle of self-preservation for a liberal democracy that it be concerned with its political preconditions. One of the few places it can still effectively do so is in the field of public school regulations.

This argument contains two parts: a (self-)praise of Christianity – and for the purposes of political correctness, also of Judaism – and a judgment about the (im)possibility of uniting Islam and the secular state. Regarding the self-praise first, this undoubtedly deserves an extensive response that I cannot give here. I will limit myself to only a few comments.

It is remarkable how nonchalantly most of the proponents of the theory that liberal democracy would not have been possible without Christian roots ignore the history of this religious movement(s).[21] Practically all human rights and dem-

---

19 A good overview is provided by the contributions in Werner Ende and Udo Steinbach, eds., *Der Islam in der Gegenwart*, 5th ed. (Munich: Beck, 2005).

20 As stated by Josef Isensee, 'Grundrechtseifer und Amtsvergessenheit', *Frankfurter Allgemeine Zeitung*, 8 June 2004.

21 This is the case, with due differentiation for individual authors, also for the study of Tine Stein, *Himmlische Quellen und irdisches Recht: Religiöse Voraussetzungen des freiheitlichen Verfassungsstaates* (Frankfurt am Main, New York: Campus-Verlag, 2006).

ocratic achievements had to be painstakingly fought for in old Europe in a battle with the representatives of official Christianity. The Catholic Church in particular took its time in recognizing human rights; it did so no earlier than the 1960s. And even today, its understanding of human rights contains certain peculiarities that are inconsistent with the principle of equality in a democratic constitutional state. If we are to assume that Catholic bishops take their own rhetoric seriously, then women who perform abortions are still cast as murderers, and homosexuals are accused of having unnatural inclinations that necessitate legal penalisation.

More importantly, all attempts to find the roots of the constitutional state in Christianity are explanations *ex post facto* of the following type: a normative progress such as the separation of church and state, or the equality of human rights has first been achieved and gained broad recognition against the resistance of Christian authorities; as a response, the progress in question is traced back to elements of Christian doctrine even though they were originally understood in a completely different manner. For example, the idea of being created in God's image might motivate Christians to acknowledge human rights *today*; but the idea in its original meaning was clearly not a predecessor of rights-oriented reasoning.[22]

Rather, the early idea of being created in God's image was marked by a role-specific interpretation of equal respect for all humans. According to the Pauline interpretation, equal respect was limited to a common brotherhood *in christo*. Apart from one's role within the religious community, individuals had to accept radical inequalities even including conditions of bondage, all with the explicit approval of the church. On the Protestant side, Martin Luther later established a clear distinction between the freedom of a Christian and the equality of the priesthood of all believers (*Priestertum aller Gläubigen*) on the one hand and questions of political-legal emancipation on the other.[23] Also, in the traditional-Christian interpretation, the individual was not understood as a subject of rights that may first and foremost ground the duties of others. Rather, what he or she could normatively expect was the function of an objective order of things, governed by natural law.

In both regards, the human rights-based interpretation of human dignity has changed the picture completely. Humans no longer count as equal in only one respect, even if it is a religiously significant one. As equals they have valid

22 On this point, and what follows: Christoph Menke and Arnd Pollmann, *Philosophie der Menschenrechte: Zur Einführung* (Hamburg: Junius-Verlag, 2007), 154–-158.

23 On this, see *Philosophie der Menschrechte: Grundlagen eines weltweiten Freiheitsethos* (Darmstadt: Wiss. Buchges., 1998), 122f.

claims that have consequences for all the roles they might play in life. Nobody today needs to endure torment or bondage in their business life, in scientific endeavors, or even in professional sports. And this is because now all are morally owed respect and regard. Every human is seen as a self-validating source of claims.[24] Neither one of these achievements was put into the cradle of Christianity, notwithstanding the idea of being created in God's image. Both together they formed the precondition for Christianity to give this thought a new interpretation, in which it may attempt, *today*, to anchor its own very specific interpretation of human rights. But it would be anachronistic to take it as the root of any valid interpretation of human rights.

As for Islam, it is claimed it cannot supply an independent ideological grounding for a secular, democratic constitutional state; or even further: it is claimed that Islam is conceptually opposed to such a state from the outset. One part of the argument appears much less suggestive if my above response is sound: Christianity did not make any indispensable contribution to the founding of the democratic constitutional state either. What it de facto did was to bring its doctrine into line after the fact, and this rather incompletely, as the example of Catholic attitudes towards women who abort and homosexuals illustrates.

This means that today a strict Catholic must perform the trick of considering women who perform abortions murderers, but without denying them the respect they are due as fellow citizens because of it. He must pay taxes to a state in which well-known homosexuals rank among the highest representatives. And he has to refrain from responding with violence to laws that give people freedoms which might lead them into eternal damnation. I do not wish to claim that these are easy tasks. But if we believe Catholics are able to perform them, then why not Muslims also? Like all other citizens, they too must distinguish between ambitions they consider suitable, taken from their comprehensive doctrines, and claims for which they may gain support, through public reasoning, by citizens with different ideological standpoints.[25] Only commonly shareable claims are permitted to co-determine the basic order of the political community.

What alternatives are there to trying to get Muslims to understand their citizen roles as equals among equals? One could hope for a mere *modus vivendi:* people with irreconcilable ideological standpoints agree on guidelines that are advantageous for everyone, calculated in an ego- or ethnocentric fashion. These rules would be justified for each person and each group, but not for all

24 Rawls, *Gerechtigkeit als Fairness*, 50.
25 Compare ibid., § 9.

together, not out of a commonly shared ground.[26] The problem with this solution is that it does not extend beyond a virtual state of war. Whenever one group believes the power dynamics allows for for an improvement of their positionality, they will be rationally motivated to negate any potential common ground with the other group. It is no wonder then that conservatives who are pursuing no more than a *modus vivendi* with Muslims look at birth statistics with great concern.

A second and a third solution is only mentioned here for the sake of completeness. To explicate them is tantamount to acknowledge their untenability. First, it is conceivable that all followers of the Muslim faith might emigrate away from Western societies. Second, it is conceivable that all Muslims living in the West might give up their faith. End of the thought experiment.

So, we stand confronted with the fact that Muslims are increasingly becoming citizens of Western democracies with no end in sight. If we do not wish to drive them into a condition of virtual war, we must offer them possibilities on how to perceive themselves as believers and as citizens simultaneously. I see no valid alternative to the attempt to win over as many as possible to the project of liberal democracy. What sense could it make to assume a priori, that this cannot be a project to which they can subscribe?

There is no doubt that the human rights battles fought by women such as Ayaan Hirsi Ali or Necla Kelek are admirable and carried out under great risk to their personal safety. However, they are doing a disservice to the democracy they seek to strengthen when they suggest that all Muslims must, consistent with their faith, perceive of themselves today in basically the same way as the fundamentalists among them. If there is no space in 'Islam' for anything other than strategically motivated participation in the public life of Western societies, then it stands to reason that many Muslims will privilege their faith over their role as members of the citizenry. This second role needs some form of grounding that is not inherently alien to Muslims from the outset. But that is incompatible with the claim that the grounding is and must forever be exclusively Christian-Occidental.

The Cultural Significance of Christianity

This brings me directly to the fifth and last argument for privileging Christianity. It finds expression in all those veiling laws that make exceptions for Christianity

26 Ibid., 293.

based on its cultural importance. In contrast to the last argument however, it does not presume that the liberal constitutional state has a particular ideological origin. Rather, it claims that symbols and expressions of Christian origin are, in contrast to the veil, separable from their religious meaning and thus generally acceptable. They merely symbolise the historically configured space that any citizen of the country inhabits. Crucifixes in offices and hanging from walls in schools, crosses on the necks of teachers, maybe even nuns in their habits, all are just as much a part of the occidental community as the holiday calendar which is also formed by Christianity.

The argument evokes two responses. First, it does not take seriously what Christian items of clothing and symbols mean to those wearing them. It assumes the position of a detached outsider who can perform a supposedly objective cultural scientific evaluation. It is only from this perspective that the religious content of these symbols can be moved as far into the background as the argument needs it to be. But a nun does surely attach a religious meaning to her habit, as does a Muslim to her veil. To each of them these items of clothing signify different things, and for each of them they are likely to represent more than some blurred cultural oppositional boundaries of Occident versus Orient. At the same time, the specific meaning of each item also makes it exclusive. The cross will appear to a Muslim as Christian, in the same way that a veil will appear Islamic to a nun. That is after all, how they are intended to be perceived.

Of course, one could try to make all symbols or expressions at stake completely devoid of their religious content. However, this would raise the question why we need them at all. Why the cross and not the German flag? Surely religious persons will not agree with this interpretation of the symbols that carry such importance for them. Alternatively, we could take seriously the religious content of these symbols. But then we have to accept that they are also exclusionary. One cannot have both, specific statements through means of expression that have direct religious connotations, *and* the inclusion of all citizens, across all religious and ideological divides. The price of specificity is exclusion; the price of inclusion, vagueness.

The second response is that symbols that are already expressive of a hegemonic culture do not need reinforcement in the form of legal favouritism in the public space. A Muslim woman living here will in any case already be confronted with testimonies of the Christian Occident wherever she goes. The typical townscape is one of church towers whose bells toll at predetermined hours. Every community will be formed by its specific history, and the resulting cultural dominance will generally be that of the majority population. Thus, complete cultural neutrality is already an illusion. We need not be concerned for the Christian heritage of this country anytime soon. It does not stand and fall with the readiness to reinforce it in those spaces that are supposed to be equally accessible to all citizens, regardless of origin and conviction.

Thus, if someone can raise truly impartial justifications for exceptions, it is the Muslim and not the Christian woman. A Muslim woman can make the case that renouncing the veil would be especially hard on her since she is already forced to inhabit a culturally foreign world, surrounded by beliefs and practices of a different cultural universe. An understanding of equal respect and regard that is somewhat sensitive to differences will thus be moderately multi-cultural. It will allow for members of minorities to also wear their symbols in public spaces.[27] Their complete cultural neutralization, even if it were achievable, would only magnify the cultural inequality in the pre-political sphere.

As a result, a basic objection to the quasi-laic solution, as put forth by the federal state of Berlin, can be raised. Its charm of apparent neutrality conceals its decisive disadvantage. It demands people who already have to overcome strong feelings of alienation to renounce all those symbols that could permit them to be themselves in public space. It would be a form of equal treatment, but at the price of regarding members of minorities not really as equals.

Another objection to the quasi-laic solution is a pragmatic one: such a solution forces Muslim women into avoidable conflicts of loyalty: they would have to decide between their belief and their desire for employment. However, precisely those people who are afraid of increased fundamentalist influence among Muslims in the country should be happiest about any Muslim woman taking up employment that is both demanding and entails her visibility in public space. Fundamentalists, after all, fear nothing more than confident and financially independent women. However, the path chosen by the state of Berlin will most likely result in some women who would have liked to become teachers deciding against that for reasons of faith. Additionally, the 'Berlin solution' signals to other employers that women who wear the veil cannot be trusted. This could have the further non-intended consequence of making it particularly difficult or even impossible for Muslim women to find employment in the private sector, even though this would have been likely to strengthen their personal independence.

Both arguments, the principled and the pragmatic one, speak in favour of permitting veiled women to work as teachers. For exceptions, there would have to be proof of a concrete danger, which, however, could not simply consist

---

27 Extensively on this: Will Kymlicka, *Multicultural Citizenship: A Liberal Theory of Minority Rights* (Oxford: Clarendon Press, 1995); Will Kymlicka, ed., *The Rights of Minority Cultures* (Oxford: Oxford University Press, 1995).

in the possibility that pupils or parents, be it out of ignorance or resentment, reject a teacher whose appearance is unfamiliar to them. In such cases, enlightened consideration and the duty of equal regard and respect are called for; not the retreat of the state from this task through the exclusion of the teacher.

Strong and Weak Evaluations

This brings me back to my earlier scenario: the teacher in Dortmund wearing a jersey of the Bayern Munich soccer club. The intuition that the educational authority may forbid him from wearing the jersey, I believe, will find a sufficient basis in the concrete danger that it represents to disrupting the peace and making orderly class instruction impossible. Now it could look as if there is no fundamental difference between the jersey and the veil. The state could also prohibit veils if there is no other possibility for orderly class instruction and if the disturbances are not based in ignorance or morally untenable motivations.

Some liberals thus also argue that we should not differentiate between religiously significant and other items of clothing. We should instead treat all clothing as though it stood solely for preferences in taste that do not concern the state. Whether earrings, t-shirts, jerseys, jeans, long or short or dyed hair, or no hair at all, berets, Jewish skull-caps, crosses, or veils: the state should abstain from any hermeneutic of the appearance that its employees may present. And it must consider that each of them has a right to the free development of their personality and that any interference in that right requires justification. In that regard, it cannot suffice for an educational authority to dislike a religious message. Otherwise, it would consequently also be free to prohibit other items of clothing, say the Prada brand, if it found it to be pretentious. So, aside from emergency cases: hands off from any clothing regulations in the public sector!

Ethical liberalism cannot make it so easy on itself. Even from its perspective, as I have attempted to show, there are good reasons for allowing women to wear the veil at public schools. But the reasons have to do with the special significance of religious convictions. An ethical liberal would posit that whoever equates such convictions with preferences in taste, or arbitrary likes and dislikes, misunderstands the kind of neutrality that liberals call for. It is not their job to level the differences between strong and weak valuations.[28]

28 On this distinction: Charles Taylor, 'Was ist menschliches Handeln?', in *Negative Freiheit? Zur Kritik des neuzeitlichen Individualismus*, ed. Charles Taylor (Frankfurt am Main: Suhrkamp, 2008), 9 ff.

Why, for example, should the British state be generally receptive to the rights claim of a Sikh[29] to wear the traditional turban while serving on the police force? The best answer is that this item of clothing represents a conviction that is central for the person's self-understanding. It would be a misunderstanding to suppose that the state is being partial to the Sikh religious community by making an exception for them. It only takes party for the possibility to live in accordance with whatever reasoned convictions determine one's identity. It takes party not for a What, but to a How; namely: how people can lead their lives. And the state is thereby treating them if not equally, then still as equals.

A liberal state should thus take some freedoms much more seriously than others. And it must weigh the obligations to justifying any interference into the realm of personal liberties quite differently. While the state is not seriously offending the autonomy of its citizens when designating a road a one-way street, it is a much more serious affair when it meddles in citizens' freedom of belief. This second freedom stands, *pars pro toto*, for any and all such practices and beliefs that give meaning to a person's life. Equality of regard and respect includes being sensitive to differences that affect practices and beliefs concerning a person's self-understanding, given that these differences are morally defensible and that citizens can abide by them without therefore being irrational.

This appears to me to be the best basis for arguing that federal state legislators and their educational authorities should opt for a moderately multiculturalist treatment in all veil cases. Solutions that are moderately multi-cultural are not based on blindness to the possibility of irrational and morally wrong practices and convictions. A *laissez-faire* policy that effectively fosters disintegration and exposes Muslim girls to fundamentalists in schools would surely be the wrong response to the fact of religious pluralism. But until the opposite is proven, we should assume that an adult Muslim woman knows what she is doing if she wears the veil and that she means what she says when she states that she is not wearing it for missionary or Islamist purposes.

Bibliography

Brandom, Robert B. *Making it Explicit: Reasoning, Representing, and Discursive Commitment.* Cambridge, MA: Harvard University Press, 1998.

Dworkin, Ronald. *Bürgerrechte ernstgenommen.* Frankfurt am Main: Suhrkamp, 1990.

29 The Sikhs are a religious community, originating in Northern India. The turban bears a sacred/holy meaning for them.

—. 'Foundations of Liberal Equality'. In *The Tanner Lectures on Human Values, vol. 11.* Edited by Grethe B. Peterson, 1–119. Salt Lake City: University of Utah Press, 1990.

—. *Sovereign Virtue: The Theory and Practice of Equality.* Cambridge, MA, London: Harvard University Press, 2002.

Ende, Werner and Udo Steinbach, eds. *Der Islam in der Gegenwart.* 5th ed. München: Beck, 2005.

Forst, Rainer. *Toleranz: Philosophische Grundlagen und gesellschaftliche Praxis einer umstrittenen Tugend.* Frankfurt am Main: Campus-Verlag, 2000.

—. *Toleranz im Konflikt: Geschichte, Gehalt und Gegenwart eines umstrittenen Begriffs.* Frankfurt am Main: Suhrkamp, 2003.

Gosepath, Stefan. *Gleiche Gerechtigkeit: Grundlagen eines liberalen Egalitarismus.* Frankfurt am Main: Suhrkamp, 2004.

Habermas, Jürgen. 'Anerkennungskämpfe im demokratischen Rechtsstaat'. In *Multikulturalismus und die Politik der Anerkennung.* Edited by Charles Taylor and Jürgen Habermas, 147–96. Frankfurt am Main: Fischer, 1997.

Hahn, Henning. *Moralische Selbstachtung: Zur Grundfigur einer sozialliberalen Gerechtigkeitstheorie.* Berlin: De Gruyter, 2008.

Heyd, David, ed. *Toleration: An Elusive Virtue.* Princeton: Princeton University Press, 1996.

Huster, Stefan. *Die ethische Neutralität des Staates: Eine liberale Interpretation der Verfassung.* Tübingen: Mohr Siebeck, 2002.

Isensee, Josef. 'Grundrechtseifer und Amtsvergessenheit'. *Frankfurter Allgemeine Zeitung,* June 8, 2004.

Jessen, Frank, and Ulrich von Wilamowitz-Moellendorff. 'Das Kopftuch: Entschleierung eines Symbols'. Accessed July 31, 2008. http://www.kas.de/wf/de/33.9095/.

Kymlicka, Will. *Multicultural Citizenship: A Liberal Theory of Minority Rights.* Oxford: Clarendon Press, 1995.

—, ed. *The Rights of Minority Cultures.* Oxford: Oxford University Press, 1995.

—. 'Two Models of Pluralism and Tolerance'. In *Toleration: An Elusive Virtue.* Edited by David Heyd, 81–105. Princeton: Princeton University Press, 1996.

Ladwig, Bernd. *Ladwig, Gerechtigkeit und Verantwortung: Liberale Gleichheit für autonome Personen.* Berlin: Akademie-Verlag, 2000.

—. 'Begründung von Normen'. In *Einführung in die Politische Theorie und Methodenlehre.* Edited by Sven-Uwe Schmitz and Klaus Schubert, 255–70. Opladen: Barbara Budrich, 2006.

—. 'Der Wert der Wahlfreiheit: Eine Kritik von Isaiah Berlins Verständnis von negativer Freiheit'. *Deutsche Zeitschrift für Philosophie* 55, no. 6 (2007): 877–87.

Lohmann, Georg. 'Unparteilichkeit in der Moral'. In *Die Öffentlichkeit der Vernunft und die Vernunft der Öffentlichkeit: Festschrift für Jürgen Habermas.* Edited by Lutz Wingert and Klaus Günther, 434–455. Frankfurt am Main: Suhrkamp, 2001.

Menke, Christoph, and Arnd Pollmann. *Philosophie der Menschenrechte: Zur Einführung.* Hamburg: Junius-Verlag, 2007.

Moller-Okin, Susan. 'Konflikte zwischen Grundrechten: Frauenrechte und die Probleme religiöser und kultureller Unterschiede'. In *Philosophie der Menschenrechte.* Edited by Stefan Gosepath and Georg Lohmann, 310–342. Frankfurt am Main: Suhrkamp, 1998.

Philosophie der Menschrechte: Grundlagen eines weltweiten Freiheitsethos. Darmstadt: Wiss. Buchges., 1998.

Rawls, John. *Gerechtigkeit als Fairness: Ein Neuentwurf.* Frankfurt am Main: Suhrkamp, 2006.
Raz, Joseph. *The Morality of Freedom.* Oxford: Clarendon Press, 1986.
Schwarzer, Alice. 'Die Islamisten meinen es so ernst wie Hitler'. *Frankfurter Allgemeine Zeitung*, July 4, 2006, Interview with Alice Schwarzer.
Stein, Tine. *Himmlische Quellen und irdisches Recht: Religiöse Voraussetzungen des freiheitlichen Verfassungsstaates.* Frankfurt am Main, New York: Campus-Verlag, 2006.
Taylor, Charles. 'Was ist menschliches Handeln?' In *Negative Freiheit? Zur Kritik des neuzeitlichen Individualismus.* Edited by Charles Taylor, 9–51. Frankfurt am Main: Suhrkamp, 2008.

Name Index

ʿAbd al-Jabbār, Qāḍī 46
Abou El Fadl 112
Abū Ḥanīfa 17, 20–23, 25, 30–33
Abū Yūsuf 31, 120
Amin, Qasim 81f.
Aquinas, Thomas 2, 47
Aristotle 2f., 47, 105f.
ʿAshʿarī, al-, Abū al-Ḥasan 40
Atay, Hüseyin 125
Augustinus 105
ʿAzm, al-, Rafiq 67

Balić, Smail 124, 128

Erdogan, Recep Tayyip 69

Ghazālī, al- 65, 111, 121

Haddad, Tahir 11, 75, 81–90, 95, 98, 100
Hashmi, Taj 128

Ibn Abī al-Rabīʿ 112
Ibn Jamāʿa 113
Ibn Khaldūn 112
Ibn Qayyim al-Jawziyya 5, 10, 73, 112
Ibn Rushd 78, 108
Ibn Sīnā, Abū ʿAlī 46
Ibn Taymiyya 1, 40, 113f.

Jalāl al-Dawla 44

Khayyam, Omar 39

Ludin, Fereshta 152f., 161, 166

Mahdī / Mahdi 4, 41, 61, 65f.
Māturīdī, al-, / Maturidi, Abū Manṣūr 17–20, 23–29, 33, 40
Māwardī, al-, Abū al-Ḥasan 4, 9f., 41–55, 108, 111, 113
Muṭahharī, Murtaḍā 6, 8, 40

Naʿim, an-, Abdullahi 108, 124
Nasser 69

Qādir, al- 44, 121
Qāʾim, al- 44
Quṭb, Sayyid 4

Radbruch 106, 114
Rahman, Fazlur 11, 42, 75, 80f., 89–95, 100, 124, 126, 128

Samarqandī, al-, Abū al-Layth 17, 19f., 22–25, 28
Sarakhsī, al- 3, 5–7, 9, 14, 32, 42, 106, 114f., 119
Shāfiʿī, al- 43, 44, 118
Shāṭibī, al- / Shatibi, al- 121f.
Shaybānī, al- / Shaybani, al-, Muḥammad 17, 30–33
Surūsh, ʿAbdulkarīm / Soroush, Abdolkarim 6

ʿUmar 61f., 68

https://doi.org/10.1515/9783110574593-009

Subject Index

ʿAdala / ʿAdāla 69, 108
ʿAdl / ʿādil 3–5, 41, 48, 50 f., 105, 107, 109, 130
Ḥanafi / Ḥanafī / Hanafite 9, 16–35, 120, 137, 139
Ḥanbali 1, 5, 10
ʿAql 47, 48, 122
Ashʿarī 40, 43
Ashʿarites / Ashʿariyya 1, 4, 40, 55, 109
Autonomy 116, 157–159, 162, 174
Awqāf 109, 116, 123

Bayʿ 77
Būyid 44, 49

Caliph 1, 32, 44 f., 49, 59, 61–64, 68, 108, 111, 113, 120
Comprehensive justice 39, 41, 47 f., 50 f., 53, 55
Crime 11, 27 f., 30, 32 f., 119

Din / dīn 5, 41, 43, 45, 46 f., 48, 96, 115, 122

Fiqh 5, 9–14, 18–20, 23, 25, 42 f., 73–75, 77–83, 85–87, 95 f., 99 f., 109, 119 f.
Fuqaha 80, 97

Haqq 20, 62

Imam 8, 13, 63, 65 f., 68, 111, 113 f., 121 f.
ʿIrḍ 93, 122, 145
Islamic feminism 74, 90 f., 98
Islamism 164 f.
Istiḥsān 5

Jihād / Jihad 11, 111, 125, 135, 137, 138, 139–149

Kemalism 69
Khalifa 62
Khārijīs 41
Kharijites 4

Liberalism 92, 151 f., 155, 158–160, 162, 173

Maẓālim 110, 120
Mahr 93
Maṣlaḥa 5, 18, 121
Malik 42, 61–63
Maqāṣid 121 f., 125
Māturīdiyya 40
Mecelle 108
Metaphysics 46
Mulk 61
Multiculturalism 120, 151
Muruwwa 93
Muʿtazilites / Muʿtazila 1, 4, 39 f., 41, 43 f., 45, 46, 55, 109

Nafaqa 77 f., 99
Nikah 77
Nushuz 75–78

Polygamy 6, 75, 78–80, 84, 87 f., 95, 110
Punishment 1, 6, 11, 27–30, 32, 48, 63, 68, 114 f., 123

Qadar 3
Qisṭ / Qist 3 f., 62
Qiwama 75, 77 f., 97, 99 f.

Shafiʿī 9, 43
Sharʿ 48
Sharia / Shariah / Sharīʿa 1, 2, 5 f., 8, 10, 40, 59, 61–65, 67 f., 70, 73–75, 77, 80, 83, 84, 86, 87, 90, 96, 97, 99, 109, 111, 112, 113, 121 f., 124, 128, 130, 135, 140, 146, 148, 167
Shia 63, 65, 107
Shiite 4, 40 f., 61, 65 f., 112, 121
Shura 67
Social contract 9, 13, 26, 29–33
Sunna 5, 20, 27, 29, 59, 83 f., 91, 118

Taghut 66

https://doi.org/10.1515/9783110574593-010

Short Biographies

Rumee Ahmed (PhD, University of Virginia) is Associate Professor of Islamic Law and Associate Dean of Communications and Innovation at the University of British Columbia. He is the author of *Narratives of Islamic Legal Theory* (Oxford University Press, 2012) and co-editor of the Oxford Handbook on Islamic Law.

Werner Ende is professor emeritus of Islamic Studies. He served as research associate at the German Orient Institute in Beirut from 1969 to 1971, as professor of Islamic Studies at the University of Hamburg from 1977 onwards, and between 1983 and 2002 at the University of Freiburg. Since his retirement in 2002 he has lived in Berlin. Ende is editor of the series Freiburger Islamstudien and was co-edited the journal *Die Welt des Islams* between 1981 and 2011.

Bernd Ladwig is professor of political theory and philosophy at the Free University Berlin. His research focuses on theories of justice and human rights. He is currently writing a book on the political philosophy of human-animal-relations. Selected publications: 'Human Rights, Institutions and the Division of Moral Labor', in: *World Political Science 2016*; 12 (1); 'Against Wild Animal Sovereignty: An Interest-based Critique of "Zoopolis"', in *Journal of Political Philosophy*, Volume 23, Issue 3, September 2015.

Ziba Mir-Hosseini is a legal anthropologist, specializing in Islamic law, gender and development, and a founding member of the Musawah Global Movement for Equality and Justice in the Muslim Family (www.musawah.org). Currently a Professorial Research Associate at the Centre for Islamic and Middle Eastern Law, University of London, she has held numerous research fellowships and visiting professorships. She has published books on Islamic family law in Iran and Morocco, Iranian clerical discourses on gender, Islamic reformist thinkers.

Abbas Poya heads the junior research group 'Norm, Normativity and Norm Changing' at the University of Erlangen-Nürnberg. He has researched and taught varies aspects of Islamic Studies (e.g. Islamic Law, Islamic intellectual history, and the idea of justice in Islam) at the Universities of Hamburg, Freiburg, Zurich, and Erlangen-Nürnberg.

Mathias Rohe is full professor of Civil Law, Private International Law and Comparative Law at the University of Erlangen-Nürnberg, where he is also the founder and head of the Erlangen Centre for Islam and the Law in Europe. Rohe has published intensely on Islamic law and on the development of Islam in Europe (e.g. *Islamic Law in Past and Present*, Leiden 2015) and regularly advises European governments and administrations.

https://doi.org/10.1515/9783110574593-011

www.ingramcontent.com/pod-product-compliance
Lightning Source LLC
Chambersburg PA
CBHW031433150426
43191CB00006B/500